SUMMER: FROM THE JOURNAL OF HENRY D. THOREAU

EDITED BY H. G. O. BLAKE

To the great seeking of the heart, God gives nature and himself
as answer beyond thought, . . . JOSEPH BROWNLEE BROWN

BOSTON
HOUGHTON, MIFFLIN AND COMPANY
New York: 11 East Seventeenth Street
The Riverside Press, Cambridge
1884

The Riverside Press, Cambridge:
Electrotyped and Printed by H. O. Houghton & Co.

INTRODUCTORY.

To those who are interested in Thoreau's life
and thoughts — a company already somewhat
large, and which, I trust, is becoming larger —
a second volume of selections from his Journal
is now offered. The same arrangement of dates
has been followed, for the most part, as in
"Early Spring in Massachusetts," in order to
give here a picture of summer as there of spring.
Thoreau seems himself to have contemplated
some work of this kind, as appears on page 99
of this volume, where he speaks of "a book of
the seasons, each page of which should be written in its own season and out-of-doors, or in its
own locality, wherever it may be." Had his life
continued, very likely he would have produced
some such work from the materials and suggestions contained in his Journal, and this would
have been doubtless far more complete and
beautiful than anything we can now construct
from fragmentary passages.

Thoreau has been variously criticised as a nat-
uralist, one writer speaking of him as not by

nature an observer, as making no discoveries, as
being surprised by phenomena familiar to other
people, though he adds that this " is one of his
chief charms as a writer," since "everything
grows fresh under his hand." Another, whose
criticism is generally very favorable, says he was
too much occupied with himself, not simple
enough to be a good observer, that " he did not
love nature for her own sake," " with an unmixed, disinterested love, as Gilbert White did,
for instance," even " cannot say that there was
any felicitous " " seeing." This last statement
seems surprising. Still another is puzzled to
explain how a man who was so bent upon self-
improvement, who could so little forget himself
and the conventions of society, could yet study
nature so intelligently. But the very fact that
Thoreau " did not love nature for her own sake "
" with an unmixed, disinterested love," rather
looked beyond and above, whither she points,
to "a far Azore," to

" The cape never rounded, nor wandered o'er,"

and was not specially bent upon being an intel-
ligent student of nature, an accurate scientific
observer or natural historian, but sometimes la-
mented that his observation was taking too exclusively that turn ; the very fact that he aimed
rather at self-improvement, if one pleases to call

it so (though this seems a somewhat prosaic account of the matter), that he was bent upon ever exploring his own genius and obeying its most delicate intimations, and in his love of nature found the purest encouragement in that direction, this constitutes to me the great charm of his Journal, as it does of all his writings, — as it did also of his life and conversation.

I desire to express here my obligations to Mr. W. E. Channing, and Mr. F. B. Sanborn, of Concord, both of them friends and biographers of Thoreau, for indicating to me the position of places on the accompanying map, most of which are referred to in the Journal.

THE EDITOR.

WORCESTER, *May*, 1884.

SUMMER.

June 1, 1852. Evening. To the Lee place. The moon about full. The sounds I hear by the bridge : the midsummer frog (I think it is not the toad), the night-hawk, crickets, the peet-weet (it is early), the hum of dor-bugs, and the whippoorwill. The boys are coming home from fishing, for the river is down at last.

June 1, 1853. Quite a fog this morning. Does it not always follow the cooler nights after the first really warm weather about the end of May ? Saw a water-snake yesterday with its tail twisted about some dead-weed stubble, and quite dry and stiff, as if it were preparing to shed its skin. . . .

Bees are swarming now, and those who keep them often have to leave their work in haste to secure them.

P. M. To Walden. Summer begins now, about a week past, with the expanded leaves, the shade, and warm weather. Cultivated fields, too, are leaving out, that is, corn and potatoes

1

coming up. Most trees have leaved and are now forming fruit. Young berries, too, are forming, and birds are being hatched. Dor-bugs and other insects have come forth the first warm evening after showers. The birds have now [all ?] come, and no longer fly in flocks. The hylodes are no longer heard ; the bull-frogs begin to trump. Thick and extensive fogs in the morning begin. Plants are rapidly growing, shooting. Hoeing corn has commenced. The first bloom of the year is over. It is now the season of growth. Have not wild animals now henceforth their young, and fishes, too ?

The pincushion galls on young white oaks are now among the most beautiful objects in the woods, — coarse, woolly, white, spotted with bright red or crimson on the exposed side. It is remarkable that a mere gall, which at first we are inclined to regard as something abnormal, should be made so beautiful, as if it were the flower of the tree ; that a disease, an excrescence, should prove, perchance, the greatest beauty, as the tear of the pearl ; beautiful scarlet sins they may be. Through our temptations, aye, and our falls, our virtues appear. As in many a character, many a poet, we see that beauty exhibited in a gall which was meant to have bloomed in a flower, unchecked. Such, however, is the accomplishment of the world.

The poet cherishes his chagrin and sets his sighs to music. This gall is the tree's " Ode to Dejection." How oft it chances that the apparent fruit of a shrub, its apple, is merely a gall or blight! How many men, meeting with some blast in the moist, growing days of their youth, so that what should have been a sweet and palatable fruit in them becomes a mere puff and excrescence, say that they have experienced religion! Their fruit is a gall, a puff, an excrescence, for want of moderation and continence. So many plants never ripen their fruit. . . .

The news of the explosion of the powder mills was not only carried seaward by the cloud which its smoke made, but more effectually, though more slowly, by the fragments which were floated thither by the river. M—— yesterday showed me quite a pile of fragments and short pieces of large timber, still black with powder, which he had saved as they were drifting by. . . . Some, no doubt, were carried down to the Merrimack, and by the Merrimack to the ocean, till, perchance, they got into the Gulf Stream and were cast upon the coast of Norway, covered with barnacles, — or who can tell on what more distant strand? — still bearing traces of burnt powder, still capable of telling how and where they were launched, to those who can read their signs. Mingling with wrecks of vessels, which told a different tale, this wreck of a powder-mill was cast up on some outlandish strand, and went to swell the pile of drift-wood — collected by some native — shouldered by whales, alighted on at first by the musk-rat and the peet-weet, and finally, perhaps, by the stormy petrel and other beach birds. It is long before nature forgets it. How slowly the ruins are being dispersed. . . .

I am as white as a miller — a rye-miller, at least — with the lint from the young leaves and twigs. The tufts of pinks on the side of the peak by the pond grow raying out from a centre, somewhat like a cyme, on the warm, dry side hill, — some a lighter, some a richer and darker shade of pink. With what a variety of colors we are entertained! Yet most colors are rare or in small doses, presented to us as a condiment or spice; much of green, blue, black, and white, but of yellow and the different shades of red, far less. The eyes feast on the colors of flowers as on tidbits.

I hear now, at five o'clock, a farmer's horn calling the hands in from the field to an early tea. Heard afar by the walker, over the woods, at this hour, or at noon, bursting upon the stillness of the air, putting life into some portion of the horizon, this is one of the most suggestive and pleasing of the country sounds produced by man. I know not how far it is peculiar to New

England or the United States. I hear two or three prolonged blasts, as I am walking along, some sultry noon, in the midst of the still woods, — a sound which I know to be produced by human breath, the most sonorous parts of which alone reach me ; and I see in my mind's eye the hired men and master dropping the implements of their labor in the field, and wending their way with a sober satisfaction toward the house. I see the well-sweep rise and fall. I see the preparatory ablutions, and the table laden with the smoking meal. It is a significant hum in a distant part of the hive. . . .

How much lupine is now in full bloom on bare sandy brows or promontories, running into meadows where the sod is half worn away and the sand exposed! The geraniums are now getting to be common. *Hieracium venosum* just out on this peak, and the snapdragon catchfly is here, abundantly in blossom a little after five P. M., — a pretty little flower, the petals dull crimson beneath or varnished mahogany color, and rose-tinted white within or above. It closed on my way home, but opened again in water in the evening. Its opening in the night chiefly is a fact which interests and piques me. Do any insects visit it then? — Lambkill just beginning, — the very earliest. . . . New, bright, glossy, light-green leaves of the umbelled wintergreen are shooting on this hill-side, but the old leaves are particularly glossy and shining, as if varnished and not yet dry, or most highly polished. Did they look thus in the winter? I do not know any leaf so wet-glossy.

While walking up this hill-side I disturbed a night-hawk eight or ten feet from me, which went half fluttering, half hopping, the mottled creature, like a winged toad (as Nuttall says the French of Louisiana call it) down the hill as far as I could see. Without moving I looked about and saw its two eggs on the bare ground on a slight shelf of the hill, on the dead pine needles and sand, without any cavity or nest whatever; very obvious when once you had detected them, but not easily detected from their color, a coarse gray, formed of white spotted with bluish or slaty brown or amber, — a stone-granite color, like the places it selects. I advanced and put my hand on them, and while I stooped, seeing a shadow on the ground, looked up and saw the bird, which had fluttered down the hill so blind and helpless, circling low and swiftly past over my head, showing the white spot on each wing in true night-hawk fashion. When I had gone a dozen rods it appeared again, higher in the air, with its peculiar limping kind of flight, all the while noiseless, and suddenly descending it dashed at me within ten feet of my head, like an imp of darkness ; then swept away high over the pond, dashing now to this side, now to that, on different tracks, as if, in pursuit of its prey, it had already forgotten its eggs on the earth. I can see how it might easily come to be regarded with superstitious awe. — A cuckoo very plainly heard.

Within little more than a fortnight the woods, from bare twigs, have become a sea of verdure, and young shoots have contended with one another in the race. The leaves are unfurled all over the country. Shade is produced, the birds are concealed, their economies go forward uninterruptedly, and a covert is afforded to animals generally. But thousands of worms and insects are preying on the leaves while they are young and tender. Myriads of little parasols are suddenly spread all the country over to shield the earth and the roots of the trees from the parching heat, and they begin to flutter and to rustle in the breeze.

From Bare Hill there is a mist on the landscape, giving it a glaucous appearance. Now I see gentlemen and ladies sitting in boats at anchor on the lakes, in the calm afternoons, under parasols, making use of nature. The farmer, hoeing, is wont to look with scorn and pride on a man sitting in a motionless boat a whole half day, but he does not realize that the object of his own labor is perhaps merely to add another dollar to his heap, nor through what coarseness and inhumanity to his family and servants he often accomplishes this. He has an Irishman or a Canadian working for him by the month, and what, probably, is the lesson he is teaching him by precept and example? Will it make that laborer more of a man? this earth more like heaven?

A redwing's nest, four eggs, low in a tuft of sedge in an open meadow. What Champollion can translate the hieroglyphics on these eggs? It is always writing of the same character, though much diversified. While the bird picks up the material and lays this egg, who determines the style of the marking? When you approach, away dashes the dark mother, betraying her nest, and then chatters her anxiety from a neighboring bush, where she is soon joined by the red-shouldered male, who comes scolding over your head, chattering and uttering a sharp " phe phee-e."

I hear the note of a bobolink concealed in the top of an apple-tree behind me. Though this bird's full strain is ordinarily somewhat trivial, this one appears to be meditating a strain as yet unheard in meadow or orchard. *Paulo majora canamus.* He is just touching the strings of his theorbo, his glassichord, his water organ, and one or two notes globe themselves and fall in liquid bubbles from his tuning throat. It is as if he touched his harp within a vase of liquid melody, and when he lifted it out the notes fell like bubbles from the trembling strings. Methinks they are the most liquidly sweet and melodious sounds I ever heard. They are as refreshing to my ear as the first distant tinkling and gurgling of a rill to a thirsty man. Oh, never advance farther in your art; never let us hear your full strain, sir! But away he launches, and the meadow is all bespattered with melody. Its notes fall with the apple blossoms in the orchard. The very divinest part of his strain drops from his overflowing breast *singultim*, in globes of melody. It is the foretaste of such strains as never fell on mortal ears, to hear which we should rush to our doors and contribute all that we possess and are. Or it seemed as if in that vase full of melody some notes sphered themselves, and from time to time bubbled up to the surface, and were with difficulty repressed.

June 2, 1853. Half past three A. M. When I awake I hear the low, universal chirping or twittering of the chip-birds, like the bursting head on the surface of the uncorked day. First come, first served. You must taste the first glass of the day's nectar if you would get all the spirit of it. Its fixed air begins to stir and escape. Also the robin's morning song is heard, as in the spring, — earlier than the notes of most other birds, thus bringing back the spring; now rarely heard or noticed in the course of the day.

Four A. M. To Nashawtuck. I go to the river in a fog — through which I cannot see more than a dozen rods — three or four times as deep as the houses. As I row down the stream, the dark, dim outlines of the trees on the banks appear coming to meet me on the one hand, while they retreat and are soon concealed in it on the other. My strokes soon bring them behind me. The birds are wide awake, as if knowing that this fog presages a fair day. I ascend Nashawtuck from the north side. I am aware that I yield to the same influence which inspires the birds and the cockerels whose hoarse courage I hear now vaunted. I would crow like chanticleer in the morning, with all the lustiness that the new day imparts, without thinking of the evening, when I and all of us shall go to roost; with all the humility of the cock that takes his perch upon the highest rail and wakes the country with his clarion brag. Shall not men be inspired as much as cockerels? My feet are soon wet with fog. It is indeed a vast dew. Are not the clouds another kind of dew?

Cool nights produce them. Now I have reached
the hill-top above the fog at a quarter to five,
about sunrise, and all around me is a sea of fog,
level and white, reaching nearly to the top of
this hill, only the tops of a few high hills appearing as distant islands in the main. Wachusett is a more distant and larger island, an
Atlantis in the west; there is hardly one to
touch at between me and it. It is just like
the clouds beneath you as seen from a mountain. It is a perfect level in some directions,
cutting the hills near their summits with a geometrical line, but puffed up here and there, and
more and more toward the east, by the influence
of the sun. An early freight train is heard, not
seen, rushing through the town beneath it. You
can get here the impression which the ocean
makes, without ever going to the shore. The
sea-shore exhibits nothing more grand, or on a
larger scale. How grand where it rolls off over
Ball's Hill, like a glorious ocean after a storm,
just lit by the rising sun. It is as boundless
as the view from the highlands of Cape Cod.
These are exaggerated billows, the ocean on a
larger scale, the sea after some tremendous and
unheard-of storm, for the actual sea never appears so tossed up and universally white with
foam and spray as this, now, far in the north-
eastern horizon, where mountain billows are

breaking on some hidden reef or bank. It is tossed up toward the sun and by it into the most boisterous of seas, which no craft, no ocean steamer, is vast enough to sail on. Meanwhile, my hands are numb with cold, and my feet ache with it. Now, at quarter past five, before this southwest wind, it is already grown thin as gossamer in that direction, and woods and houses are seen through it, while it is heaped up toward the sun, and finally becomes so thick there that for a short time it appears in one place a dark, low cloud, such as else can only be seen from mountains; and now long, dark ridges of wood appear through it, and now the sun reflected from the river makes a bright glow in the fog, and now, at half past five, I see the green surface of the meadows, and the water through the trees sparkling with bright reflections. Men will go further and pay more to see a tawdry picture on canvas, a poor, painted scene, than to behold the fairest or grandest scene that nature ever displays in their immediate vicinity, although they may never have seen it in their lives. . . .

Cherry birds are the only ones I see in flocks now. I can tell them afar by their peculiar fine Spring-y note. . . .

Four P. M. To Conantum. . . . Arethusas are abundant in what I may call Arethusa

Meadow. They are the more striking for growing in such green localities in meadows where
the brilliant purple, more or less red, contrasts
with the green grass. Found four perfect ar-
rowheads, and one imperfect, in the potato field
just plowed up for the first time that I remember, at the Hubbard bathing place. . . .

Clintonia borealis a day or two. Its beauty
at present consists chiefly in its commonly three
very handsome, rich, clear, dark-green leaves,
which Bigelow describes truly as " more than
half a foot long, oblanceolate, smooth, and shining." They are perfect in form and color,
broadly oblanceolate, with a deep channel down
the middle, uninjured by insects, arching over
from a centre at the ground; and from their
midst rises the scape, a foot high, with one or
more umbels of " green, bell-shaped flowers," —
yellowish-green, nodding or bent downward, but
without fragrance. In fact, the plant is all
green, both leaves and corolla. The leaves
alone — and many have no scape — would detain
the walker. Its berries are its flower. A single
plant is a great ornament in a vase, from the
beauty of its form and the rich, unspotted green
of its leaves.

The sorrel now reddens the fields far and
wide. As I look over the fields thus reddened
in extensive patches, now deeper, now passing

into green, and think of the season now in its
prime and heyday, it looks as if it were the
blood mantling in the cheek of the beautiful
year, — the rosy cheek of its health, its rude
June health. The *medeola* has been out a day
or two, apparently, — another green flower. . . .

June 2, 1854. p. m. Up Assabet to Castil-
leja and Anursnack. While waiting for ——
and S—— I look now from the yard to the waving and slightly glaucous-tinged June meadows,
edged by the cool shade of shrubs and trees, —
a waving shore of shady bays and promontories,
yet different from the August shades. It is
beautiful and Elysian. The air has now begun
to be filled with a bluish haze. These virgin
shades of the year, when everything is tender,
fresh, and green, how full of promise! — promising bowers of shade in which heroes may repose themselves. I would fain be present at the
birth of shadow. It takes place with the first
expansion of the leaves. . . . The black willows are already beautiful, and the hemlocks
with their bead-work of new green. Are these
not king-bird-days, — these clearer first June
days, full of light, when this aerial, twittering
bird flutters from willow to willow, and swings
on the twigs, showing his white-edged tail? The
Azalea nudiflora is about done, or there was
apparently little of it. — I see some breams'

nests near my old bathing place above the stone heaps, with sharp, yellow, sandy edges, like a milk pan from within. . . . Also there are three or four small stone heaps formed. . . .

The painted-cup meadow is all lit up with ferns on its springy slopes. The handsome flowering fern, now rapidly expanding and fruiting at the same time, colors these moist slopes afar with its now commonly reddish fronds; and then there are the interrupted and the cinnamon ferns in very handsome and regular tufts, and the brakes standing singly, and more backward. . . .

June 2, 1855. From that cocoon of the *Attacus cecropia* which I found — I think it was on the 24th of May — came out this forenoon a splendid moth. I had pinned the cocoon to the sash at the upper part of my window, and quite forgotten it. About the middle of the forenoon S—— came in, and exclaimed that there was a moth on my window. My *Attacus cecropia* had come out and dropped down to the window-sill, where it hung on the side of a slipper, to let its wings hang down and develop themselves. At first the wings were not only not unfolded laterally, but not longitudinally, the thinner ends of the foremost ones for perhaps three fourths of an inch being very feeble, and occupying very little space. It was surprising to see the creature unfold and expand before our eyes, the wings gradually elongating, as it were, by their own gravity, and from time to time the insect assisting this operation by a slight shake. It was wonderful how it waxed and grew, revealing some new beauty every fifteen minutes, which I called S—— to see, but never losing its hold on the shoe. It looked like a young emperor just donning the most splendid ermine robes, the wings every moment acquiring greater expansion, and their at first wrinkled edge becoming more tense. At first, they appeared double, one within the other. But at last it advanced so far as to spread its wings completely, but feebly, when we approached. This process occupied several hours. It continued to hang to the shoe, with its wings ordinarily closed erect behind its back, the rest of the day, and at dusk, when apparently it was waving them preparatory to its evening flight, I gave it ether, and so saved it in a perfect state. As it lies, not outspread to the utmost, it is five and nine tenths inches by two and one fourth. . . .

The *Azalea nudiflora* now in its prime. What splendid masses of pink, with a few glaucous green leaves sprinkled here and there, — just enough for contrast!

June 2, 1858. Half past eight A. M. Start for Monadnock. Between Shirley Village and Lunenburg I notice, in a meadow on the right hand, close to the railroad, the *Kalmia glauca* in bloom, as we are whirled past. Arrived at Troy station at five minutes past eleven, and shouldered our knapsacks, steering northeast to the mountain, its top some four miles off. It is a pleasant, hilly road, leading past a few farmhouses, where you already begin to sniff the mountain or at least up-country air. Almost without interruption we had the mountain in sight before us, its sublime gray mass, that antique, brownish-gray, Ararat color. Probably these crests of the earth are for the most part of one color in all lands, — that gray color of antiquity which nature loves, the color of unpainted wood, weather stain, time stain ; not glaring nor gaudy ; the color of all roofs, the color of all things that endure, the color that wears well ; color of Egyptian ruins, of mummies, and all antiquity, baked in the sun, done brown, — not scarlet, like the crest of the bragging cock, but that hard, enduring gray, a terrene sky color, solidified air with a tinge of earth.

We left the road at a school-house, and, crossing a meadow, began to ascend gently through very rocky pastures. . . . The neighboring hills began to sink, and entering the wood we soon passed Fassett's shanty, he so busily at work inside that he did not see us, and we took our dinner by the rocky brookside in the woods just

2

above. A dozen people passed us early in the afternoon while we sat there, — men and women on their way down from the summit, this suddenly very pleasant day after a lowering one, having attracted them. . . .

Having risen above the dwarfish woods (in which mountain ash was very common) which reached higher up along the ravine we had traversed than elsewhere, and nearly all the visitors having descended, we proceeded to find a place for and to prepare our camp at mid P. M. We wished it to be near water, out of the way of the wind — which was northwest — and of the path, and also near to spruce-trees, for a bed. There is a good place, if you would be near the top, within a stone's-throw of it, on the north side, under some spruce-trees. We chose a sunken yard in a rocky plateau on the southeast side of the mountain, perhaps half a mile from the summit by the path, a rod and a half wide by many more in length, with a mossy and bushy floor about five or six feet beneath the general level, where a dozen black spruce-trees grew, though the surrounding rock was generally bare. There was a pretty good spring within a dozen rods, and the western wall shelved over a foot or two. We slanted two scraggy spruce-trees, long since bleached, from the western wall, and, cutting many spruce boughs with our knives, made a thick bed and walls on the two sides, to keep out the wind. Then, putting several poles transversely across our two rafters, we covered them with a thick roof of spruce twigs, like shingles. The spruce, though harsh for a bed, was close at hand, we cutting away one tree to make room. We crawled under the low eaves of this roof, about eighteen inches high, and our extremities projected about a foot.

Having left our packs here, and made all ready for the night, we went up to the summit to see the sun set. Our path lay through a couple of small swamps, and then up the rocks. Forty or fifty rods below the very apex, or quite on the top of the mountain, I saw a little bird flit from beneath a rock close by the path, where there were only a very few scattered dwarf black spruces about, and looking I found a nest with three eggs. It was the *Fringilla hiemalis*, which soon disappeared around a projecting rock. The nest was sunk in the ground by the side of a tuft of grass, and was pretty deep, made of much fine, dry grass or [sedge?]. The eggs were three, of a regular oval form, faint bluish-white, sprinkled with fine pale-brown dots, in two of the three condensed into a ring about the larger end. They had just begun to develop. The nest and tuft were covered by a projecting rock. Brewer says that only one nest is known to naturalists.

We saw many of these birds flitting about the summit, perched on the rocks and the dwarf spruces, and disappearing behind the rocks. It is the prevailing bird now on the summit. They are commonly said to go to the fur countries to breed, though Wilson says that some breed in the Alleghanies. The New York Reports make them breed in the Catskills and some other mountains of that State. This was a quite interesting discovery. They probably are never seen in the surrounding low grounds at this season. The ancestors of this bird had evidently perceived in their flight northward that here was a small piece of arctic region containing all the conditions they require, coolness and suitable food, etc., etc., and so for how long have builded here. For ages they have made their home here with the *Arenaria Groenlandica* and *Potentilla tridentata*. They discerned arctic isles sprinkled in our southern sky. I did not see any of them below the rocky and generally bare portion of the mountain. It finds here the same conditions as in the north of Maine and in the far countries, Labrador mosses, etc. . . . Now that the season is advanced, migrating birds have gone to the extreme north or to the mountain tops. By its color it harmonized with the gray and brownish-gray rocks. We felt that we were so much nearer to perennial spring and winter. . . .

We heard the hylodes peeping from a rain-water pool, a little below the summit, toward night. As it was quite hazy we could not see the shadow of the mountain well, and so returned just before sunset to our camp. We lost the path coming down, for nothing is easier than to lose your way here, where so little trail is left upon the rocks, and the different rocks and ravines are so much alike. Perhaps no other equal area is so bewildering in this respect as a rocky mountain summit, though it has so conspicuous a central point. Notwithstanding the newspaper and egg-shell left by visitors, these parts of nature are still peculiarly unhandseled and untracked. The natural terraces of rock are the steps of this temple, and it is the same whether it rises above the desert or a New England village. Even the inscribed rocks are as solemn as most ancient grave-stones, and nature reclaims them with bog and lichen. These sculptors seemed to me to court such alliance with the grave as they who put their names over tomb-stones along the highway. One, who was probably a blacksmith, had sculptured the emblems of his craft, an anvil and hammer, beneath his name. Apparently, a part of the regular outfit of mountain climbers is a hammer and cold chisel, and perhaps they allow themselves a supply of garlic also. But no Old Mortality will ever be caught renewing their epitaphs. It reminds one what kind of steep do climb the false pretenders to fame, whose chief exploit is the carriage of the tools with which to inscribe their names. For speaking epitaphs they are, and the mere name is a sufficient revelation of the character. They are all of one trade, — stone-cutters, defacers of mountain tops. "Charles and Lizzie!" Charles carried the sledge-hammer, and Lizzie the cold chisel. Some have carried up a paint pot, and painted their names on the rocks.

We returned to our camp, and got our tea in our sunken yard. While one went for water to the spring, the other kindled a fire. The whole rocky part of the mountain, except the extreme summit, is strewn with the relics of spruce-trees a dozen or fifteen feet long, and long since dead and bleached, so that there is plenty of dry fuel at hand. We sat out on the brink of the rocky plateau, near our camp, taking our tea in the twilight, and found it quite dry and warm there, though you would not have thought of sitting out at evening in the surrounding valleys. I have often perceived the warm air high on the sides of hills, while the valleys were filled with a cold, damp night-air, as with water, and here the air was warmer and drier the greater part of the night. We perceived no dew there this or the next night. This was our parlor and supper-room; in another direction was our wash-room. The chewink sang before night, and this, as I have before observed, is a very common bird on mountain tops; the wood-thrush sang, too, indefinitely far or near, a little more distant and unseen, as great poets are. It seems to love a cool atmosphere, and sometimes lingers quite late with us. Early in the evening the night-hawks were heard to spark and boom over these bare gray rocks, and such was our serenade at first as we lay on our spruce bed. We were left alone with the night-hawks. These withdrawn, bare rocks must be a very suitable place for them to lay their eggs, and their dry and unmusical, yet supra-mundane and spirit-like, voices and sounds gave fit expression to the rocky mountain solitude. It struck the very key-note of that stern, gray, and barren region. It was a thrumming of the mountain's rocky chords; strains from the music of chaos, such as were heard when the earth was rent and these rocks heaved up. Thus they went sparking and booming while we were courting the first access of sleep, and I could imagine their dainty, limping flight, inclining over the kindred rocks with a spot of white quartz in their wings. No sound could be more in harmony with that scenery. Though common below, it seemed peculiarly proper here. But ere long the night-hawks are stilled, and we hear

only the sound of our companion's breathing, or
of a bug in our spruce roof. I thought I heard
once, faintly, the barking of a dog far down under the mountain.

A little after one A. M. I woke and found that
the moon had risen, and heard some little bird
near by sing a short strain of welcome to it,
song-sparrow-like. Before dawn the night-hawks
commenced their sounds again, which were as
good as a clock to us, telling how the night got
on. At length, by three o'clock, June 3d, the
signs of dawn appear, and soon we hear the
robin and the *Fringilla hiemalis* (its prolonged
jingle as it sat on the top of a spruce), the
chewink, and the wood-thrush. Whether you
have slept soundly or not, it is not easy to lie
abed under these circumstances, and we rose at
half past three, in order to see the sun rise from
the top and get our breakfast there. It was
still hazy, and we did not see the shadow of the
mountain until it was comparatively short, nor
did we get the most distant views, as of the
Green and White mountains, while we were
there. . . .

We concluded to explore the whole rocky part
of the mountain in this wise : to saunter slowly
around it at about the height and distance from
the summit, of our camp, or say half a mile,
more or less, first going north, and returning by

the western semicircle, and then exploring the
east side, completing the circle, and returning
over the summit at night. . . .

During this walk, in looking toward the summit, I first observed that its steep, angular pro-
jections and the brows of the rocks were the
parts chiefly covered with dark brown lichens,
umbilicaria, etc., as if they were to grow on the
ridge and slopes of a man's nose only. It was
the steepest and most exposed parts of the high
rocks alone on which they grew, where you
would think it most difficult for them to cling.
They also covered the more rounded brows on
the sides of the mountain, especially on the east
side, where they were very dense, fine, crisp, and
firm, like a sort of shagreen, giving a firm hold
to the feet where it was needed. It was these
that gave that Ararat brown color of antiquity
to these portions of the mountain, which a few
miles distant could not be accounted for, compared with the more prevalent gray. From the
sky blue you pass through the misty gray of the
rocks to this darker and more terrene color.
The temples of the mountain are covered with
lichens, which color it for miles. . . .

We had thus made a pretty complete survey
of the top of the mountain. It is a very unique
walk, and would be almost equally interesting to
take if it were not elevated above the surround-

ing valleys. It often reminded me of my walks on the beach, and suggested how much both depend for their sublimity on solitude and dreariness. In both cases we feel the presence of some vast, titanic power. The rocks and valleys and bogs and rain pools of the mountain are so wild and unfamiliar still that you do not recognize the one you left fifteen minutes before. This rocky region, forming what you may call the top of the mountain, must be more than two miles long by one wide in the middle, and you would need to ramble round it many times before it would begin to be familiar. . . .

We proceeded to get our tea on the summit, in the very place where I had made my bed for a night some fifteen years before. . . . It was interesting to watch from that height the shadows of fair-weather clouds passing over the landscape. You could hardly distinguish them from forests. It reminded me of similar shadows seen on the sea from the high bank of Cape Cod beach. There the perfect equality of the sea atoned for the comparatively slight elevation of the bank. . . . In the valley or on the plain you do not commonly notice the shadow of a cloud unless you are in it, but on a mountain top or on a lower elevation in a plane country, or by the sea-side, the shadows of clouds flitting over the landscape are a never - failing source of

amusement. It is commonly easy enough to refer a shadow to its cloud, since in one direction
its form is perceived with sufficient accuracy.
Yet I was surprised to observe that a long, straggling, downy cumulus, extending north and south
a few miles east of us, when the sun was perhaps
an hour high, cast its shadow along the base of
the Peterboro hills, and did not fall on the other
side, as I should have expected. It proved the
clouds not so high as I had supposed. . . . It
was pleasant enough to see one man's farm in
the shadow of a cloud, which perhaps he thought
covered all the Northern States, while his neighbor's farm was in sunshine.

June 4th. At six A. M. we began to descend.
As you are leaving a mountain and looking back
at it from time to time, it is interesting to see
how it gradually gathers up its slopes and spurs
to itself into a regular whole, and makes a new
and total impression.

June 2, 1859. Found, within three rods of
Flint's Pond, a rose-breasted grossbeak's nest,
and one fresh egg (three on the 4th). It was
in a thicket where there was much catbriar, in
a high blueberry bush, some five feet from the
ground, in the forks of the bush, and of very
loose construction, being made of the dead gray
extremities of the catbriar with its tendrils (and

some of them had dropped on the ground beneath), and this was lined, lined merely, with fine brown stems of weeds, like pinweeds, without any leaves or anything else, a slight nest on the whole. Saw the birds. The male uttered a very peculiar sharp clicking or squeaking note of alarm while I was near the nest. The egg is thickly spotted with reddish brown on a pale blue ground (not white ground, as Buonaparte and the New York ornithologist says), like a hermit thrush's, but rounder, very delicate.

June 2, 1860. A boy brought me yesterday a nest with two Maryland yellow-throat's eggs and two cow-bird's eggs in it, and said that they were all found together.

You see now in suitable shallow and warm places, where there is a sandy bottom, the nests of the bream begun, circular hollows recently excavated, weeds, *confervæ*, and other rubbish neatly removed, and many whitish root fibres of weeds left bare and exposed.

8 P. M. Up Assabet. Bats go over, and a king-bird very late. . . . Ever and anon we hear the stake-driver from a distance. There is a more distinct sound from animals than by day, and an occasional bull-frog's trump is heard. Turning the island, I hear a very faint and slight screwing or working sound once, and suspect a screech owl, which I afterwards see on an oak. I

soon hear its mournful scream, probably to its mate ; not loud now, but though within thirty or thirty-two rods, sounding a mile off. I hear it louder from my bed at night.

June 3, 1838. Walden.

" True, our converse a stranger is to speech ;
Only the practised ear can catch the surging words
That break and die upon thy pebbled lips.
Thy flow of thought is noiseless as the lapse of thy own
    waters,
Wafted as is the morning mist up from thy surface,
So that the passive soul doth breathe it in,
And is infected with the truth thou wouldst express."

June 3, 1853. p. m. To Anursnack. By way of the Linnæa, which I find is not yet out. That thick pine wood is full of birds. . . . The painted cup is in its prime. It reddens the meadow, Painted Cup Meadow. It is a splendid show of brilliant scarlet, the color of the cardinal flower and surpassing it in mass and profusion. They first appear on the side of the hill, on dryer ground, half a dozen inches high, and the color is most striking then, when it is most rare and precious ; but they now cover the meadow mingled with buttercups, etc., and many are more than eight inches high. I do not like the name. It does not remind me of a cup, rather of a flame when it first appears. It might be called flame flower, or scarlet tip. Here is a large meadow full of it, and yet very

few in the town have ever seen it. It is startling to see a leaf thus brilliantly painted, as if
its tip were dipped into some scarlet tincture,
surpassing most flowers in intensity of color.

Seen from Anursnack the woods now appear
full-leafed, smooth green, no longer hoary, and
the pines a dark mulberry, not green. But you
are still covered with lint as you go through the
copses. Summer begins when the hoariness dis-
appears from the forest as you look down on it,
and gives place thus to smooth green, full and
universal.

The song of the robin and the chirp (?) of the
chip-bird now begin prominently to usher in and
to conclude the day. The robin's song seems
not so loud as in the early spring, perhaps because there are so many other sounds at present.

June 3, 1854. 9 A. M. To Fair Haven. Going up Fair Haven Hill, the blossoms of the
huckleberries and blueberries imparted a sweet
scent to the whole hillside. . . . On the pond
played a long time with the bubbles which we
made with our paddles on the smooth, perhaps
unctuous surface, in which little hemispherical
cases we saw ourselves and boat, small, black, and
distinct, with a fainter reflection on the opposite
side of the bubble (head to head). These lasted
sometimes a minute before they burst. They reminded me more of Italy than of New Eng-

land. . . . Thought how many times other similar bubbles, which had now burst, had reflected here the Indian, his canoe and paddle, with the same faithfulness that they now image me and my boat.

June 3, 1856. While running a line in the woods close to the water on the southwest side of Loring's Pond, I observed a chickadee sitting quietly within a few feet. Suspecting a nest, I looked and found it in a small, hollow maple stump, which was about five inches in diameter and two feet high. I looked down about a foot, and could just discern the eggs. Breaking off a little, I managed to get my hand in and took out some eggs. There were seven, making by their number an unusual figure, as they lay in the nest, a sort of egg rosette, a circle around, with one or more in the middle. In the meanwhile the bird sat silent, though rather restless, within three feet. The nest was very thick and warm, of average depth, and made of the bluish slate rabbit's (?) fur. The eggs were a perfect oval, five-eighths of an inch long, white, with small reddish-brown or rusty spots, especially about larger end, partly developed. The bird sat on the remaining eggs next day. I called off the boy in another direction that he might not find it.

Picked up a young wood tortoise about an

inch and a half long, but very orbicular. Its
scales very distinct, and, as usual, very finely and
distinctly sculptured ; but there was no orange
on it, only buff or leather color on the sides beneath. So the one of similar rounded form and
size, and with distinct scales, but faint yellow
spots on back, must have been a young spotted
turtle, I think, after all.

June 3, 1857. P. M. To White Cedar Swamp.
. . . I see a branch of *Salix lucida* which has
been broken off, probably by the ice in the winter, and come down from far up stream, and
lodged, butt downward, amid some bushes, where
it has put forth pink fibres from the butt end in
the water, and is growing vigorously, though
not rooted in the bottom. Thus detained, it begins to sprout and send its pink fibres down to
the mud, and finally the water, getting down
to the summer level, leaves it rooted in the
bank. . . .

The pitch pine at Hemlocks is in bloom. The
sterile flowers are yellowish, while those of the
Pinus resinosa are dark purple. As usual, when
I jar them, the pollen rises in a little cloud
about the pistillate flowers and the tops of the
twigs, there being a little wind. . . .

I have several friends and acquaintances who
are very good companions in the house, or for
an afternoon walk, but whom I cannot make up

my mind to make a longer excursion with, for I
discover all at once that they are too gentle-
manly in manners, dress, and all their habits.
I see in my mind's eye that they wear black
coats, considerable starched linen, glossy boots
and shoes, and it is out of the question. It is a
great disadvantage for a traveler to be a gentleman of this kind, he is so ill-treated, only a prey
to landlords. It would be too much of a circumstance to enter a strange town or house with
such a companion. You could not travel incog-
nito. You might get into the papers. You
should travel as a common man. If such a one
were to set out to make a walking journey, he
would betray himself at every step. Every one
would see that he was trying an experiment, as
plainly as they see that a lame man is lame by
his limping. The natives would bow to him,
other gentlemen would invite him to ride, conductors would warn him that this was the second-
class car, and many would take him for a clergy-
man, and so he would be continually pestered
and balked and run upon. He could not see the
natives at all. Instead of going in quietly and
sitting by the kitchen fire, he would be shown
into a cold parlor, there to confront a fire-board
and excite a commotion in a whole family. The
women would scatter at his approach, and the
husbands and sons would go right off to hunt up

3

their black coats, for they all have them. They
are as cheap as dirt. He would go trailing his
limbs along the highways, mere bait for corpu-
lent innholders, as a frog's leg is trolled along a
stream to catch pickerel, and his part of the
profits would be the frog's. No, you must be a
common man, or at least travel as one, and then
nobody will know you are there or have been
there. I could not undertake a simple pedes-
trian excursion with one of these, because to enter a village or a hotel or a private house with
such a one would be too great a circumstance,
would create too great a stir. You would not
go half as far with the same means, for the price
of board and lodging would rise everywhere; so
much you have to pay for wearing that kind of
coat. Not that the difference is in the coat at
all, for the character of the scurf is determined
by that of the true liber beneath. Innkeepers,
stablers, conductors, clergymen, know a true way-
faring man at first sight, and let him alone. It
is of no use to shove your gaiter shoes a mile further than usual. Sometimes it is mere shiftless-
ness or want of originality; *the clothes wear
them.* Sometimes it is egoism that cannot afford
to be treated like a common man; *they wear
the clothes.* They wish to be at least fully appreciated by every stage-driver and school-boy.
They would like well enough to see a new place,

perhaps, but then they would like to be regarded
as important public personages. They would
consider it a misfortune if their names were left
out of the published list of passengers, because
they came in the steerage, an obscurity from
which they might never emerge.

June 3, 1860. These are the clear breezy
days of early June, when the leaves are young
and few, and the sorrel not yet in its prime.
Perceive the meadow fragrance. . . . The roads
are strewn with red maple seed. The pine
shoots have grown generally from three to six
inches, and begin to make a distinct impression,
even at some distance, of white and brown above
their dark green. The foliage of deciduous
trees is still rather yellow-green than green.
Tree-toads heard. There are various sweet
scents in the air now. Especially as I go along
an arbor-vitæ hedge, I perceive a very distinct
fragrance like strawberries from it.

June 4, 1852. The birds sing at dawn.
What sounds to be awakened by ! If only our
sleep, our dreams are such as to harmonize with
the song, the warbling of the birds ushering in
the day. They appear comparatively silent an
hour or two later.

The dandelions are almost all gone to seed,
and children may now see if "your mother
wants you." . . . Lupines in prime. The Can-

ada snapdragon, that little blue flower that lasts so long, grows with the lupines under Fair Haven. The early chickweed? with the star-shaped flower, cerastium? is common in fields now.

June 4, 1853. The date of the introduction of the *Rhododendron maximum* into Concord is worth preserving, May 16, 1853. They were small plants one to four feet high, some with large flower buds, twenty-five cents apiece, and I noticed the next day one or more in every front yard on each side of the street, and the inhabitants out watering them. Said to be the most splendid native flower in Massachusetts. In a swamp in Medfield. I hear to-day that one in town has blossomed. . . . The clintonia is abundant in Hubbard's shady swamp, along by the foot of the hill, and in its prime. Look there for its berries. Commonly four leaves there with an obtuse point. — The lady's slipper leaf out, so rich, dark green and smooth, having several channels. The bull-frog now begins to be heard at night regularly, has taken the place of the hylodes.

Looked over the earliest town records at the clerk's office this evening, the old book containing grants of land. Am surprised to find such names as " Wallden Pond " and " Fair Haven " as early as 1653, and apparently '52; also under

the first date, at least, "2d Division," the rivers
as North and South rivers (not Assabet at that
date), "Swamp Bridge," apparently on Back
road, "Goose Pond," "Mr. Flint's Pond,"
"Nutt Meadow," "Willow Swamp," "Spruce
Swamp," etc., etc. . . . It is pleasing to read
these evergreen wilderness names, now, perchance, cleared fields and meadows, said to be
redeemed. The 2d Division appears to have
been a very large tract between the two rivers.

June 4, 1854. 8 A. M. Up Assabet with
B—— and B——.

These warm and dry days which put Spring
far behind, the sound of the crickets at noon has
a new value and significance, so severe and cool.
It is the *iced* cream of song. It is modulated
shade.

I see now, here and there, deep furrows in the
sandy bottom, two or three inches wide, leading
from the middle of the river toward the side,
and a clam on its edge at the end of each.
There are distinct white lines. Plainly, then,
about these times the clams are coming up to
the shore, and I have caught them in the act.

P. M. To Walden. Now is the time to observe the leaves, so fair in color and so perfect
in form. I stood over a sprig of chokeberry
with fair and perfect glossy, green, obovate and
serrate leaves in the woods this P. M., as if it

were a rare flower. Now the various forms of
oak leaves in sproutlands, wet-glossy, as if newly
painted green and varnished, attract me. The
chinquapin and black shrub oaks have such
leaves as I fancy crowns were made of. And
in the washing breeze the lighter under-sides begin to show, and a new light is flashed upon the
year, lighting up and enlivening the landscape.
Perhaps, on the whole, as most of the undersides
are of a glaucous hue, they add to the glaucous
mistiness of the atmosphere which now has begun to prevail. The mountains are hidden. The
first drought may be beginning. The dust is
powdery in the street, and we do not always
have dew in the night.

In some cases Fame is perpetually false and
unjust. Or rather I should say that she never
recognizes the simple heroism of an action, but
only as connected with its apparent consequence.
She praises the interested energy of the Boston
Tea Party, but will be comparatively silent
about the more bloody and disinterestedly heroic
attack on the Boston Court House, simply because the latter was unsuccessful. Fame is not
just.. She never finely or discriminatingly
praises, but coarsely hurrahs. The truest acts
of heroism never reach her ear, are never published by her trumpet.

June 4, 1855. P. M. To Hubbard's Close.

White clover out probably some days; also red, as long. . . . It has just cleared off after this first rain of consequence for a long time, and now I observe the shadows of massive clouds still floating here and there in the peculiarly blue sky. These dark shadows on field and wood are the more remarkable by contrast to the light, yellow-green foliage, and where they rest on evergreens, they are doubly dark, like dark rings about the eyes of June. Great white-bosomed clouds, darker beneath, float through the clearest sky, and are seen against its delicious blue, such a sky as we have not had before. This is after the first important rain at this season. The song of birds is more lively and seems to have a new character; a new season has commenced. In the woods I hear the tanager, the chewink, and the redeye. It is fairly summer, and mosquitoes begin to sting in earnest. . . . There are now many potentillas ascendant, and the *Erigeron bellidifolium* I see sixteen inches high and quite handsome. . . . Now the crimson velvety leaves of the black oak, showing also a crimson edge on the downy undersides, are beautiful as a flower, and the more salmon-colored white oak.

The *Linnœa borealis* has grown an inch, but are not the flowers winter-killed? I see dead and blackened flower-buds. Perhaps it should have opened before.

June 4, 1857. P. M.   To Bare Hill. . . .
One thing that chiefly distinguishes this season
from three weeks ago is that fine serene under-
tone or earth-song, as we go by sunny brooks
and hillsides, the creak of crickets, which affects
our thoughts so favorably, imparting its own
serenity.   It is time now to bring our philosophy
out of doors.   Our thoughts pillow themselves
unconsciously in the trough of this serene rippling sea of sound.   Now first we begin to be
peripatetics.   No longer our ears can be content
with the bald echoing earth, but everywhere
recline on the spring-cushion of a cricket's
chirp.   These rills that ripple from every hill-
side become at length a universal sea of sound,
nourishing our ears when we are most unconscious. . . . In the high pasture behind Jacob
Baker's, soon after coming out of the wood, I
scare up a baywing.   She runs several rods
close to the ground through the thin grass, and
then lurks behind tussocks, etc.   The nest has
four eggs, dull pinkish white with brown spots.
It is low in the ground, made of stubble lined
with white horse-hair.

June 4, 1860.   The foliage of the elms over
the street is dense and heavy already, comparatively.   The black-poll warblers appear to have
left, and some others, if not the warblers generally, with this first clear, bright, and warm

peculiarly June weather, immediately after the May rain. About a month ago, after the stormy and cold winds of March and April, and the (in common years) rain and high water, the ducks, etc., left us for the north. Now there is a similar departure of the warblers, on the expansion of the leaves and advent of yet warmer weather. Their season with us, *i. e.*, the season of those that go further, is when the buds are bursting, till the leaves are about expanded, and probably they follow these phenomena northward till they get to their breeding places, flying from tree to tree, *i. e.*, to the next tree north which contains their insect prey. . . .

The clear brightness of June was well represented yesterday by the buttercups (*Ranunculus bulbosus*) along the roadside. Their yellow cups are glossy and varnished within, but not without. Surely there is no reason why the new butter should not be yellow now.

The time has now come when the laborers, having washed and put on their best suits, walk into the fields on the Sabbath, and lie on the ground at rest.

A cat-bird has her nest in our grove. We cast out strips of white cotton cloth, all of which she picked up and used. I saw a bird flying across the street with so long a strip of cloth, or the like, the other day, and so slowly, that at first I thought it was a little boy's kite, with a long tail. The cat-bird sings less now while its mate is sitting, or may be taking care of her young, and probably this is the case with robins and birds generally.

At the west spring of Fair Haven Hill I cast a bit of wood against a pitch-pine in bloom (perhaps not yet in bloom generally), and I see the yellow pollen dust blown away from it in a faint cloud, distinctly for three rods at least, and gradually rising all the while (rising five or six feet perhaps).

You may say that now, when most trees have fully expanded leaves, and the black ash fairly shows green, that the leafy season has commenced. (I see that I so called it May 27 and 31, 1853.)

June 5, 1850. To-night, after a hot day, I hear the first peculiar summer breathing of the frogs.

The other day, when I walked to Goodman's Hill, it seemed to me that the atmosphere was never so full of fragrance and spicy odors. There is a great variety in the fragrance of the apple blossoms as well as in their tints. Some are quite spicy. The air seemed filled with the odor of ripe strawberries, though it is quite too early for them. The earth was not only fragrant, but sweet and spicy, reminding us of Arabian gales, and what mariners tell of the Spice Islands.

The first of June, when the lady's slipper and the wild pink have come out in sunny places on the hill-sides, then the summer is begun according to the clock of the seasons.

June 5, 1852. The medeola has blossomed in a tumbler. I seem to perceive a pleasant fugacious fragrance from its rather delicate, but inconspicuous, green flower. Its whorls of leaves of two stages are the most remarkable. I do not perceive the smell of the cucumber in its root.

To Harrington's. P. M. The silvery cinquefoil, *Potentilla argentea*, now. A delicate spring yellow, sunny yellow (before the dog-days) flower. None of the fire of autumnal yellows in it. Its silvery leaf is as good as a flower. White weed.

The constant inquiry which Nature puts is, " Are you virtuous ? Then you can behold me." Beauty, fragrance, music, sweetness, and joy of all kinds are for the virtuous. That I thought when I heard the telegraph harp to-day.

The *Viola lanceolata* now, instead of the *Viola blanda*. In some places the leaves of the last are grown quite large. The side-saddle flower. The *Thalictrum* anemonoides still. The dwarf cornel by Harrington's road looks like large snow-flakes on the hill-side, it is so thick. It is a neat, geometrical flower, of a pure white, sometimes greenish, or green.

Some poet must sing in praise of the bulbous *Arethusa*.

The lupine is now in its glory. It is the more important, because it occurs in such extensive patches, even an acre or more together, and of such a pleasing variety of colors, purple, pink or lilac, and white, especially with the sun on it, when the transparency of the flower makes its color changeable. It paints a whole hill-side with its blue, making such a field (if not meadow) as Proserpine might have wandered in. Its leaf was made to be covered with dew-drops. I am quite excited by this prospect of blue flowers in clumps, with narrow intervals, such a profusion of the heavenly, the Elysian color, as if these were the Elysian Fields. . . . That is the value of the lupine. The earth is blued with it. Yet a third of a mile distant I do not detect their color on the hill-side. Perchance because it is the color of the air. It is not distinct enough. You may have passed along here a fortnight ago, and the hill-side was comparatively barren, but now you come, and these glorious redeemers appear to have flashed out here all at once. Who plants the seeds of lupines in the barren soil? Who watereth the lupines in the fields?

De Kay of the New York Report says the bream " is of no value as an article of food, but is often caught for amusement." I think it is the sweetest fish in our river.

June 5, 1853. 5 A. M. By river to Nashawtuck. For the most part we are inclined to
doubt the prevalence of gross superstition among
the civilized ancients ; whether the Greeks, for
instance, accepted literally the mythology which
we accept as matchless poetry. But we have
only to be reminded of the kind of respect paid to
the Sabbath as a *holy* day here in New England,
and the fears which haunt those who break it, to
see that our neighbors are the creatures of an
equally gross superstition with the ancients. I
am convinced that there is no very important
difference between a New Englander's religion
and a Roman's. We both worship in the shadow
of our sins. They erect the temples for us. Je-
hovah has no superiority to Jupiter. The New
Englander is " a pagan suckled in a creed out-
worn." Superstition has always reigned. It is
absurd to think that these farmers, dressed in
their Sunday clothes, proceeding to church, differ
essentially in this respect from the Roman peas-
antry. They have merely changed the name and
number of their gods. Men were as good then
as they are now, and loved one another as much
or as little. . . .

P. M. To Mason's Pasture.

The world is now full of verdure and fragrance, and the air comparatively clear (not yet
the constant haze of the dog-days), through

which the distant fields are seen, reddened with sorrel, the meadows wet - green, full of fresh grass, and the trees in their first beautiful, bright, untarnished, and unspotted green. May is the bursting into leaf and early flowering with much coolness and wet, and a few decidedly warm days ushering in summer; June, verdure and growth, with not intolerable, but agreeable heat.

The young pitch pines in Mason's Pasture are a glorious sight now, most of the shoots grown six inches, so soft and blue-green, nearly as wide as high. It is Nature's front yard. The mountain laurel shows its red flower buds, but many shoots have been killed by frost.

There is a tract of pasture and wood land, orchard, and swamp in the north part of the town through which the old Carlisle road runs, which is nearly two miles square, without a single house, and with scarcely any cultivated land, four square miles. . . .

I perceive some black birch leaves with a beautiful crimson kind of sugaring along the furrows of the nerves, giving them a bright crimson color, either a fungus or the deposit of an insect. Seen through a microscope it sparkles like a ruby.

Nature is fair in proportion as the youth is pure. The heavens and the earth are one flower. The earth is the calyx; the heavens, the corolla.

June 5, 1854.   6 P. M.   To Cliffs.   Now, just
before sundown, a night-hawk is circling imp-
like with undulating, irregular flight over the
sproutland on the Cliff Hill with an occasional
squeak, and showing the spot on his wings.   He
does not circle away from this place, and I associate him with two gray eggs somewhere on the
ground beneath, and a mate there sitting.   This
squeak and occasional booming is heard in the
evening air, while the stillness on the side of the
village makes more distinct the increased hum
of insects.

I see at a distance a king-bird, or blackbird,
pursuing a crow lower down the hill, like a satel-
lite revolving about a black planet.   I have come
to the hill to see the sun go down, to recover san-
ity, and put myself again in relation with Nature.
I would fain drink a draught of Nature's serenity.   Let deep answer to deep.   Already I see
reddening clouds reflected in the smooth mirror
of the river, a delicate tint, far off and elysian,
unlike anything in the sky as yet.   The evergreens now look even black by contrast with the
sea of fresh and light green foliage which sur-
rounds them.   Children have been to the cliffs
and woven wreaths or chaplets of oak leaves
which they have left, unconsciously attracted by
the beauty of the leaves now.   The sun goes
down red and shorn of his beams, a sign of hot

weather, as if the western horizon or the lower stratum of the air were filled with the hot dust of the day. The dust of his chariot eclipses his beams. I love to sit here and look off into the broad deep vale in which the shades of night are beginning to prevail. When the sun has set, the river becomes more white and distinct in the landscape. . . . I return by moonlight.

June 5, 1855. P. M.   To Clam Shell by river.
. . . I am much interested to see how Nature proceeds to heal the wounds where the turf was stripped off this meadow. There are large patches where nothing remained but pure black mud, nearly level, or with slight hollows like a plate in it. This the sun and air had cracked into irregular polygonal figures, a foot, more or less, in diameter. The whole surface of these patches is now covered with a short, soft, and pretty dense moss-like vegetation springing up and clothing it. The little hollows and the cracks are filled with a very dense growth of reddish grass or sedge, about an inch high, the growth in the cracks making pretty regular figures as in a carpet, while the intermediate spaces are very evenly, but much more thinly covered with minute sarothra and whitish *Gnaphalium uliginosum.* Thus the wound is at once scarred over. Apparently the seeds of that grass were heavier and were washed into the hol-

lows and cracks. It is not likely that the owner
has sprinkled seed here.

June 5, 1856. Everywhere now in dry pitch-
pine woods stand the red lady's slippers over the
red pine leaves on the forest floor, rejoicing in
June, with their two broad, curving green leaves
(some even in swamps), upholding their rich,
striped, drooping sack.

A cuckoo's nest with three light bluish-green
eggs, partly developed, short, with rounded ends,
nearly of a size; in a black cherry-tree that had
been lopped three feet from the ground, amid the
thick sprouts; of twigs, lined with *green* leaves,
pine needles, etc., and edged with some dry,
branchy weeds. The bird stole off silently at
first.

[*June* 10. The cuckoo of June 5 has deserted
her nest, and I find the fragments of eggshells in
it; probably because I found it.]

June 5, 1857. I am interested in each contemporary plant in my vicinity, and have attained to a certain acquaintance with the larger
ones. They are cohabitants with me of this part
of the planet, and they bear familiar names.
Yet how essentially wild they are, as wild really
as those strange fossil plants whose impression I
see on my coal. Yet I can imagine that some
race gathered those too with as much admiration and knew them as intimately as I do these,

4

that even they served for a language of the sentiments. Stigmariæ stood for a human sentiment in that race's flower language. Chickweed or a pine-tree is but little less wild. I assume to be acquainted with these, but what ages between me and the tree whose shade I enjoy. It is as if it stood substantially in a remote geological period.

June 5, 1860. . . . When I open my window at night, I hear the peeping of the hylodes distinctly through the rather cool rain (as also some the next A. M.), but not of toads ; more hylodes than in the late very warm evenings when the toads were heard most numerously. The hylodes evidently love the cooler nights of spring. The toads, the warm days and nights of May. Now it requires a cool (and better if wet) night, which will silence the toads, to make the hylodes distinct.

June 6, 1852. First devil's needles in the air, and some smaller bright green ones on flowers. The earliest blueberries are now forming as green berries. The wind already injures the just expanded leaves, tearing them and making them turn black. . . . The side-flowering sandwort, an inconspicuous white flower like a chickweed.

June 6, 1853, 4.30 A. M. To Linnæa Woods. The Linnæa just out.

Corydalis glauca, a delicate glaucous plant rarely met with, with delicate flesh-colored and yellow flowers, covered with a glaucous bloom, on dry rocky hills. Perhaps it suggests gentility. Set it down as early as middle of May or earlier. . . .

This morning I hear the note of young bluebirds in the air, which have recently taken wing, and the old birds keep up such a warbling and twittering as remind me of spring.

According to S——'s account, she must have seen an emperor moth, " pea-green with something like maple keys for tail," in a lady's hand in Cambridge to-day. So one may have come out of the chrysalid seen May 23d.

P. M. To Conantum by boat. . . . Blue-eyed grass now begins to give that slaty blue tint to meadows.

The deep shadow of Conantum Cliff and of mere prominences in the hills, now at mid-afternoon as we row by, is very interesting. It is the most pleasing contrast of light and shade that I notice. Methinks that in winter a shadow is not attractive. The air is very clear, at least as we look from the river valley, and the landscape all swept and brushed. We seem to see to some depth into the side of Fair Haven Hill.

The side-saddle flowers are now in their prime. There are some very large ones hereabouts, five inches in diameter when you flatten out their petals, like great dull-red roses. Their petals are of a peculiar red, and the upper sides of their calyx leaves, of a shiny leather red or brown red, are agreeable.

A slippery elm, *Ulmus fulva*, on Lee's Cliff, red elm. Put it with the common. It has large rough leaves and straggling branches, a rather small, much-spreading tree, with an appearance between the common elm and ironwood.

The aspect of the dry rocky hills already indicates the rapid revolution of the seasons. The spring, that early age of the world, following hard on the reign of winter, and the barren rocks yet dripping with it, is past. How many plants have already dried up, lichens and algæ, which we can still remember as if belonging to a former epoch, saxifrage, crowfoot, anemone, columbine for the most part, etc. It is Lee's Cliff I am on. There is a growth confined to the damp and early spring. How dry and crisp the turf feels there now, not moist with melted snows, remembering, as it were, when it was the bottom of the sea. How wet-glossy the leaves of the red oak now, fully expanded. They shine as when the sun comes out after rain.

I find on a shelf of the rock the *Turritis stricta*, now gone to seed, two feet two inches high, . . . pods upright and nearly three inches long, linear and flat, leaves decidedly lanceolate or linear. Some minute, imperfect, unexpanded flowers, still on it, appear as if they would have been yellowish.

In the very open park in rear of the rocks on the hill-top, where lambkill and huckleberries and grass alternate, came to one of those handsome, round, mirror-like pools, a rod or two in diameter, and surrounded with a border of fine weeds, such as you frequently meet with on the top of springy hills. Though warm and muddy at bottom, they are very beautiful and glassy, and look as if they were cool springs, so high, exposed to the light, yet so wild and fertile ; as if the fertility of the lowlands was transferred to the summit of the hills. They are the kind of mirrors at which the huntresses in the golden age arranged their toilets, which the deer frequented and contemplated their branching horns in.

June 6, 1854. I perceive the sweetness of the locust blossoms fifteen or twenty rods off, as I go down the street. P. M. To Assabet bathing place and return by Stone Bridge. . . . The painted tortoises are now-a-days laying their eggs. I see where they have just been digging in the sand or gravel in a hundred places on the southerly sides of hills and banks near the river, but they have laid their eggs in very few. I find none whole. Here is one which has made its hole with the hind part of its shell and its tail, apparently. . . . They are remarkably circumspect, and it is difficult to see one working. They stop instantly and draw in their heads, and do not move till you are out of sight, and then probably try a new place. They have dabbled in the sand and left the marks of their tails all around.

The black oaks, birches, etc., are covered with ephemeræ of various sizes and colors, with one, two, or three, or no streamers, ready to take wing at evening, *i. e.*, about seven. I am covered with them and much incommoded.

The air over the river meadows is saturated with sweetness, but I look round in vain for the source, on the yellowish sensitive fern and the reddish eupatorium springing up.

From time to time at mid-afternoon, is heard the trump of a bull-frog, like a triton's horn.

I am struck now by the large, light-purple, *Viola palmatas* rising above the grass near the river.

Of oak leaves, there is the small, firm, few-lobed, wholesome, dark-green shrub oak leaf, light beneath.

The more or less deeply cut, and more or less dark green, or sometimes reddish, black oak, not light beneath. These two, bristle-pointed.

The very wet-glossy, obovatish, sinuate-edged swamp white oak, light beneath.

The small narrower, sinuated, and still more chestnut-like chinquapin, a little lighter beneath.

All these, more or less glossy, especially the swamp-white and shrub.

Then the dull green, *sometimes* reddish, more or less deeply cut or fingered, unarmed, round-lobed white oak, not light beneath.

The last three without bristles.

I remember best the sort of rosettes made by the wet-glossy leaves at the ends of some swamp white oak twigs; also the wholesome and firm dark green shrub oak leaves, and some glossy and finely cut light green, black? or red? or scarlet? oak leaves.

I see some devil's needles, a brilliant green with white and black, or open work and black wings, some with clear black wings, some with white bodies and black wings, etc.

6.30 A. M. Up Assabet. . . . Beautiful the hemlock fans now, broad at the ends of the lower branches which slant down, seen in the shade against the dark hillside; such is the contrast of the very light green just put forth on their edges, with the old, very dark. I feast my eyes on it.

Sphynx moths about the flowers at evening, a night or two.

June 6th, 1855. You see the dark eye and shade of June on the river as well as on land, and a dust-like lint on river, apparently from the young leaves and bud scales, covering the waters which begin to be smooth, and imparting a sense of depth.

Blue-eyed grass, may be several days, in some places.

White weed, two or three days.

June 6, 1856. P. M. To Andromeda Ponds. Cold, mizzling weather. In the large circular hole or cellar at the turn-table on the railroad, which they are repairing, I see a star-nosed mole endeavoring in vain to bury himself in the sandy and gravelly bottom. Some inhuman fellow has cut off his tail. He is blue-black, with much fur, a very thick, plump animal, apparently some four inches long, but he occasionally shortens himself one third or more; looks as fat as a fat hog. His fore-feet are large, and set side-wise, or on their edges, and with these he shovels the earth aside, while his large, long, starred snout is feeling the way and breaking ground. I see deep indentations in his fur, where his eyes are situated, and once I saw distinctly his eye open, a dull, blue?-black bead, not very small; and he very plainly noticed my movements two feet off. He was using his eye as plainly as any creature that I ever saw. Yet it is said to be a question

whether their eyes are not merely rudimentary.
. . . I carried him along to plowed ground where
he buried himself in a minute or two.

How well-suited the lining of a bird's nest not
only to the comfort of the young, but to keep
the eggs from breaking, fine elastic grass stems
or root fibres, pine needles, hair, or the like.
These tender and brittle things, which you can
hardly carry in cotton, lie there without harm.

June 6, 1857. 8 A. M. To Lee's Cliff by
river. . . . This is June, the month of grass
and leaves. Already the aspens are trembling
again, and a new summer is offered me. I feel
a little fluttered in my thoughts, as if I might
be too late. Each season is but an infinitesimal
point. It no sooner comes than it is gone. It
has no duration. It simply gives a tone and hue
to my thought. Each annual phenomenon is a
reminiscence and prompting. Our thoughts and
sentiments answer to the revolutions of the seasons as two cog-wheels fit into each other. We
are conversant with only one point of contact
at a time, from which we receive a prompting
and impulse, and instantly pass to a new season
or point of contact. A year is made up of a
certain series and number of sensations and
thoughts, which have their language in nature.
Now I am ice, now I am sorrel. Each experience reduces itself to a mood of the mind. I see

a man grafting, for instance. What this imports chiefly is not apples to the owner or bread to the grafter, but a certain mood or train of thought to my mind. That is what the grafting is to me. Whether it is anything at all, even apples or bread, to anybody else, I cannot swear, for it would be worse than swearing through glass. I only see those other facts as through a glass, darkly. . . .

Krigias, with their somewhat orange yellow, spot the dry hills all the forenoon, and are very common, but as they are closed in the afternoon, they are but rarely noticed by walkers.

June 6, 1860. . . . 6.30 P. M. Up Assabet.

. . . Not only the foliage begins to look dark and dense, but many ferns are fully grown, as the cinnamon and interrupted, and being curved over the bank and shore, add to the leafy impression of the season. The *Osmunda regalis* looks later and more tender, reddish brown still. It preserves its habit of growing in circles, though it may be on a steep bank, and one half the circle in the water. . . .

The trees commonly are not yet so densely leaved but that I can see through them, *e. g.*, I see through the red oak and the bass (below Dome Rock), looking toward the sky. They are a mere network of light and shade after all. The oak may be a little the thicker.

The white ash is considerably thinner than either. . . .

How full is the air of sound at sunset and just after! Especially at the end of a rain storm. Every bird seems to be singing in the wood across the stream, and there are the hylodes and the sounds of the village. Beside, sounds are more distinctly heard. Ever and anon we hear a few sucks or strokes from the bittern or stake driver, whenever we lie to, as if he had taken the job of extending all the fences up the river, to keep the cows from straying. We hear but three or four toads in all, to-night, but as many hylodes as ever. It is too cool, both water and air (especially the first), after the rain, for the toads. . . .

As the light is obscured after sunset, the birds rapidly cease their songs, and the swallows cease to flit over the river. Soon the bats are seen taking the places of the swallows, and flying back and forth like them, and commonly a late king-bird will be heard twittering still in the air. After the bats, or half an hour after sunset, the water bugs begin to spread themselves over the stream (though fifteen minutes earlier not one was seen without the pads), now when it is difficult to see them or the dimples they make, except you look toward the reflected western sky. It is evident that they dare not come out thus by day for fear of fishes, and probably the nocturnal or vespertinal fishes, as eels and pouts, do not touch them. I think I see them all over Walden by day, and if so, it may be because there is not much danger from fishes in that very deep water.

June 7, 1841. . . . We are accustomed to exaggerate the immobility and stagnation of those eras [the early Oriental], as of the waters which leveled the steppes; but those slow revolving "years of the gods" were as rapid to all the needs of virtue as these bustling and hasty seasons. Man stands to revere, he kneels to pray. Methinks history will have to be tried by new tests to show what centuries were rapid and what slow. Corn grows in the night. Will this bustling era detain the future reader longer? Will the earth seem to have conversed more with the heavens during these times? Who is writing better Vedas? How science and art spread and flourished, how trivial conveniences were multiplied, that which is the gossip of the world is not recorded in them, and if they are left out of our scriptures, too, what will remain?

Since the battle of Bunker Hill we think the world has not been at a stand-still.

June 7, 1851. My practicalness is not to be trusted to the last. To be sure, I go upon my legs for the most part, but being hard pushed and dogged by a superficial common sense which is bound to near objects by beaten paths, I am off the handle, as the phrase is; I begin to be transcendental and show where my heart is. I am like those Guinea fowl which Charles Darwin saw at the Cape de Verde Islands. He says: "They avoided us like partridges on a rainy day in September, running with their heads cocked up, and if pursued they readily took to the wing." Keep your distance, do not impinge on the interval between us, and I will pick up lime and lay real terrestrial eggs for you, and let you know by cackling when I have done it. When I have been asked to speak at a temperance meeting, my answer has been, I am too transcendental to serve you in your way. They would fain confine me to the rum-sellers and rum-drinkers, of whom I am not one, and whom I know little about. . . . There are few so temperate that they can afford to remind us even at table that they have a palate and a stomach.

We believe that the possibility of the future far exceeds the accomplishments of the past. We review the past with the common sense, but we anticipate the future with transcendental senses. In any sanest moments we find ourselves naturally expecting or prepared for far greater changes than any which we have experi-

enced within the period of distinct memory, only
to be paralleled by experiences which are forgotten. Perchance there are revolutions which
create an interval impossible to the memory.

One of those gentle, straight-down rainy days,
when the rain begins by spotting the cultivated
fields, as if shaken down from a pepper-box; a
fishing day, when I see one neighbor after another, having donned his oil-cloth suit, walking
or riding past with a fish-pole, having struck
work, a day and an employment to make philosophers of them all.

June 7, 1853. P. M. To Walden. Clover begins to redden the fields generally. The quail is
heard at a distance. Buttercups of various kinds
mingled, yellow the meadows, the tall, the bulbous, the repens. The cinquefoil, in its ascending state, keeping pace with the grass, is now
abundant in the fields. Saw it one or two weeks
ago. This is a feature of June. Still both
high and low blueberry and huckleberry blossoms abound. The hemlock woods, their fan-
like sprays edged or spotted with short, yellowish-
green shoots, tier above tier, shelf above shelf,
look like a cool bazaar of rich embroidered
goods. How dense their shade, dark and cool
beneath them, as in a cellar. No plants grow
there, but the ground is covered with fine red
leaves. It is oftenest on a side hill they grow.

The oven-bird runs from her covered nest, so
close to the ground, under the lowest twigs and
leaves, even the loose leaves on the ground, like
a mouse, that I cannot get a fair view of her.
She does not fly at all. Is it to attract me, or
partly to protect herself?

Visited my night-hawk on her nest. Could
hardly believe my eyes when I stood within
seven feet and beheld her sitting on her eggs, her
head towards me; she looked so Saturnian, so
one with the earth, so sphynx-like, a relic of the
reign of Saturn which Jupiter did not destroy,
a riddle that might well cause a man to go dash
his head against a stone. It was not an actual
living creature, far less a winged creature of
the air, but a figure in stone or bronze, a fanciful
production of art, like the gryphon or phœnix.
In fact, with its breast toward me, and, owing to
its color or size, no bill perceptible, it looked like
the end of a brand, such as are common in a
clearing, its breast mottled, or alternately waved
with dark brown and gray, its flat, grayish,
weather-beaten crown, its eyes nearly closed,
purposely, lest these bright beads should betray
it, with the stony cunning of the sphynx. A
fanciful work in bronze to ornament a mantel.
It was enough to fill one with awe. The sight
of this creature sitting on its eggs impressed me
with the venerableness of the globe. There was

nothing novel about it. All the while this seemingly sleeping bronze sphynx, as motionless as
the earth, was watching me with intense anxiety
through those narrow slits in its eyelids. Another step, and it fluttered down the hill, close
to the ground, with a wabbling motion, as if
touching the ground now with the tip of one
wing, now with the other, so ten rods to the
water, which it skimmed close over a few rods,
and then rose and soared in the air above me.
Wonderful creature, which sits motionless on its
eggs, on the barest, most exposed hills, with its
eyes shut and its wings folded; and after the
two days' storm, when you think it has become
a fit symbol of the rheumatism, it suddenly rises
into the air, a bird, one of the most aerial, sup-
ple, and graceful of creatures, without stiffness
in its wings or joints. It was a fit prelude
to meeting Prometheus bound to his rock on
Caucasus.

June 7, 1854. . . . P. M. To Dugan Desert
via Linnæa Hills. Linnæa abundantly out some
days, say three or four.

The locusts so full of pendulous white racemes
five inches long, filling the air with their sweetness, and resounding with the hum of humble
and honey-bees, are very interesting. These racemes are strewn along the path by children.

I am struck by the rank, dog-like scent of the
rue budded to blossom.

I am surprised at the size of green berries, shad-bush, low blueberries, choke-cherries, etc., etc. It is but a step from flower to fruit.

As I expected, I find the desert scored by the tracks of turtles, made evidently last night, though the rain of this morning has obliterated the marks of their tails. The tracks are about seven eighths of an inch in diameter, half an inch deep, two inches apart (from centre to centre) in each row, and the rows four or five inches apart. They have dabbled in the sand in many places, and made some small holes. Yesterday it was hot and dusty, and this morning it rained. Did they choose such a time? Yesterday I saw the painted and the wood tortoise out. Now I see a snapping turtle, its shell about a foot long, out here on the damp sand, with its head out, disturbed by me. It had just been excavating, and its shell, especially the fore part and sides, and still more its snout, were deeply covered with earth. It appears to use its shell as a kind of spade, whose handle is within, tilting it now this way, now that, and perhaps using its head and claws as a pick. It was in a little cloud of mosquitoes, which were continually settling on its head and flippers, but which it did not mind. Its sternum was slightly depressed. It seems that they are frequently found fighting in the water, and sometimes dead in the spring, perhaps killed by the ice.

Common iris some days, one withered.

Saw again what I have pronounced the yellow-winged sparrow, *Fringilla passerina*, with white line down head, and yellow over eyes, and my seringo note. But this time the yellow of wings is not apparent; ochreous throat and breast. Quite different from the bay-wing and smaller.

This muggy evening I see fire-flies, the first I have seen or heard of this year.

June 7, 1855. . . . I have heard no musical gurgle-ee from blackbirds for a fortnight. They are now busy breeding.

June 7, 1858. P. M. To Walden. Warm weather has suddenly come, beginning yesterday. To-day it is yet warmer, 87° at 3 P. M., compelling me to put on a thin coat, and I see that a new season has arrived. June shadows are moving over waving grass fields, the crickets chirp uninterruptedly, and I perceive the agreeable acid scent of high blueberry bushes in bloom. The trees having leaved out, you notice their rounded tops suggesting shade. The night-hawk booms over arid hill-sides and sproutlands.

It is evidence enough against crows, hawks, and owls, proving their propensity to rob birds' nests of eggs and young, that smaller birds pursue them so often. You do not need the testi-

mony of so many farmers' boys when you can
see and hear the small birds daily crying "Thief
and murder" after these spoilers. What does it
signify, the kingbird, blackbird, swallow, etc.,
pursuing a crow. They say plainly enough, " I
know you of old, you villain ; you want to devour my eggs or young. I have often caught
you at it, and I 'll publish you now." And
probably the crow, pursuing the fish-hawk and
eagle, proves that the latter sometimes devour
their young.

As I was wading in this Wyman meadow, looking for bull-frog spawn, I saw a hole at the bottom where it was six or eight inches deep, by the
side of a mass of mud and weeds, which rose
just to the surface three or four feet from the
shore. It was about five inches in diameter, with
some sand at the mouth, just like a musquash's
hole. As I stood there within two feet, a pout
put her head out, as if to see who was there, and
directly came forth, and disappeared under the
target weed ; but as I stood perfectly still, waiting for the water which I had disturbed to settle
about the hole, she circled round and round several times between me and the hole cautiously,
stealthily approaching the entrance, but as often
withdrawing, and at last mustered courage to
enter it. I then noticed another similar hole in
the same mass, two or three feet from this. I

thrust my arm into the first, running it down about fifteen inches. It was a little more than a foot long, and enlarged somewhat at the end, the bottom also being about a foot beneath the surface, for it slanted downward. But I felt nothing within. I only felt a pretty regular and rounded apartment with firm walls of weedy or fibrous mud. I then thrust my arm into the other hole, which was longer and deeper, at first discovering nothing. But, trying again, I found that I had not reached the end, for it turned a little and descended more than I supposed. Here I felt a similar apartment or enlargement some six inches in diameter horizontally, but not quite so high, nor nearly so wide at its throat. Here, to my surprise, I felt something soft like a gelatinous mass of spawn, but, feeling a little further, felt the horns of a pout. I deliberately took hold of her by the head, and lifted her out of the hole and the water, having run my arm in two thirds of its length. She offered not the slightest resistance from first to last, even when I held her out of water before my face, and only darted away suddenly when I dropped her into the water. The entrance to the apartment was so narrow that she could hardly have escaped, if I had tried to prevent her. Putting in my arm again, I felt under where she had been, a flattish mass of ova, several inches in diameter,

resting on the mud, and took out some. Feeling
again in the first hole, I found as much more
there. Though I had been stepping round and
over the second nest for several minutes, I had
not scared the pout. The ova of the first nest
already contained *white* wiggling young. I saw
no motion in the others. The ova in each case
were dull yellowish, and the size of small buck-
shot. These nests did not communicate with
each other, and had no other outlet.

Pouts then make their nests in shallow mud-
holes or bays in masses of weedy mud, or probably in the muddy bank, and the old pout hovers
over the spawn or keeps guard at the entrance.
Where do the Walden pouts breed when they
have not access to the meadow? The first pout,
whose eggs were most developed, was the largest,
and had some slight wounds on the back. The
other may have been the male, in the act of fertilizing the ova.

I sit in my boat in the twilight, by the edge
of the river. Bull-frogs now are in full blast.
I do not hear other frogs. Their notes are probably drowned. . . . Some of these great males
are yellow, or quite yellowish over the whole
back. Are not the females oftenest white-
throated? What lungs, what health, what ter-
renity (if not serenity) their note suggests! At
length I hear the faint stertoration of a *Rana
palustris* (if not halecina?)

Seeing a large head with its prominent eyes projecting above the middle of the river, I found it was a bull-frog coming across. It swam under water a rod or two, and then came up to see where it was, on its way. It is thus they cross when sounds or sights attract them to more desirable shores. Probably they prefer the night for such excursions, for fear of large pickerel, etc.

June 7, 1860. White clover already whitens some fields, and resounds with bees.

June 8, 1850. Not till June can the grass be said to be waving in the fields. When the frogs dream and the grass waves, and the buttercups toss their heads, and the heat disposes one to bathe in the ponds and streams, then is summer begun.

June 8, 1851. I found the white pine top full of staminate blossom buds, not yet fully grown or expanded, with a rich red tint, like a tree full of fruit, but I could find no pistillate blossom.

June 8, 1853. P. M. To Well Meadow. . . . As I stood by the last small pond near Well Meadow, I heard a hawk scream, and looking up, saw a pretty large one circling not far off, and incessantly screaming, as I at first supposed to scare and so discover its prey. But its screaming was so incessant, and it circled from time to time so near me as I moved southward, that I began to think it had a nest near by, and was angry at my intrusion into its domains. As I moved, the bird still followed and screamed, coming sometimes quite near, or within gunshot, then circling far off or high into the sky. At length, as I was looking up at it, thinking it the only living creature within view, I was singularly startled to behold, as my eye by chance penetrated deeper into the blue, — the abyss of blue above which I had taken for a solitude, — its mate silently soaring at an immense height, and seemingly indifferent to me. We are surprised to discover that there can be an eye on us on that side, and so little suspected, that the heavens are so full of eyes, though they look so blue and spotless. Then I knew that it was the female that circled and screamed below. At last the latter rose gradually to meet her mate, and they circled together there, as if they could not possibly feel any anxiety on my account. When I drew nearer to the tall trees where I suspected the nest to be, the female descended again, swept by screaming, still nearer to me, just over the tree tops, and finally, while I was looking for the orchis in the swamp, alighted on a white pine twenty or thirty rods off. (The great fringed orchis just open.) At length I detected the nest about eighty feet from the ground, in a very large white pine by the edge of the swamp. It was about three feet in diameter, of dry sticks, and a young hawk, apparently as big as its mother, stood on the edge looking down at me, and only moving its head when I moved.

In its imperfect plumage, and the slow motion of its head, it reminded me strongly of a vulture, so large and gaunt. It appeared a tawny brown on its neck and breast, and dark brown or blackish on wings. The mother was light beneath, and apparently lighter still on the rump.

White pine in flower. All the female flowers on the very top of the tree, a small crimson cone upright on the ends of its peduncles, while the last year's, now three or four inches long, and green, are curved downward like scythes. Best seen looking down on the tops of lower pines from the top of a higher one. Apparently just beginning.

June 8, 1854. The *Rosa nitida* bud, which I plucked yesterday, has blossomed to-day, so that notwithstanding the rain, I will put it down for to-day. *Erigeron strigosum* slowly opening, perhaps to-morrow.

Meadow rue, with its rank, dog-like scent. Ribwort plantain is abundantly in bloom, fifteen or sixteen inches high. How long ?

Herndon in his " Exploration of the Amazon," says that " There is wanting an industrious and

active population, who know what the comforts
of life are, and who have artificial wants, to draw
out the great resources of the country." But
what are the "artificial wants" to be encouraged,
and the " great resources " of a country? surely
not the love of luxuries, like the tobacco and
slaves of his native (?) Virginia, or that fertility
of soil which produces these. The chief want is
ever a life of deep experiences, *i. e.*, character,
which alone draws out " the great resources " of
Nature. When our wants cease to be chiefly
superficial and trivial, which is commonly meant
by artificial, and begin to be wants of character,
then the great resources of a country are taxed
and drawn out, and the result, the staple production, is poetry. Have the great resources of
Virginia been drawn out by such artificial wants
as there exist? Was that country really designed
by its maker to produce slaves and tobacco? or
something more than freemen, and food for freemen? Wants of character, aspirations, this is
what is wanted, but what is called civilization
does not always substitute this for the barren
simplicity of the savage.

June 8, 1860. 2 P. M. To Well Meadow
via Walden. Within a day or two has begun
that season of summer when you see afternoon
showers — perhaps with thunder — or the threat
of them dark in the horizon, and are uncertain

whether to venture far away or without an umbrella. I noticed the very first such cloud on the 25th of May ; the dark iris of June. When you go forth to walk at 2 P. M. you see perhaps, in the southwest or west, or may be eastern horizon, a dark and threatening mass of cloud, showing itself just over the woods, its base horizontal and dark, with lighter edges where it is rolled up to the light, while all beneath is a dark skirt of falling rain. These are summer showers, come with the heat of summer.

What delicate fans are the great red - oak leaves, now just developed, so thin, and of so tender a green. They hang loosely, flaccidly down, at the mercy of the wind, like a new-born butterfly or dragon fly. A strong, cold wind would blacken and tear them now. They remind me of the frailest stuffs hung around a dry-goods shop. They have not been hardened by exposure yet, these raw and tender lungs of the tree. The white-oak leaves are especially downy and lint your clothes.

This is truly June when you begin to see brakes (dark green) fully expanded in the wood paths.

In early June, methinks, as now, we have clearer days, less haze, more or less breeze, especially after rain, and more sparkling water, than before. I look from Fair Haven Hill. As there is more shade in the woods, so there is more shade in the sky, *i. e.*, dark, heavy clouds contrasted with the bright sky ; not the gray clouds of spring.

The leaves generally are almost fully expanded, *i. e.*, some of each tree.

June 9–14, 1850. I see the pollen of the pitch-pine now beginning to cover the surface of the pond. Most of the pines at the north-northwest end have none, and in some there is only one pollen-bearing flower.

There are as many strata at different levels of life as there are leaves in a book. Most men have probably lived in two or three. When on the higher levels we can remember the lower, but when on the lower we cannot remember the higher.

My imagination, my love and reverence and admiration, my sense of the miraculous, is not so excited by any event as by the remembrance of my youth. Men talk about Bible miracles because there is no miracle in their lives. Cease to gnaw that crust. There is ripe fruit over your head.

Woe to him who wants a companion, for he is unfit to be the companion even of himself.

We inspire friendship in men when we have contracted friendship with the gods.

When we cease to sympathize with and to be

personally related to men, and begin to be universally related, then we are capable of inspiring others with the sentiment of love for us.

We hug the earth. How rarely we mount! How rarely we climb a tree! We might elevate ourselves. That pine would make us dizzy. You can see the mountains from it as you never did before.

Shall not a man have his spring as well as the plants?

Any reverence even for a material thing proceeds from an elevation of character. Layard, speaking of the reverence for the sun exhibited by the Yezidis, or Worshipers of the Devil, says, " They are accustomed to kiss the object on which the sun's first beams fall; and I have frequently, when traveling in their company at sunrise, observed them perform this ceremony. For fire, as symbolic, they have nearly the same reverence ; they never spit into it, but frequently pass their hands through the flame, kiss them, and pass them over their right eyebrow, or sometimes over the whole face."

Who taught the oven-bird to conceal her nest? It is on the ground, yet out of sight. What cunning there is in Nature! No man could have arranged it more artfully for the purpose of concealment. Only the escape of the bird betrays it.

June 9, 1851. Gathered the *Linnæa borealis.*
June 9, 1852. The buck-bean in Hubbard's
meadow just going out of blossom. The yellow
water ranunculus is an important flower in the
river now, rising above the white lily pads, whose
flower does not yet appear. I perceive that
their petals, washed ashore, line the sand conspicuously.

For a week past we have had washing days.
The grass is waving, and the trees having leaved
out, their boughs feel the effect of the breeze.
Thus new life and motion is imparted to the
trees. The season of waving boughs, and the
lighter under-sides of the new leaves are exposed. This is the first half of June. Already
the grass is not so fresh and liquid velvety a
green, having much of it blossomed, and some
even gone to seed, and it is mixed with reddish
ferns and other plants, but the general leafiness,
shadiness, and waving of grass and boughs
characterize the season. The wind is not quite
agreeable, because it prevents your hearing the
birds sing. Meanwhile the crickets are strength-
ening their choir. The weather is very clear,
and the sky bright. The river shines like silver.
Methinks this is a traveler's month. The locust
in bloom. The undulating rye. The deciduous
trees have filled up the intervals between the
evergreens, and the woods are bosky now.

The priests of the Germans and Britons were Druids. They had their sacred oaken groves. Such were their steeple-houses. Nature was to some extent a fane to them. There was fine religion in that form of worship, and Stonehenge remains are evidence of some vigor in the worshipers, as the pyramids perchance of the vigor of the Egyptians, derived from the slime of the Nile. Evelyn says of the oaks, which he calls "these robust sons of the earth," " 'T is reported that the very shade of this tree is so wholesome that the sleeping or lying under it becomes a present remedy to paralytics, and recovers those whom the mistaken malign influence of the walnut-tree has smitten." Which we may take for a metaphorical expression of the invigorating influence of rude, wild, robust nature compared with the effeminating luxury of civilized life. Evelyn has collected the fine exaggerations of antiquity respecting the virtues and habits of trees, and added some himself. He says, " I am told that those small young acorns which we find in the stock-doves' craws are a delicious fare, as well as those incomparable salads of young herbs taken out of the maws of partridges at a certain season of the year, which gives them a preparation far exceeding all the art of cookery." His oft-repeated glorification of the forest from age to age smacks of religion, is even Druidical. Evelyn is as good as several old Druids, and his " Sylva," is a new kind of prayer-book, a glorifying of the trees and enjoying them forever, which was the chief end of his life.

A child loves to strike on a tin pan or other ringing vessel with a stick, because its ears being fresh, attentive, and percipient, it detects the finest music in the sound at which all Nature assists. Is not the very cope of the heavens the sounding-board of the infant drummer ? So, clear and unprejudiced ears hear the sweetest and most soul-stirring melody in tinkling cowbells and the like (dogs baying the moon), not to be referred to association, but intrinsic in the sound itself ; those cheap and simple sounds which men despise because their ears are dull and debauched. Ah, that I were so much a child that I could unfailingly draw music from a quart pot. Its little ears tingle with the melody. To it there is music in sound alone.

Evelyn speaks of mel-dews attracting bees. Can mildew be corrupted from this ? He says that the alder laid under water " will harden like a very stone," and speaks of alders being used " for the draining of grounds by placing them in the trenches," which I have just seen done here under Clamshell Hill.

Peaches are the principal crop in Lincoln, and

cherries a very important one, yet Evelyn says,
" We may read that the peach was at first accounted so tender and delicate a tree as that it
was believed to thrive only in Persia; and even
in the days of Galen it grew no nearer than
Egypt of all the Roman provinces, but was not
seen in the city till about thirty years before
Pliny's time ; " but now it is the principal crop
cultivated in Lincoln in New England, and it is
also cultivated extensively in the West, and on
lands not half a dozen years vacated by the Indians.   Also, " It was six hundred and eighty
years after the foundation of Rome ere Italy
had tasted a cherry of their own, which, being
then brought thither out of Pontus, did after
one hundred and twenty years travel *ad ultimos
Britannos*," and, I may add, *Lincolnos.*   As
Evelyn says, " Methinks this should be a wonderful incitement."

He well says, " a sobbing rain."   Evelyn's
love of his subject teaches him to use many expressive words. . . . He speaks of pines " pearl-
ing out into gums."   He talks of modifying the
air as well as the soil about plants, making " the
remedy as well regional as topical."   This suggests the propriety of Shakespeare's expression,
" the region cloud," region meaning thus upper
regions relatively to the earth.   He speaks of a
" dewie sperge or brush " to be used instead of

a watering-pot which "gluts" the earth. He
calls the kitchen-garden the "Olitory garden."
In a dedication of his "Kalendarium Hortense"
to Cowley, he inserts two or three good sentences or quotations, viz., "as the philosopher in
Seneca desired only bread and herbs to dispute
felicity with Jupiter." So of Cowley's simple,
retired life. "Who would not, like you, *cacher
sa vie?*" "delivered from the gilded imperti-
nences of life."

June 9, 1853. 4.15 A. M. To Nashawtuck
by boat. A prevalent fog, though not quite so
thick as the last described. . . . Here and there
deep valleys are excavated in it, as painters imagine the Red Sea for the passage of Pharaoh's
host, wherein trees and houses appear, as it were,
at the bottom of the sea. It is interesting to see
the tops of the trees first and most distinctly before you see their trunks or where they stand on
earth. Far in the northeast there is, as before,
apparently a tremendous surf breaking on a
distant shoal. It is either a real shoal, that is,
a hill over which the fog breaks, or the effect of
the sun's rays on it.

The first white lily bud. White clover is
abundant and very sweet, on the common, filling
the air, but not yet elsewhere as last year.

8 A. M. To Orchis Swamp. Well Meadow.
Hear a goldfinch. This the second or third only

6

that I have heard. White-weed now whitens the
fields. There are many *star* flowers. I remember the anemone especially. The rue anemone
is not yet all gone, lasting longer than the true
one; above all, the trientalis, and of late the
yellow Bethlehem star, and perhaps others.

I have come with a spy-glass to look at the
hawks. They have detected me, and are already
screaming over my head more than half a mile
from the nest. I find no difficulty in looking at
the young hawk (there appears to be one only
standing on the edge of the nest); resting the
glass in the crotch of a young oak, I can see
every wink and the color of its iris. It watches
me more steadily than I it, now looking straight
down at me with both eyes and outstretched neck,
now turning its head and looking with one eye.
How its eye and its whole head express anger.
Its anger is more in its eye than in its beak. It is
quite hoary over the eye and under the chin. The
mother meanwhile is incessantly circling about,
and above its charge and me, farther or nearer,
sometimes withdrawing a quarter of a mile, but
occasionally coming to alight for a moment, almost within gun-shot, on the top of a tall white
pine; but I hardly bring my glass fairly to bear
on her, and get sight of her angry eye through
the pine needles, before she circles away again.
Thus for an hour that I lay there, screaming

every minute, or oftener, with open bill, now and
then pursued by a kingbird or a blackbird, who
appear merely to annoy her by dashing down at
her back. Meanwhile the male is soaring quite
undisturbed at a great height above, evidently
not hunting, but amusing or recreating himself
in the thinner and cooler air, as if pleased with
his own circles like a geometer, and enjoying the
sublime scene. I doubt if he has his eye fixed
on any prey on the earth. He probably descends
to hunt.

Got two or three handfuls of strawberries on
Fair Haven. They are already drying up. . . .
It is natural that the first fruit which the earth
bears should emit, and be, as it were, an embodi-
ment of, that vernal fragrance with which the
air has teemed. Strawberries are its manna,
found ere long where that fragrance has filled
the air. Little natural beds or patches on the
sides of dry hills where the fruit sometimes reddens the ground. But it soon dries up, unless
there is a great deal of rain. Well, are not the
juices of early fruit distilled from the air? Prunella out. The meadows are now yellow with
the golden senecio, a more orange-yellow mingled with the light, glossy yellow of the buttercup. The green fruit of the sweet fern now.
The *juniper repens* appears (though now dry
and effete) to have blossomed recently. The

tall, white erigeron just out. I think it is *strigo-sum*, but tinged with purple sometimes.

The bull-frogs are in full blast to-night. I do not hear a toad from my window, only the crickets beside. The toads I have but rarely heard of late. So there is an evening for the toads, and another for the bull-frogs.

June 9, 1854. P. M. To Well Meadow. The summer aspect of the river begins, perhaps, when the *utricularia vulgaris* is first seen on the surface, as yesterday.

As I go along the railroad causeway I see, in the cultivated ground, a lark flashing his white tail, and showing his handsome yellow breast with its black crescent, like an Indian locket. For a day or two I have heard the fine seringo note of the cherry birds, and seen them flying past, the only? birds, methinks, that I see in small flocks now, except swallows.

Find the great fringed orchis out apparently two or three days, two are almost fully out, two or three only budded; a large spike of peculiarly delicate, pale purple flowers growing in the luxuriant and shady swamp, amid hellebores, ferns, golden senecio, etc. It is remarkable that this, one of the fairest of all our flowers, should also be one of the rarest, for the most part, not seen at all. . . . The village belle never sees this more delicate belle of the swamp. How little

relation between our life and its! . . . The seasons go by, to us, as if it were not. A beauty
reared in the shade of a convent, who has never
strayed beyond the convent bell. Only the skunk
or owl, or other inhabitant of the swamp, be-
holds it. It does not pine because man does
not admire it. I am inclined to think of it as
a relic of the past, as much as the arrowhead
or the tomahawk.

The air is now pretty full of shad flies, and
there is an incessant sound made by the fishes
leaping for such as are struggling on the surface.
It sounds like the lapsing of a swift stream sucking amid rocks. The fishes make a business of
thus getting their evening meal, dimpling the
river like large drops, as far as I can see, sometimes making a loud plashing. Meanwhile, the
kingfishers are on the lookout for the fishes as
they rise, and I saw one dive in the twilight and
go off uttering his cr-r-ack-cr-r-rack.

Covered with disgrace, this State has sat down
coolly, to try for their lives the men who at-
tempted to do its duty for it, and this is called
justice! They who have shown that they can
behave particularly well, they alone are put under bonds for their good behavior! It behoves
every man to see that his influence is on the side
of justice, and let the courts make their own
characters. What is any political organization

worth, when it is in the service of the Devil?
While the whole military force of the State, if
need be, is at the service of a slaveholder, to enable him to carry back a slave, not a soldier is
offered to save a citizen of Massachusetts from
being kidnapped. Is this what all these arms,
all this " training " has been for, these seventy-
eight years past? . . . The marines and the mil-
itia, whose bodies were used lately, were not men
of sense nor of principle ; in a high moral sense,
they were not men at all.

June 9, 1856. P. M. To Corner Spring.
Without an umbrella, thinking the weather settled at last. There are some large cumuli with
glowing, downy cheeks, floating about. Now I
notice where an elm is in the shadow of a cloud,
the black elm tops and shadows of June. It is
a dark eyelash, which suggests a flashing eye beneath. It suggests houses that lie under the
shade, the repose and siesta of summer noons,
the thunder cloud, bathing, and all that belongs
to summer. These veils are now spread here
and there over the village. They suggest also
the creak of crickets, a June sound now fairly
begun, inducing contemplation and philosophic
thought.

June 9, 1857. P. M. To Violet, Sorrel, and
Calla Swamp. In the sproutland beyond the
red huckleberry, an indigo bird, which chirps

about me, as if it had a nest there. This is a splendid and marked bird, high-colored as is the tanager, looking strange in this latitude. Glowing indigo. It flits from the top of one bush to another, chirping as if anxious. Wilson says it sings, not like most other birds, in the morning and evening chiefly, but also in the middle of the day. In this I notice it is like the tanager, the other fiery-plumaged bird. They seem to love the heat. It probably had its nest in one of these bushes.

I had said to P—— " It will be worth the while to look for other rare plants in Calla Swamp, for I have observed that where one rare plant grows, there will commonly be others." Carrying out that thought this P. M., I had not taken three steps at this swamp bare-legged, before I found the *Naumburgia thyrsiflora* in sphagnum and water, which I had not seen growing before. (C—— brought one to me from Hubbard's Great Meadow once.) It is hardly beginning yet. (In prime June 24th.)

June 9, 1860. 6 P. M. Paddle to Flint's Bridge. The water bugs begin to venture out on to the stream from the shadow of a dark wood, as at the Island. So soon as the dusk begins to settle on the river, they begin to steal out, and to extend their circling far amid the bushes and reeds over the channel of the river.

They do not simply then, if ever, venture forth,
but then invariably and at once, the whole length
of the river, they one and all rally out, and begin to dimple its broad surface, as if it were a
necessity so to do.

June 10, 1853.   P. M.   To Mason's Pasture,
in Carlisle.   Haying begins in front yards.
Cool, but agreeable easterly winds.   The streets
now beautiful with verdure and the shade of
elms, under which you look through an air,
clear for summer, to the woods in the horizon.
. . . As C—— and I go through the town,
we hear the cool peep of the robin calling to its
young now learning to fly.   The locust bloom is
now perfect, filling the street with its sweetness,
but it is more agreeable to my eye than my nose.
. . . The fuzzy seeds or down of the black willow is filling the air over the river, and, falling
on the water, covers its surface.   By the 30th
of May, at least, white maple keys were falling.
How early then they had matured their seed.
The mountain laurel will begin to bloom to-
morrow.   The frost some weeks since killed
most of the buds and shoots, except where they
were protected by the trees or by themselves,
and now new shoots have put forth, and grow
four or five inches from the sides of what were
the leading ones.   It is a plant which plainly
requires the protection of the wood.   It is
stunted in the open pasture.

What shall this great wild tract over which we strolled be called? Many farmers have pastures there, and wood-lots and orchards. It consists mainly of rocky pastures. It contains what I call the Boulder Field, the Yellow Birch Swamp, the Black Birch Hill, the Laurel Pasture, the Hog Pasture, the White Pine Grove, the Easterbrook Place, the Old Lime Kiln, the Lime Quarries, Spruce Swamp, the Ermine Weasel Woods ; also, the Oak Meadows, the Cedar Swamp, the Kibbe Place, and the old place northwest of Brooks Clark's. Ponkawtasset bounds it on the south. There are a few frog-ponds and an old mill-pond within it, and Bateman's Pond on its edge. What shall the whole be called? The old Carlisle road which runs through the middle of it is bordered on each side with wild apple pastures, where the trees stand without order, having, many or most of them, sprung up by accident or from pomace sown at random, and are, for the most part, concealed by birches and pines. These orchards are very extensive, and yet many of these apple trees, growing as forest trees, bear good crops of apples. It is a paradise for walkers in the fall. There are also boundless huckleberry pastures, as well as many blueberry swamps. Shall we call it the Easterbrook Country? It would make a princely estate in Europe. Yet it is owned

by farmers who live by the labor of their hands
and do not esteem it much.   Plenty of huckleberries and barberries here.

A second great uninhabited tract is that on
the Marlboro' road, stretching westerly from
Francis Wheeler's to the river, and beyond
about three miles, and from Harrington's, on
the north, to Dakin's, on the south, more than a
mile in width.

A third, the Walden Woods.

A fourth, the Great Fields.   These four are
all in Concord.

There are one or two in the town who probably have Indian blood in their veins, and when
they exhibit any unusual irascibility, the neighbors say they have got their Indian blood roused.

Now methinks the birds begin to sing less
tumultuously, as the weather grows more constantly warm, with morning, noon, and evening
songs, and suitable recesses in the concert.

High blackberries are conspicuously in bloom,
whitening the sides of lanes.

Mention is made in the Town Records, as
quoted by Shattuck, p. 33, under date of 1654,
of "the Hogepen-walke about Annursnake," and
reference is at the same time made to "the old
hogepen." . . .   There is some propriety in calling such a tract a walk, methinks, from the
habit which hogs have of walking about with

an independent air, and pausing from time to time to look about from under their flapping ears and snuff the air. The hogs I saw this afternoon, all busily rooting without holding up their heads to look at us, the whole field appearing as if it had been most miserably ploughed or scarified with a harrow, with their shed to retreat to in rainy weather, affected me as more human than other quadrupeds. They are comparatively clean about their lodgings.

June 10, 1856. P. M. To Dugan Desert. — I hear the huckleberry bird now add to its usual strain *a-tea tea tea tea tea.*

A painted tortoise laying her eggs ten feet from the wheel track on the Marlboro' road. She paused at first, but I sat down within two feet, and she soon resumed her work, had excavated a hollow about five inches wide and six long in the moistened sand, and cautiously, with long intervals, she continued her work, resting always her fore feet on the same spot, and never looking round, her eye shut all but a narrow slit. Whenever I moved, perhaps to brush off a mosquito, she paused. A wagon approached, rumbling afar off, and then there was a pause till it had passed, and long after, a tedious, *naturlangsam* pause of the slow-blooded creature, a sacrifice of time such as those animals are up to which slumber half a year and live for

centuries. It was twenty minutes before I discovered that she was not making the hole, but
filling it up slowly, having laid her eggs. She
drew the moistened sand under herself, scraping
it along from behind with both feet brought
together. The claws turned inward. In the
long pauses the ants troubled her, as the mosquitoes, me, by running over her eyes, which
made her snap or dart out her head suddenly,
striking the shell. She did not dance on the
sand, nor finish covering the hollow quite so
carefully as the one observed last year. She
went off suddenly, and quickly at first, with a
slow but sure instinct through the wood toward
the swamp.

In a hollow apple tree, hole eighteen inches
deep, young pigeon woodpeckers, large and well
feathered. They utter their squeaking hiss
whenever I cover the hole with my hand, apparently taking it for the approach of the
mother.

June 10, 1857. . . . A striped snake (so-
called) was running about in a yard this forenoon, and in the afternoon it was found to have
shed its slough, leaving it half way out of a hole
which probably it used to confine it in. It was
about in its new skin. Many creatures, devil's
needles, etc., cast their sloughs now. Can't I?

F—— tells me to-day, that he has seen a reg-

ular barn swallow, with forked tail, about his
barn, which was *black*, not rufous.

June 10, 1858. . . . As we entered a rye
field, I saw what I took to be a hawk fly up
from the other end, though it may have been a
crow. It was soon pursued by small birds.
When I got there, I found an *Emys insculpta*
on its back, with its head and feet drawn in and
motionless, and what looked like the track of a
crow on the sand. Undoubtedly the bird which
I saw had been pecking at it, and perhaps they
get many of their eggs.

June 10, 1859. Surveying. . . .

June 10, 1860. 2 P. M. To Anursnack.
. . . There is much handsome interrupted fern
in the Painted Cup Meadow, and near the top
of one of the clumps we noticed something like
a large cocoon, the color of the rusty cinnamon
fern wool. It was a red bat, the New York bat,
so-called. It hung suspended, head directly
downward, with its little sharp claws or hooks
caught through one of the divisions at the base
of one of the pinnæ, above the fructification. It
was a delicate rusty brown, in color very like the
wool of the cinnamon fern, with the whiter bare
spaces, seen through it early in the season. I
thought at first glance it was a broad cocoon, then
that it was the plump body of a monstrous emperor moth. It was rusty or reddish brown,

white or hoary within, with a white, apparently
triangular spot beneath, about the insertion of
the wings. Its wings were very compactly folded
up, the principal bones (dark or reddish) lying
flat along the under side of its body, and a hook
on each, meeting its opposite under the chin of
the creature. It did not look like fur, but was
like the plush of the ripe cat-tail head, though
more loose, all trembling in the wind and with
the pulsations of the animal. I broke off the
top of the fern, and let the bat lie on its back in
my hand. I held it and turned it about for ten
or fifteen minutes, but it did not awake. Once
or twice it opened its eyes a little, and even
raised its old, baggish head, and opened its
mouth, but soon drowsily dropped the head and
fell asleep again. Its ears were nearly bare. It
was more attentive to sounds than to motions.
Finally by shaking it, and especially by hissing
or whistling, I thoroughly awakened it, and it
fluttered off twenty or thirty rods to the woods.
I cannot but think that its instinct taught it
to cling to the interrupted fern, since it might
readily be mistaken for a mass of its fruit. . . .
Unless it moved its head wide awake, it looked
like a tender infant.

June 11, 1851. Last night, a beautiful summer night, not too warm, moon not quite full,
after two or three rainy days. Walked to Fair

Haven by railroad, returning by Potter's pasture
and Sudbury road. I feared at first that there
would be too much white light, like the pale remains of daylight, and not a yellow, gloomy,
dreamier light; that it would be like a candle-
light by day; but when I got away from the
town and deeper into the night, it was better. I
saw by the shadows cast by the inequalities of
the clayey sand-bank in the Deep Cut, that it
was necessary to see objects by moonlight as well
as sunlight, to get a complete notion of them.
This bank had looked much more flat by day,
when the light was stronger, but now the heavy
shadows revealed its prominences. The prominences are light, made more remarkable by the
dark shadows they cast. . . . I hear the night-
hawks uttering their squeaking notes high in the
air, now at nine o'clock, P. M., and occasionally,
what I do not remember to have heard so late,
their booming note. It sounds more as if under
a cope than by day. The sound is not so fugacious, going off to be lost amid the spheres, but
is echoed hollowly to earth, making the low roof
of heaven vibrate. Such a sound is more confused and dissipated by day.

The whippoorwill suggests how wide asunder
are the woods and the town. Its note is very
rarely heard by those who live on the street, and
then it is thought to be of ill-omen. Only the

dwellers on the outskirts of the village hear it
occasionally. It sometimes comes into their
yards. But go into the woods in a warm night
at this season, and it is the prevailing sound. I
hear now five or six at once. It is no more of
ill-omen, therefore, here, than the night and the
moonlight are. It is a bird not only of the
woods, but of the night side of the woods. I
hear some whippoorwills on hills, others in thick
wooded vales, which ring hollow and cavernous,
like an apartment or cellar, with their note, as
when I hear the working of some artisan within
an apartment. New beings have usurped the
air we breathe, rounding nature, filling her crev-
ices with sound. To sleep where you may hear
the whippoorwill in your dreams.

I hear from this upland, whence I see Wachusett by day, a wagon crossing one of the bridges.
I have no doubt that in some places to-night I
should be sure to hear every carriage which
crossed a bridge over the river, within the limits
of Concord, for in such an hour and atmosphere
the sense of hearing is wonderfully assisted, and
asserts a new dignity. We become the Hearalls
of the story. . . . The planks of a bridge, struck
like a bell swung near the earth, emit a very res-
onant and penetrating sound. And then it is
to be considered that the bell is in this instance
hung over water, and that the night air, not only

on account of its stillness, but perhaps on account of its density, is more favorable to the transmission of sound. If the whole town were a raised plank floor, what a din there would be!

I now descend round the corner of the grain field, through the pitch-pine wood, into a lower field, more inclosed by woods, and find myself in a colder, damp, and misty atmosphere, with much dew on the grass. I seem to be nearer to the origin of things. There is something creative and primal in the cool mist. This dewy mist does not fail to suggest music to me, unaccountably, fertility, the origin of things. An atmosphere which has forgotten the sun, where the ancient principle of moisture prevails. It is laden with the condensed fragrance of plants, as it were, distilled dews.

The woodland paths are never seen to such advantage as in a moonlight night, so embowered, still opening before you almost against expectation as you walk. You are so completely in the woods, and yet your feet meet no obstacles. It is as if it were not a path, but an open, winding passage through the bushes, which your feet find. Now I go by the spring, and when I have risen to the same level as before, find myself in the warmer stratum again. These warmer veins, in a cool evening like this, do not fail to be agreeable.

7

The woods are about as destitute of inhabitants at night as the streets. In both there will be some night walkers. There are but few wild creatures to seek their prey. The greater part of its inhabitants have retired to rest.

Ah, that life that I have known! How hard it is to remember what is most memorable. We remember how we itched, not how our hearts beat. I can sometimes recall to mind the quality, the immortality of my youthful life, but in memory is the only relation to it.

I hear the night-warbler breaking out as in his dreams, made so from the first for some mysterious reason.

Our spiritual side takes a more distinct form now, like our shadow which we see accompanying us.

I do not know but I feel less vigor at night, — my legs will not carry me so far, as if the night were less favorable to muscular exertion, weakened us somewhat, as darkness turns plants pale, — but perhaps my experience is to be referred to my being already exhausted by the day; yet sometimes, after a hard day's work, I have found myself unexpectedly vigorous. I have never tried the experiment fairly.

Only the harvest and hunter's moons are famous, but I think that each full moon deserves to be, and has its own character, well-marked. One might be called the midsummer night moon.

So still and moderate is the night. No scream is heard, whether of fear or joy. No great comedy, no tragedy is being enacted. The chirping of crickets is the most universal, if not the loudest sound. There is no French revolution in Nature, no excess. She is warmer or colder by a degree or two.

My shadow has the distinctness of a second person, a certain black companion bordering on the imp, and I ask who is this that I see dodging behind me as I am about to sit down on a rock. The rocks do not feel warm to-night, for the air is warmest, nor does the sand particularly.

No one, to my knowledge, has observed the minute differences in the seasons. Hardly two nights are alike.

A book of the seasons, each page of which should be written in its own season and out of doors, or in its own locality, wherever it may be.

When you get into the road, though far from the town, and feel the sand under your feet, it is as if you had reached your own gravel walk. You no longer hear the whippoorwill nor regard your own shadow, for here you expect a fellow traveler. You catch yourself walking merely. The road leads your steps and thoughts alike to the town. You see only the path, and your thoughts wander from the objects that are presented to your senses. You are no longer in place. It is like conformity, walking in the ways of men.

June 11, 1852. — It commonly happens that a flower is considered more beautiful that is not followed by fruit. It must culminate in the flower.

The red-eye sings now in the woods perhaps more than any other bird.

As I climbed the cliffs, when I jarred the foliage, I perceived an exquisite perfume which I could not trace to its source. Ah, those fugacious, universal fragrances of the meadows and woods! odors rightly mingled!

The shrub oaks on the plain are so covered with foliage that, when I look down on them from the cliffs, I am impressed as if I looked down on a forest of oaks.

The oven-bird and the thrasher sing. The last has a sort of chuckle. The crickets begin to sing in warm, dry places.

Lupines, their pods and seeds. First, the profusion of color, spikes of flowers rising above and prevailing over the leaves; then the variety in different clumps, rose? purple, blue, and white; then the handsome palmate leaf, made to hold dew. Gray says the name is from *lupus*, wolf, because they " were thought to devour the fertility of the soil." This is scurrilous.

Under Fair Haven. First grew the *Viola pedata* here; then lupines, mixed with the delicate snapdragon. This soil must abound with the blue principle.

Utricularia vulgaris, common bladderwort, a dirty-conditioned flower, like a sluttish woman with a gaudy yellow bonnet.

Those spotted maple leaves, what mean their bright colors? Yellow, with a greenish centre and crimson border, on the green leaves, as if the great chemist had dropped some strong acid, by chance, from a phial designed for autumnal juice! Very handsome. Decay and disease are often beautiful, like the pearly tear of the shell-fish and the hectic glow of consumption.

June 11, 1853. The upland fields are already less green where the June grass is ripening its seed. They are greenest when only its blade is seen. In the sorrel fields, also, what lately was the ruddy, rosy cheek of health, now that the sorrel is ripening and dying, has become the tanned and imbrowned cheek of manhood.

Probably blackbirds were never less numerous along our river than in these years. They do not depend on the clearing of the woods and the cultivation of the orchards, etc. The streams and meadows in which they delight always existed. Most of the towns, soon after they were settled, were obliged to set a price upon their heads.

In 1672, according to the town records of Concord, instruction was given to the selectmen, "That encouragement be given for the destroying of blackbirds and jaies." Shattuck, p. 45.

I remember Helen's telling me that John Marston, of Taunton, told her that he was aboard a vessel, during the Revolution, which met another vessel, and, as I think, one hailed the other. A French name being given could not be understood; whereupon a sailor, probably aboard his vessel, ran out on the bowsprit and shouted, " La Terrible " (the vessel in which John Adams was being brought back or carried out to France), and that sailor's name was Thoreau.

My father has an idea that he stood on the wharf and cried this to the bystanders. He tells me that when the war came on, my grandfather, being thrown out of business and being a young man, went a-privateering. I find from his Diary that John Adams set sail from Port Louis at L'Orient in the French frigate Terrible, Captain Chavagnes, June 17, 1779, the Bonhomme Richard, Captain Jones, and four other vessels, being in company at first, and the Terrible arrived at Boston the 2d of August. On the 13th of November following he set out for France again in the same frigate from Boston, and he says that a few days before the 24th, being at the last date on the Grand Bank of Newfoundland, we spoke an American privateer, the General Lincoln, Captain Barnes. If the above-mentioned incident occurred at sea, it was probably on this occasion.

June 11, 1855. When I would go a-visiting, I find that I go off the fashionable street (not being inclined to change my dress) to where man meets man, and not polished shoe meets shoe.

What if we feel a yearning to which no breast answers. I walk alone. My heart is full. Feelings impede the current of my thoughts. I knock on the earth for my friend. I expect to meet him at every turn, but no friend appears, and perhaps none is dreaming of me. I am tired of frivolous society in which silence is forever the most natural and the best manners. I would fain walk on the deep waters, but my companions will only walk on shallows and puddles. I am naturally silent in the midst of twenty persons, from day to day, from year to year. I am rarely reminded of their presence. . . . One complains that I do not take his jokes. I took them before he had done uttering them, and went my way. One talks to me of his apples and pears, and I depart with my secret untold. His are not the apples that tempt me.

June 11, 1856. P. M. To Flint's Pond. It is very hot this P. M., and that peculiar stillness which belongs to summer noons now reigns in the woods. I observe and appreciate the shade, as it were the shadow of each particular leaf on the ground. I think that this peculiar darkness of the shade, of the foliage as seen between you and the sky, is not accounted for merely by saying that we have not yet got accustomed to clothed trees, but the leaves are rapidly acquiring a darker green, are more and more opaque, and, beside, the sky is lit with the intensest light. It reminds me of the thunder-cloud and the dark eyelash of summer. Great cumuli are slowly drifting in the intensest blue sky, with glowing white borders. The red-eye sings incessant, and the more indolent yellow-throated vireo, and the creeper, and perhaps the redstart? or else it is the parti-colored warbler.

I perceive that scent from the young, sweet fern shoots and withered blossoms, which made the first settlers of Concord to faint on their journey.

See a bream's nest, two and one fourth feet in diameter, laboriously scooped out, and the surrounding bottom for a diameter of eight feet! comparatively white and clean, while all beyond is mud, leaves, etc., and a very large, green, and cupreous bream, with a red spot on the operculum, is poised over the centre, while half a dozen shiners are hovering about, apparently watching a chance to steal the spawn.

A partridge with young in the saw-mill brook path. Could hardly tell what kind of a creature it was at first, it made such a noise and fluttering amid the weeds and bushes. Finally ran off, with its body flat and wings somewhat spread.

June 11, 1858. P. M. To Assabet Bath. . . . Saw a painted turtle on the gravelly bank, . . . and suspected that she had just been laying (it was mid P. M.), so, examining the ground, I found the surface covered with loose lichens, etc., about one foot behind her, and, digging, found five eggs just laid, one and one-half or two inches deep, under one side. It is remarkable how firmly they are packed in the soil, rather hard to extract, though but just laid. . . .

Saw half a dozen of the insculptæ preparing to dig now at mid P. M. (one or two had begun), at the most gravelly spot there, but they would not proceed while I watched, though I waited nearly half an hour, but either rested perfectly still, with their heads drawn partly in, or when a little further off, stood warily looking about, with their necks stretched out, turning their anxious-looking heads about. It seems a very earnest and pressing business they are upon. They have but a short season to do it in, and they run many risks.

Having succeeded in finding the *Emys picta's*

eggs, I thought I would look for the *Emys in-sculpta's* at Abel Hosmer's rye field; so, looking carefully to see where the ground had been recently disturbed, I dug with my hand, and could directly feel the passage to the eggs. So I discovered two or three nests with their large and long eggs, five in one of them. It seems then, that if you look carefully soon after the eggs are laid in such a place, you can find the nests, though rain or even a dewy night might conceal the spot.

June 11, 1860. 10.30 A. M. Sail on the river. . . . The evergreens are now invested by the deciduous trees, and you get the full effect of their dark-green contrasting with the yellowish-green of the deciduous trees. . . .

I see from time to time a fish, scared by our sail, leap four to six feet through the air above the waves. . . .

Just within the edge of the wood, . . . I see a small painted turtle on its back, with its head stretched out as if to turn over. Surprised by the sight, I stooped to investigate the case. It drew in its head at once, but I noticed that its shell was partially empty. I could see through it from side to side, as it lay, its entrails having been extracted through large openings just before the hind legs. The dead leaves were flattened for a foot around where it had been oper-

ated on, and were a little bloody. Its paunch
lay on the leaves, and contained much vegetable
matter, old cranberry leaves, etc. Judging by
the striae, it was not more than five or six years
old (or four or five). Its fore-parts were quite
alive, its hind legs apparently dead, its inwards
gone, apparently its spine perfect. The flies
had entered it in numbers. What creature had
done this which it would be difficult for a man
to do? I thought of a skunk, weasel, mink, but
I do not believe they could have got their snouts
into so small a space as that in front of the hind
legs, between the shells. The hind legs themselves had not been injured, nor the shell
scratched. I thought it likely that this was done
by some bird of the heron kind which has a long
and powerful bill. This may account for the
many dead turtles which I have found, and
thought died from disease. Such is Nature, who
gave one creature a taste or yearning for another's entrails as its favorite tid-bit! I thought
the more of a bird, for just as we were shoving
away from this isle, I heard a sound *just like a
small dog barking hoarsely*, and looking up saw
it was made by a bittern (*Ardea minor*), a pair
of which were flapping over the meadows, and
probably had a nest in some tussock thereabouts.
No wonder the turtle is wary, for notwithstanding its horny shell, when it comes forth to lay its

eggs, it runs the risk of having its entrails plucked out. That is the reason that the box turtle, which lives entirely on the land, is made to shut itself up entirely within its shell, and I suspect that the mud tortoise only comes forth by night. What need the turtle has of some horny shield over those weaker parts, avenues to its entrails. I saw several of these painted turtles dead on the bottom.

Already I see those handsome fungi on the red maple leaves, yellow within, with a green centre, then the light red ring deepening to crimson.

On our way up, we eat our dinner at Rice's shore, and looked over the meadows covered there with waving sedge, light glaucous as it is bent by the wind, reflecting a grayish or light glaucous light from its under-side.

Looking at a hill-side of young trees, what various shades of green. The oaks generally are a light, tender, and yellowish-green. The white birches dark green now. The maples dark and silvery.

The white lily-pads, reddish, and showing their crimson under-sides from time to time, when the wind blows hardest.

June 12, 1851. Listen to music religiously, as if it were the last strain you might hear.

There would be this advantage in traveling in

your own country, even in your own neighborhood, that you would be so thoroughly prepared
to understand what you saw. You would make
fewer traveler's mistakes.

Is not he hospitable who entertains thoughts?
June 12, 1852. P. M. To Lupine Hill *via*
Depot Field Brook. The meadows are yellow
with golden senecio. Marsh speedwell, *Veronica
scutellata*, lilac tinted, rather pretty. The mouse-
ear forget-me-not, *Myosotis laxa*, has now extended its racemes? very much, and hangs over
the edge of the brook. It is one of the most
interesting minute flowers. It is the more beautiful for being small and unpretending; even
flowers must be modest. The blue flag, *Iris
versicolor*. Its buds are a dark, indigo-blue tip
beyond the green calyx. It is rich, but hardly
delicate and simple enough. A very handsome, sword-shaped leaf. The blue-eyed grass
is one of the most beautiful of flowers. It might
have been famous from Proserpine down. It
will bear to be praised by poets.

The blue flag, notwithstanding its rich furni-
ture, its fringed, re-curved parasols over its an-
thers, and its variously streaked and colored
petals, is loose and coarse in its habit. How
completely all character is expressed by flowers.
This is a little too showy and gaudy, like some
women's bonnets. Yet it belongs to the meadow

and ornaments it much. Ever it will be some obscure, small, and modest flower that will most please us.

How difficult, if not impossible, to do the things we have done, as fishing and camping out. They seem to me a little fabulous now. Boys are bathing at Hubbard's Bend, playing with a boat, I at the willows. The color of their bodies in the sun at a distance is pleasing, the not often seen flesh color. I hear the sound of their sport borne over the water. As yet we have not man in Nature. What a singular fact for an angel visitant to this earth to carry back in his note-book, that men were forbidden to expose their bodies under the severest penalties! A pale pink which the sun would soon tan. White man! There are no white men to contrast with the red and the black. They are of such colors as the weaver gives them. I wonder that the dog knows his master when he goes in to bathe, and does not stay by his clothes.

Small white-bellied (?) swallows in a row (a dozen) on the telegraph wire over the water by the bridge. This perch is little enough departure from unobstructed air to suit them. Pluming themselves. If you could furnish a perch aerial enough, even birds of paradise would alight. They do not alight on trees, methinks, unless on dead and bare boughs, but stretch a

wire over water, and they perch on it. This is
among the phenomena that cluster about the telegraph. The swallow has a forked tail, and
wings and tail are of about the same length. . . .

Some fields are almost wholly covered with
sheep's sorrel, now turned red, its valves (?). It
helps thus agreeably to paint the earth, contrasting even at a distance with the greener fields,
blue sky, and dark or downy clouds. It is red,
marbled, watered, mottled, or waved with greenish, like waving grain, three or four acres of it.
To the farmer or grazier it is a troublesome
weed, but to the landscape viewer, an agreeable
red tinge laid on by the painter. I feel well
into summer when I see this red tinge. It appears to be avoided by the cows. The petals
of the side-saddle flower, fully expanded, hang
down. How complex it is, what with flowers
and leaves! It is a wholesome and interesting
plant to me, the leaf especially.

. . . The glory of Dennis's lupines is departed, and the white now shows in abundance
beneath them. So I cannot walk longer in those
fields of Enna in which Proserpine amused herself gathering flowers.

The steam whistle at a distance sounds even
like the hum of a bee in a flower. So man's
works fall into Nature. The flies hum at mid-
afternoon, as if peevish and weary at the length

of the days. The river is shrunk to summer width, on the sides smooth, whitish water, or rather it is the light from the pads ; in the middle, dark blue or slate, rippled. The color of the earth at a distance where a wood has been cut off is a reddish brown. . . .

It is day, and we have more of that same light that the moon sent us, not reflected now, but shining directly. The sun is a fuller moon. Who knows how much lighter day there may be !

June 12, 1853. P. M. To Bear Hill. . . . The laurel probably by day after to-morrow.

The note of the wood-thrush answers to some cool, unexhausted morning vigor in the hearer.

The leaf of the rattlesnake plantain now surprises the walker amid the dry leaves on cool hill-sides in the woods ; of very simple form, but richly veined with longitudinal and transverse white veins. It looks like art.

Going up Pine Hill, disturbed a partridge and her brood. She ran in dishabille directly to me, within four feet, while her young, not larger than chickens just hatched, dispersed, flying along a foot or two from the ground, just over the bushes, for a rod or more. The mother kept close at hand to attract my attention, and mewed and clucked, and made a noise as when a hawk is in sight. She stepped about and held her head above the bushes, and clucked just like a hen. What a remarkable instinct, that which keeps the young so silent, and prevents their peeping and betraying themselves! This wild bird will run almost any risk to save her young. The young, I believe, make a fine sound at first, in dispersing, something like a cherry-bird.

Visited the great orchis which I am waiting to have open completely. It is emphatically a flower (within gunshot of the hawk's nest); its great spike, six inches by two, of delicate, pale purple flowers which begin to expand at bottom, rises above and contrasts with the green leaves of the hellebore, skunk-cabbage, and ferns (by which its own leaves are concealed), in the cool shade of an alder swamp. It is the more interesting for its variety and the secluded situations in which it grows, owing to which it is seldom seen, not thrusting itself upon the observation of men. It is a pale purple, as if from growing in the shade. It is not remarkable in its stalk and leaves, which, indeed, are commonly concealed by other plants.

A wild moss rose in Arethusa Meadow where are arethusas lingering still. The side-saddle flowers are partly turned up now, and make a great show with their broad red petals flapping like saddle ears (?). . . . I visited my hawk's nest, and the young hawk was perched now four or five feet above the nest, still in the shade. It

8

will soon fly. So now in secluded pine woods
the young hawks sit high on the edges of their
nests, or on the twigs near by, in the shade, waiting for their pinions to grow, while their parents
bring to them their prey. Their silence also is
remarkable, not to betray themselves, nor will
the old bird go to the nest while you are in
sight. She pursues me half a mile when I withdraw.

The buds of young white oaks which have
been frost-bitten are just pushing forth again.
Are these such as were intended for next year, at
the base of the leaf stalk?

June 12, 1854. P. M. To Walden. Clover
now reddens the fields, grass in its prime. . . .
With the roses now fairly begun, I associate
summer heats. . . .

Hear the evergreen forest note, and see the
bird on the top of a white pine, somewhat
creeper-like along the boughs. A golden head,
except a black streak from eyes, black throat,
slate-colored back, forked tail, white beneath,
er te, ter ter te. Another bird with *yellow*
throat, near by, may have been of the other sex.

Scared a kingfisher on a bough over Walden.
As he flew off, he hovered two or three times
thirty or forty feet above the pond, and at last
dove and apparently caught a fish with which he
flew off low over the water to a tree.

Mountain laurel at the pond.

June 12, 1855. Down river to swamp east of Poplar Hill. I hear the toad still, which I have called *spray frog* falsely. He sits close to the edge of the water, and is hard to find. Hard to tell the direction though you may be within three feet. I detect him chiefly by the motion of the great swelling bubble on his throat. A peculiarly rich sprayey dreamer now at 2 P. M. How serenely it ripples over the water! What a luxury life is to him! I have to use a little geometry to detect him. Am surprised at my discovery at last, while C. sits by incredulous. Had turned our prow to shore to search. This rich sprayey note possesses all the shore. It diffuses itself far and wide over the water, and enters into every crevice of the noon, and you cannot tell whence it proceeds.

Young redwings now begin to fly feebly amid the button bushes, and the old ones chatter their anxiety.

In the thick swamp behind the hill I look at the vireo's nest which C. found. . . . He took one cow-bird's egg from it, and I now take the other which he left. There is no vireo's egg, and it is said they always desert their nest when there are two cow-bird's eggs laid in it.

Nuttall says of the cow-bird's egg: "If the egg be deposited in the nest alone, it is uniformly

forsaken;" — has seen " sometimes two of these
eggs in the same nest, but in this case one of
them commonly proves abortive," — " is almost
oval, scarcely larger than that of the bluebird."
He says it is " thickly sprinkled with points and
confluent touches of olive brown, of two shades,
somewhat more numerous at the greater end, on
a white ground tinged with green. But in some
of these eggs the ground is almost pure white,
and the spots nearly black."

June 12, 1859. p. m. To Gowing's Swamp.
I am struck with the beauty of the sorrel now.
What a wholesome red! It is densest in parallel lines, according to the plowing or cultivation. There is hardly a more agreeable sight at
this season.

June 12, 1860. p. m. Up Assabet. I find
several *Emys insculpta* nests and eggs, and see
two painted turtles going inland to lay, at 2 p. m.
At this moment these turtles are on their way
inland, to lay their eggs, all over the State, warily drawing in their heads and waiting when you
come by. Here is a painted turtle just a rod
inland, its back all covered with the fragments
of green leaves blown off and washed up yesterday, which now line the shore. It has come out
through this wrack. As the river has gone
down, these green leaves mark the bank in lines,
like saw-dust.

June 13, 1851. Walked to Walden last night (moon not quite full). I noticed night before last from Fair Haven how valuable was some water by moonlight, like the river and Fair Haven, though far away, reflecting the light with a faint glimmering sheen, as in the spring of the year. The water shines with an inward light, like a heaven on earth. The silent depth and serenity and majesty of water! Strange that men should distinguish gold and diamonds, when these precious elements are so common. I saw a distant river by moonlight, making no noise, yet flowing, as by day, still to the sea, like melted silver, reflecting the moonlight. Far away it lay encircling the earth. How far away it may look in the night! Even from a low hill, miles away down in the valley! As far off as Paradise and the delectable country! There is a certain glory attends on water by night. By it the heavens are related to the earth, undistinguishable from a sky beneath you. After I reached the road, I saw the moon suddenly reflected from a pool, the earth, as it were, dissolved beneath my feet. The magical moon, with attendant stars, suddenly looking up with mild lustre from a window in the dark earth. I observed also, the same night, a halo about my shadow in the moonlight, which I referred to the accidentally lighter color of the surrounding

surface, but on transferring it to the darkest
patches I saw the halo there equally. It serves
to make the outline of the shadow more distinct.
But now for last night. A few fire-flies in
the meadow. Do they shine, though invisibly,
by day? Is their candle lighted by day?— It
is not night-fall till the whippoorwills begin to
sing.

As I entered the Deep Cut, I was affected by
beholding the first faint reflection of genuine,
unmixed moonlight on the eastern sand-bank,
while the horizon, yet red with day, was tinging
the western side. What an interval between
these two lights! The light of the moon, in
what age of the world does that fall upon the
earth? The moonlight was as the earliest and
dewy morning light, and the daylight tinge reminded me much more of the night. There
were the old and new dynasties contrasted, and
an interval between, not recognized in history,
which time could not span. Nations have flourished in that light.

When I had climbed the sand-bank on the
left, I felt the warmer current or stratum of air
on my cheek, like a blast from a furnace.

The white stems of the pines which reflected
the weak light, standing thick and close together,
while their lower branches were gone, reminded
me that the pines are only longer grasses, which

rise to a chaffy head, and we the insects that
crawl between them. They are particularly
grass-like.

I heard the partridge drumming to-night as
late as nine o'clock. What a singularly space-
penetrating and filling sound! Why am I never
nearer to its source ?

We do not commonly live our life out and
full; we do not fill all our extremities with our
blood; we do not inspire and expire fully and
entirely enough, so that the wave, the comber of
each inspiration, shall break upon our extremest
shores, rolling till it meets the sand which
bounds us, and the sound of the surf come back
to us. Might not a bellows assist us to breathe ?
. . . Why do we not let on the flood, raise the
gates, and set all our wheels in motion ? He
that hath ears to hear, let him hear. Employ
your senses.

The newspapers tell us of news not to be
named even with that in its own kind, which an
observing man can pick up in a solitary walk,
as if it gained some importance and dignity by
its publicness. Do we need to be advertised
each day that such is still the routine of life ?

The tree-toad's, too, is a summer-sound. I
hear, just as the night sets in, faint notes from
time to time, from some sparrow (?) falling
asleep, a vesper hymn ; and later, in the woods,

the chuckling, rattling sound of some unseen
bird on the near trees. — The night-hawk booms
wide awake.

As I approached the pond down Hubbard's
path, after coming out of the woods into a
warmer air, I saw the shimmering of the moon
on its surface; and in the near, now flooded
cove, the water bugs, now darting, circling about,
made streaks or curves of light. The moon's
inverted pyramid of shimmering light commenced about twenty rods off, like so much micaceous sand. But I was startled to see midway
in the dark water, a bright flame like more than
phosphorescent light, crowning the crests of the
wavelets, which at first I mistook for fire-flies.
. . . It had the appearance of a pure smokeless
flame, half a dozen inches long, rising from the
water and bending flickeringly along its surface.
I thought of St. Elmo's lights and the like. But
coming near to the shore of the pond itself, these
flames increased, and I saw that even this was
so many broken reflections of the moon's disk,
though one would have said they were of an intenser light than the moon herself. From contrast with the surrounding water they were.
Standing up close to the shore and nearer the
rippled surface, I saw the reflections of the moon
sliding down the watery concave, like so many
lustrous burnished coins poured from a bag with

inexhaustible lavishness, and the lambent flames
on the surface were much multiplied, seeming to
slide along a few inches with each wave before
they were extinguished ; and I saw from farther
and farther off, they gradually merged in the
general sheen, which in fact was made up of a
myriad little mirrors reflecting the disk of the
moon with equal brightness to an eye rightly
placed. The pyramid or sheaf of light which
we see springing from near where we stand is in
fact only that portion of the shimmering surface
which our eye takes in. To a myriad eyes suit-
ably placed, the whole surface of the pond would
be seen to shimmer, or rather it would be seen,
as the waves turned up their mirrors, to be covered with those bright flame-like reflections of
the moon's disk, like a myriad candles everywhere arising from the waves. . . .

As I climbed the hill again toward my old
bean-field, I listened to the ancient, familiar, immortal, cricket sound under all others, hearing
at first some distinct chirps. But when these
ceased, I was aware of the general earth song
which I had not before perceived, and amid
which these were only taller flowers in a bed,
and I wondered if behind or beneath this there
was not some other chant yet more universal.
Why do we not hear when this begins in the
spring? and when it ceases in the fall? or is it

too gradual? — After getting into the road I
have no thought to record. All the way home
the walk is comparatively barren.

June 13, 1852. 3 P. M. To Conantum. . . .
The river has a summer mid-day look, smooth,
with green shores, and shade from the trees on
its banks.

What a sweetness fills the air now in low
grounds or meadows, reminding me of times
when I went strawberrying years ago. It is as
if all meadows were filled with some sweet mint.

The *Dracaena borealis* (Bigelow), *Clintonia
borealis* (Gray), amid the Solomon's-seals in
Hubbard's Grove Swamp, a very neat and handsome liliaceous flower, with three large, regular,
spotless green convallaria leaves, making a triangle from the root, and sometimes a fourth from
the scape, linear, with four drooping, greenish-
yellow, bell-shaped (?) flowers. It is a handsome and perfect flower, though not high-colored.
I prefer it to some more famous. But Gray
should not have named it from the Governor of
New York. What is he to the lovers of flowers
in Massachusetts? If named after a man, it
must be a man of flowers. Rhode Island may
as well name the flowers after her governors as
New York. Name your canals and railroads
after Clinton, if you please, but his name is not
associated with flowers.

The buckbean grows in Conant's meadow. Lambkill is out. I remember with what delight I used to discover this flower in dewy mornings. All things in this world must be seen with the morning dew on them, must be seen with youthful, early opened, hopeful eyes.

Saw four cunning little woodchucks, about one-third grown, that live under Conant's old house, nibbling the short grass. Mistook one for a piece of rusty iron.

The *Smilax herbacea*, carrion flower, a rank green vine, with long peduncled umbels, small greenish or yellowish flowers, and tendrils, just opening, at the Miles swamp. It smells exactly like a dead rat in the wall, and apparently attracts flies like carrion. I find small gnats in it. A very remarkable odor. A single minute flower, in an umbel, open, will scent a whole room. Nature imitates all things in flowers. They are at once the most beautiful and the ugliest objects, the most fragrant, and the most offensive to the nostrils.

The great leaves of the bass attract one now, six inches in diameter.

The delicate maiden-hair fern forms a cup or dish, very delicate and graceful. Beautiful, too, its glossy black stem and its wave-edged, fruited leaflets.

I hear the feeble, plaintive note of young

bluebirds, just trying their wings or getting used to them. Young robins peep.

I think I know four kinds of cornel beside the dogwood and bunchberry. One now in bloom, with rather small leaves, which have a smooth, silky feeling beneath, and a greenish gray spotted stem, old stocks all gray (*Cornus alternifolia?* or *sericea?*). The broad-leaved cornel in Laurel Glen, yet green in the bud (*Cornus circinata?*). The small-leaved cornel, with a small cyme or corymb as late as the last (*Cornus paniculata*), and the red osier by the river (*Cornus stolonifera*), which I have not seen this year.

June 13, 1853. 9 A. M. To Orchis Swamp. — I find that there are two young hawks. One has left the nest, and is perched on a small maple seven or eight rods distant. It appears much smaller than the former one. I am struck by its large naked head, so vulture-like, and large eyes, as if the vulture's were an inferior stage through which the hawk passed. Its feet, too, are large, remarkably developed, by which it holds to its perch securely, like an old bird, before its wings can perform their office. It has a buff breast, striped with dark brown. P——, when I told him of this nest, said he would like to carry one of his rifles down there. But I told him that I should be sorry to have them killed, I would rather save one of these hawks than have a hundred hens and chickens. It was worth more to see them soar, especially now that they are so rare in the landscape. It is easy to buy eggs, but not to buy hen-hawks. My neighbors would not hesitate to shoot the last pair of hen-hawks in the town to save a few of their chickens! But such economy is narrow and groveling. I would rather never taste chickens' meat nor hens' eggs than never to see a hawk sailing through the upper air again. The sight is worth incomparably more than a chicken soup or boiled egg. So we exterminate the deer and substitute the hog. It was amusing to observe the swaying to and fro of the young hawk's head to counterbalance the gentle action of the bough in the wind.

Violets appear to be about done generally. Four-leaved loosestrife just out; also, the smooth wild rose yesterday. The pogonia at Forget-me-not Brook.

What was that rare and beautiful bird in the dark woods under the Cliffs, with black above and white spots and bars, a large triangular blood-red spot on breast, and sides of breast and beneath, white? Note, a warble, like the oriole, but softer and sweeter. It was quite tame. Probably a rose-breasted grossbeak. At first I thought it was a chewink, as it sat side-

ways to me, and was going to call Sophia to
look at it, but then it turned its breast full
toward me, and I saw the large, triangular,
blood-red spot occupying the greater part of it.
. . . It is a memorable event to meet with so
rare a bird. Birds answer to flowers, both in
their abundance and their rareness. The meeting with a rare and beautiful bird like this is
like meeting with some rare and beautiful
flower, which you may never find again perchance, like the great purple-fringed orchis, at
least. How much it enhances the wildness and
the richness of the forest.

June 13, 1854. 2 p. m. By boat to Bittern
Cliff, and so to Lee's Cliff. I hear the muttering of thunder and see a dark cloud in the
horizon ; am uncertain how far up stream I
shall get.

Now in shallow places near the bends the large
and conspicuous spikes of the broad-leaved potamogeton rise thickly above the water. . . .

I see the yellow water ranunculus in dense
fields now in some places on the side of the
stream, two or three inches above water, and
many gone to seed.

The flowering fern is reddish and yellowish-
green on the meadows.

It is so warm that I stop to drink wherever
there is a spring.

The little globular, drooping, reddish buds of the *Chimaphila umbellata* (*pipsissewa*) are now very pretty.

How beautiful the solid cylinders of the lamb-kill now just before sunset, small ten-sided rosy-crimson basins, about two inches above the re-curved, drooping, dry capsules of last year, and sometimes those of the year before, two inches lower.

When I have stayed out thus till late, many miles from home, and have heard a cricket be-ginning to chirp louder near me in the grass, I have felt that I was not far from home after all. Began to be weaned from my village home.

I see over the bream nests little schools of countless minute minnows (can they be young breams?), the breams being still in their nests.

It is surprising how thickly-strewn our soil is with arrow heads. I never see the surface broken in sandy places but I think of them. I find them on all sides, not only in corn, grain, potato, and bean fields, but in pastures and woods, by woodchucks' holes and pigeon beds, and, as to-night, in a pasture where a restless cow had pawed the ground.

Is not the rosa lucida paler than the nitida?

June 13, 1860. 2 P. M. To Martial Miles's *via* Clamshell. I see at Martial Miles's two young woodchucks taken sixteen days ago, when

they were perhaps a fortnight old. There were
four in all, and they were dug out by the aid of
a dog. The mother successively *pushed out* her
little ones to the dog to save herself, and one
was at once killed by the dog. These two are
now nearly one third grown. They have found
a hole within the house, into which they run, and
whither they have carried shavings, etc., and
made a nest. Thence they run out doors and
feed close about the house, lurking behind barrels, etc. They eat yarrow, clover, catnip, etc.,
and are fed with milk and bread. They do not
drink the milk like a dog or a cat, but simply
suck it, taking the sharp edge of the shallow tin
dish in their mouths. They are said to spit like
a cat. They eat bread sitting upright on their
haunches, and holding it in their forepaws just
like a squirrel. That is their common and
natural mode of eating. They are as gray
(hoary) as the old, or grayer. Mrs. Miles says
they sleep on their heads, *i. e.*, curling their
heads under them ; also, that they can back as
straight into their hole as if they went head
foremost. I saw a full-grown one this P. M.
which stood so erect and still (its paws hanging
down and inobvious as its ears) that it might be
mistaken for a short and very stout stake.

This P. M. the streets are strewn with the
leaves of the button-wood, which are still fall-

ing. Looking up, I see many more half-formed leaves hanging wilted or withered. I think that the leaves of these trees were especially injured by the cold wind of the 10th, and are just now falling in consequence. I can tell when I am under a button-wood by the number of leaves on the ground. With the other trees it was mainly a mechanical injury, done rather by the wind than the cold, but the tender shoots of this tree were killed.

June 14, 1840.

> " In glory and in joy,
> Behind his plough, upon the mountain side."
>
> (Wordsworth.)

I seemed to see the woods wave on a hundred mountains, as I read these lines, and the distant rustling of their leaves reached my ear.

June 14, 1851. Full moon last night. Set out on a walk to Conantum at 7 P. M. A serene evening, the sun going down behind clouds. A few white or slightly-shaded piles of clouds floating in the eastern sky, but a broad, clear, mellow cope left for the moon to rise into. An evening for poets to describe. As I proceed along the back road I hear the lark still singing in the meadow, and the bobolink, the golden robin on the elms, and the swallows twittering about the barns. All Nature is in an expectant attitude. Before Goodwin's house at the open-

9

ing of the Sudbury road, the swallows are diving
at a tortoise-shell cat who cavorts rather awkwardly as if she did not know whether to be
scared or not. And now, the sun having buried
himself in the low cloud in the west and hung
out his crimson curtain, I hear, while sitting by
the wall, the sound of the stake-driver at a distance, like that made by a man pumping in a
neighboring farm-yard, watering his cattle, or
like chopping wood before his door on a frosty
morning, and I can imagine it like driving a
stake in a meadow. The pumper. I immediately went in search of the bird, but after going one third of a mile, it did not sound much
nearer, and the two parts of the sound did not
appear to proceed from the same place. What
is the peculiarity of these sounds which pene-
trate so far on the key-note of Nature? At last
I got near to the brook in the meadow behind
Hubbard's wood, but I could not tell if it were
farther or nearer than that. When I got within
half a dozen rods of the brook, it ceased, and I
heard it no more. I suppose that I scared it.
As before I was farther off than I thought, so
now I was nearer than I thought. It is not
easy to understand how so small a creature can
make so loud a sound by merely sucking or throwing out water with pump-like lungs. It was a
sound as of gulping water.

Where my path crosses the brook in the meadow there is a singularly sweet scent in the heavy air where the brakes grow, the fragrance of the earth, as if the dew were a distillation of the fragrant essences of Nature.

And now, as I enter the embowered willow causeway, my senses are captivated again by a sweet fragrance. I know not if it be from a particular plant, or all together, sweet-scented vernal grass, or sweet briar. Now the sun is fairly gone, I hear the dreaming toad (?), and the whippoorwill from some darker wood, and the cuckoo. It is not far from eight. The song-sparrows sing quite briskly among the willows as if it were spring again, the blackbird's harsher note resounds over the meadow, and the veery's comes up from the wood. Fishes are dimpling the surface of the river, seizing the insects which alight. A solitary fisherman in his boat inhabits the scene. As I ascended the hill, I found myself in a cool, fragrant, dewy, up-country, mountain, morning air. The moon was now seen rising over Fair Haven, and at the same time reflected in the river, pale and white, like a silvery cloud barred with a cloud. In Conant's orchard I hear the faint cricket-like song of a sparrow, saying its vespers, as if it were a link between the cricket and the bird. The robin sings now, though the moon shines silvery, and the veery jingles its trill.

* I hear the fresh and refreshing sound of falling water as I have heard it in New Hampshire. It is a sound we do not commonly hear.

How moderate, deliberate is Nature, how gradually the shades of night gather and deepen, giving man ample leisure to bid farewell to day, conclude his day's affairs, and prepare for slumber. The twilight seems out of proportion to the length of the day.

I see, indistinctly, oxen asleep in the fields, silent, in majestic slumber, reclining statuesque, Egyptian, like the Sphinx. What solid rest! How their heads are supported!

From Conant's summit I hear as many as fifteen whippoorwills, or whip-or-I-wills, at once, the succeeding cluck sounding strangely foreign, like a hewer at work elsewhere.

How sweet and encouraging it is to hear the sound of some artificial music from the midst of woods or from the top of a hill at night, borne on the breeze from some distant farm-house, the human voice, or a flute. That is a civilization one can endure, worth having. I could go about the world listening for the strains of music. Men use this gift but sparingly, nevertheless. What should we think of a bird which had the gift of song, but used it only once in a dozen years! like the plant which blossoms only once in a century.

Peabody says that the night-hawk retires to rest about the time the whippoorwill begins its song. The whippoorwill begins now at half-past seven. I hear the night-hawk after nine o'clock. He says the latter flies low in the evening, but it also flies high, as it must needs do to make the booming sound.

Not much before ten o'clock does the moonlight night begin, when man is asleep and day fairly forgotten. Then is the beauty of moonlight seen upon lonely pastures where cattle are silently feeding. Then let me walk in a diversified country of hill and dale, with heavy woods on one side, and copses and scattered trees enough to give me shadows. As I return, a mist is on the river, which is thus taken into the bosom of Nature again.

June 14, 1852. Saw a wild rose from the cars in Weston. The early red roses are out in gardens at home.

June 14, 1853. P. M. To White's Pond. Heard the first locust from amid the shrubs by the roadside. He comes with heat.

Snake sloughs are found nowadays, bleached and whitish.

I observed the cotton of aphides on the alders yesterday and to-day. How regularly these phenomena appear, even the stains or spots or galls on leaves, as that bright yellow on blackberry leaves and those ring spots on maple leaves I see to-day, exactly the same pattern with last year's, and the crimson frosting on the black birch leaves I saw the other day. Then there are the huckleberry apples and the large green puffs on the panicled andromeda, and also I see now the very light or whitish solid and juicy apples on the swamp pink with a fungus-like smell when broken.

Erigeron strigosum. Some white, some purplish, common now, and daisy-like. I put it rather early on the 9th.

Instead of the white lily which requires mud or the sweet flag, here grows the blue flag in the water, thinly about the shore. The color of the flower harmonizes singularly with the water. With our boat's prow to the shore, we sat half an hour this evening, listening to the bull-frogs. What imperturbable fellows ! One sits perfectly still behind some blades of grass while the dog is chasing others within two feet. Some are quite handsome, large, and spotted. We see here and there light - colored, greenish, or white spots on the bottom, where a fish — a bream, perhaps — has picked away all the dead wood and leaves for her nest over a space of eighteen inches or more. Young bream, from one to three inches long, light - colored and transparent, are swimming about, and here and there a leech in the shallow water, moving as serpents are represented to do. Large devil's needles are buzzing back and forth. They skim along the edge of the blue flags, apparently quite round this cove or further, like hen-harriers beating the bush for game. And now comes a humming-bird, humming from the woods, and alights on the blossom of a blue flag. The bull-frogs begin with one or two notes, and with each peal add another trill to their trump, *er roonk* — er-er-roonk — er-er-er-roonk, etc. I am amused to hear one after another, and then an unexpectedly deep and confident bass, as if he had charged himself with more wind than the rest. And now, as if by a general agreement, they all trump together, making a deafening noise. Sometimes one jumps up a foot out of water in the midst of these concerts. What are they about? Suddenly a tree-toad in the overhanging woods begins, and another answers, and another, with loud ranging notes, such as I never heard before, and in three minutes they are all silent again. A red-eye sings on a tree top, and a cuckoo is heard from the wood. These are the evening sounds.

As we look over the water now, the opposite woods are seen dimly through what appears not so much the condensing dew and mist as the dry

haziness of the afternoon now settled and condensed. The woods on the opposite shore have
not the distinctness they had an hour before, but
perhaps a more agreeable dimness, a sort of
gloaming, or settling and thickening of the haze
over the water, which melts tree into tree, they
being no longer bright and distinct, and masses
them agreeably, a bluish mistiness. This appears
to be an earlier gloaming before sunset. . . .

This seems the true hour to be abroad, saun-
tering far from home. Your thoughts being
already turned toward home, your walk in one
sense ended, you are in that favorable frame of
mind described by De Quincey, open to great
impressions, and you see those rare sights with
the unconscious side of the eye, which you could
not see by a direct gaze before. Then the dews
begin to descend in your mind, and its atmosphere is strained of all impurities. Home is farther away than ever ; here is home. The beauty
of the world impresses you. There is a coolness
in your mind as in a well. Life is too grand
for ripples. The wood-thrush launches forth his
evening strains from the midst of the pines. I
admire the moderation of this master. There is
nothing tumultuous in his song. He launches
forth one strain of pure, unmatchable melody,
and then he pauses and gives the hearer and
himself time to digest this, and then another and

another at suitable intervals. Men talk of the
rich song of other birds, the thrasher, mocking-
bird, nightingale. But I doubt, I doubt. They
know not what they say. There is as great an
interval between the thrasher and the wood-
thrush as between Thompson's " Seasons " and
Homer. The sweetness of the day crystallizes
in this morning coolness.

June 14, 1854. Caught a locust, properly
harvest fly, drumming on a birch, which ——
and —— think like the *septendecim*, except that
ours has not red eyes, but black ones. Harris
says of the other kind, the dog-day cicada (*canic-
ularis*) or harvest fly, that it begins to be heard
invariably at the beginning of dog days ; that he
has heard it for many years in succession, with
few exceptions, on the 25th of July.

June 14, 1857. [Plymouth.] B. M. W——
tells me that he learns from pretty good authority that Webster once saw the sea serpent. It
seems it was first seen in the bay between Manomet and Plymouth Beach by a perfectly reli-
able witness (many years ago) who was accustomed to look out on the sea with his glass every
morning the first thing, as regularly as he ate
his breakfast. One morning he saw this mon-
ster, with a head somewhat like a horse's, raised
some six feet above the water, and his body, the
size of a cask, trailing behind. He was career-

ing over the bay, chasing the mackerel, which
ran ashore in their fright, and were washed up
and died in great numbers. The story is that
Webster had appointed to meet some Plymouth
gentlemen at Manomet and spend the day fishing with them. After the fishing was over he set
out to return to Duxbury in his sail-boat with
Peterson, as he had come, and on the way they
saw the sea serpent, which answered to the common account of this creature. It passed directly
across the bows only six or seven rods off, and
then disappeared. On the sail homeward, Webster, having had time to reflect on what had occurred, at length said to Peterson, "For God's
sake never say a word about this to any one, for
if it should be known that I have seen the sea
serpent, I should never hear the last of it, but,
wherever I went, should have to tell the story to
every one I met." So it has not leaked out till
now.

W—— also tells me (and E. W—— confirms
it, his father having probably been of the party)
that many years ago a party of Plymouth gentlemen rode round by the shore to the Gurnet, and
there had a high time. When they set out to
return, they left one of their number, a General
Winslow, asleep, and, as they rode along homeward, amused themselves with conjecturing what
he would think when he waked up and found

himself alone. When at length he awoke, he comprehended his situation at once, and, being somewhat excited by the wine he had drunk, he mounted his horse and rode along the shore to Saquish Head in the opposite direction. From here to Plymouth Beach is about a mile and a quarter, but, it being low tide, he waded his horse as far as the Beacon, north of the channel at the entrance to Plymouth Harbor, about three quarters of a mile, and then boldly swam him across to the end of Plymouth Beach, about half a mile further, notwithstanding a strong current. Having landed safely, he whipped up and soon reached the town, having come only about eight miles, and having ample time to warm and dry himself at the tavern before his companions arrived, who had at least twenty miles to ride about through Marshfield and Duxbury. When they found him sitting by the tavern fire, they at first thought it was his ghost.

June 14, 1859. P. M. To Flint's Pond. — Pout's nest with a straight entrance some twenty inches long and a simple round nest at end. The young, just hatched, all head, light colored, under a mass of weedy hummocks which is all under water.

The rose-breasted grossbeak is common now in the Flint's Pond woods. It is not at all shy, and our richest singer, perhaps, after the wood-

thrush. The rhythm is very like that of the tanager, but the strain is perfectly clear and sweet.
One sits on the bare dead twig of a chestnut
high over the road at Gourgas wood, and over
my head, and sings clear and loud at regular intervals, the strain about ten or fifteen seconds
long, rising and swelling to the end with various
modulations. Another, singing in emulation,
regularly answers it, alternating with it, from
a distance, at least a quarter of a mile off. It
sings thus long at a time, and I leave it singing
there, regardless of me.

June 14, 1860. P. M. To 2d Division. . . .
The white water ranunculus is abundant in the
brook, out, say a week, and well open in the sunshine. It is a pretty white flower, with yellow
centre, seen above the dark-brown green leaves
in the rapid water, its peduncle recurved so as to
present the flower erect half an inch to an inch
above the surface, while the buds are submerged.

June 15, 1840. I stood by the river to-day,
considering the forms of the elms reflected in
the water. For every oak and birch, too, growing on the hill-top, as well as for these elms and
willows, there is a graceful, ethereal, and ideal
tree making down from the roots, and sometimes
Nature in high tides brings her mirror to its foot
and makes it visible. Anxious Nature sometimes
reflects from pools and puddles the objects which

our groveling senses may fail to see relieved against the sky, with the pure ether for background.

It would be well if we saw ourselves as in perspective always, impressed with distinct outline on the sky, side by side with the shrubs on the river's brim. So let our life stand to heaven as some fair sun-lit tree against the western horizon, and by sunrise be planted on some eastern hill to glisten in the first rays of the dawn.

June 15, 1851. Saw the first wild rose to-day. The white weed has suddenly appeared, the clover gives whole fields a rich and florid appearance. The rich red and the sweet-scented white. The fields are blushing with the red as the western sky at evening.

The blue-eyed grass, well-named, looks up to heaven, and the yarrow, with its persistent dry stalks and heads, is now ready to blossom again. The dry stems and heads of last year's tansy stand high above the new green leaves.

I sit in the shade of the pines to hear a wood-thrush at noon; the ground smells of dry leaves; the heat is oppressive. The bird begins in a low strain, *i. e.*, it first delivers a strain on a lower key, then, a moment after, another a little higher, then another still varied from the others, no two successive strains alike, but either ascending or descending. He confines himself to his few notes in which he is unrivaled, as if his kind had learned this and no more, anciently.

I perceive, as formerly, a white froth dripping from the pitch pines just at the base of the new shoots. It has no taste.

The pollywogs in the pond are now full-tailed.

The hickory leaves are blackened by a recent frost, which reminds me that this is near their northern limit.

The rapidity with which the grass grows is remarkable. The 25th of May I walked to the hills in Wayland, and when I returned across lots do not remember that I had much occasion to think of the grass, or to go round any fields to avoid treading on it. But just a week afterward, at Worcester, it was high and waving in the fields, and I was to some extent confined to the road, and the same was the case here. Apparently in a month you get from fields which you can cross without hesitation, to haying time. It has grown you hardly know when, be the weather what it may, sunshine or storm.

I start up a solitary woodcock in the shade of some copse ; it goes off with a startled, rattling, hurried note.

After walking by night several times, I now walk by day, but I am not aware of any crowning advantage in it. I see small objects better, but it does not enlighten me any. The day is more trivial.

What a careful gardener Nature is! She
does not let the sun come out suddenly with all
his intensity after rain and cloudy weather, but
graduates the change to suit the tenderness of
plants.

I see the tall crowfoot now in the meadows,
Ranunculus acris, with a smooth stem. I do
not notice the *bulbosus* which was so common a
fortnight ago. The rose-colored flowers of the
Kalmia angustifolia, lambkill, just opened and
opening. The *Convallaria bifolia* growing stale
in the woods. The *Hieracium venosum*, veiny-
leaved hawk-weed, with its yellow blossoms, in
the woodland path. The *Hypoxis erecta*, yellow
Bethlehem star, where there is a thick wiry grass
in open paths, might well be called yellow-eyed
grass. The *Pyrola asarifolia*, with its pagoda-
like stem of flowers, *i. e.*, broad-leaved winter-
green. The *Trientalis Americana*, like last, in
the woods, with its star-like white flower and
pointed, whorled leaves. The prunella, too, is
in blossom, and the rather delicate *Thesium um-
bellatum*, a white flower. The Solomon's-seal,
with a greenish, drooping raceme of flowers at
the top, I do not identify.

I find I postpone all actual intercourse with
my friends to a certain real intercourse which
takes place commonly when we are actually at a
distance from one another.

June 15, 1852. Yesterday we smelt the sea strongly. The sea breeze alone made the day tolerable. This morning, a shower. The robin only sings the louder for it. He is inclined to sing in foul weather.

To Clematis Brook. 1.30 P. M.

Very warm. This melting weather makes a stage in the year. The crickets creak louder and more steadily. The bull-frogs croak in earnest. The dry z-ing of the locust is heard. The drouth begins. Bathing cannot be omitted. The conversation of all boys in the streets is whether they will or will not, or who will, go in a-swimming. . . . You lie with open windows and hear the sounds in the streets. The seringo sings now *at noon* on a post, has a light streak over eye. The autumnal dandelion. Leontodon or Apargia. *Erigeron integrifolium* or *strigosum, i. e.,* narrow-leaved daisy fleabane of Gray, very common, like a white aster.

Men are inclined to be amphibious, to sympathize with fishes now. I desire to get wet, saturated with water. The North River, Assabet, by the old stone bridge, affords the best bathing-place I think of, — a pure, sandy, uneven bottom, with a swift current, a grassy bank, and overhanging maples, transparent water, deep enough, where you can see every fish in it. Though you stand still, you feel the rippling current about you.

Young robins, dark-speckled, and the pigeon woodpecker flies up from the ground and darts away.

The farm-houses under their shady trees look as if their inhabitants were taking their siesta at this hour. I pass Baker's in the rear through the open pitch-pine wood. . . . No scouring of tubs or cans now. They eat and all are gone to sleep preparing for an early tea, excepting the indefatigable, never-resting hoers in the cornfield, who have carried a jug of molasses and water to the field, and will wring their shirts to-night. I shall ere long hear the horn blow for their early tea. The wife or the hired Irish woman steps to the door and blows the long tin horn, a cheering sound to the laborers in the field.

The motive of the laborer should be not to get his living, to get a good job, but to perform well a certain work. A town must pay its engineers so well that they shall not feel they are working for low ends, as for a livelihood mainly, but for scientific ends. Do not hire a man who does your work for money, but him who does it for love, and pay him well.

On Mount Misery, panting with heat, looking down the river. The haze an hour ago reached to Wachusett ; now it obscures it.

Methinks there is a male and female shore to the river, one abrupt, the other flat and mead-

10

owy. Have not all streams this contrast more or less, — on the one hand eating into the bank, on the other depositing their sediment?

The year is in its manhood now. The very river looks warm, and there is none of that light celestial blue seen in far reaches in the spring.

I see fields a mile distant reddened with sorrel.

The very sight of distant water is refreshing, though a bluish steam appears to rise on it.

How refreshing the sound of the smallest waterfall in hot weather. I sit by that on Clematis Brook, and listen to its music. The very sight of this half stagnant pond-hole drying up and leaving bare mud, with the pollywogs and turtles making off in it, is agreeable and encouraging to behold, as if it contained the very seeds of life, the liquor, rather, boiled down. The foulest water will bubble purely. They speak to our blood, even these stagnant, slimy pools. Even this water has, no doubt, its falls nobler than Montmorenci, grander than Niagara, in the course of its circulations.

Cattle walk along now in a brook or ditch for coolness, lashing their tails, and browse the edges; or they stand concealed for shade amid thick bushes. How perfectly acquainted they are with man.

I hear the scream of a great hawk sailing

with a ragged wing against the high wood side,
apparently to scare his prey, and so detect it,
shrill, harsh, fitted to excite terror in sparrows,
and to issue from his split and curved bill, spit
with force from his mouth with an undulatory
quaver imparted to it from his wings or motion
as he flies. I see his open bill the while against
the sky. A hawk's ragged wing will grow whole
again, but so will not a poet's.

Here at Well Meadow head I see the fringed
purple orchis, unexpectedly beautiful, though a
pale lilac purple, a large spike of purple flowers.
I find two [of the same species], the grandiflora
of Bigelow and fimbriata of Gray. Bigelow
thinks it the most beautiful of all the orchises.
. . . Why does it grow there only, far in a
swamp, remote from public view? It is somewhat fragrant, reminding me of the lady's slipper. Is it not significant that some rare and delicate and beautiful flowers should be found only
in unfrequented wild swamps? . . . Yet I am
not sure but this is a fault in the flower. It is
not quite perfect in all its parts. A beautiful
flower must be simple, not spiked. It must
have a fair stem and leaves. The stem is rather
naked, and the leaves are for shade and moisture. It is fairest seen rising from amid brakes
and hellebore, its lower part, or rather naked
stem, concealed. Where the most beautiful wild

flowers grow, there man's spirit is fed and poets grow. It cannot be high-colored, growing in the shade. Nature has taken no pains to exhibit it, and few that bloom are ever seen by mortal eyes.

There are few really cold springs. How few men can be believed when they say one is cold. I go out of my way to the Boiling Spring. It is as cold as the coldest well water. What a treasure is such a spring! Who *divined* it?

8 P. M. On river. No moon. A deafening sound from toads, and intermittingly from bull-frogs. What I have thought to be frogs prove to be toads, sitting by thousands along the shore, and trilling short and loud, not so long a quaver as in the spring. And I have not heard them in those pools, now indeed mostly dried up, where I heard them in the spring. (I do not know what to think of my midsummer frog now.) The bull-frogs are very loud, of various degrees of baseness and sonorousness, answering each other across the river with two or three grunting croaks. They are not now so numerous as the toads. It is candle light. The fishes leap. The meadows sparkle with the coppery light of fire-flies. The evening star, multiplied by undulating water, is like bright sparks of fire continually ascending. The reflections of the trees are generally indistinct. There is a low mist slightly enlarging the river, through

which the arches of the stone bridge are just
visible, as in a vision. The mist is singularly
bounded, collected here while there is none there,
close up to the bridge on one side and none on
the other, depending apparently on currents of
air. . . . There is a low crescent of northern
light, and shooting stars from time to time. . . .
I paddle with a bough, the Nile boatman's oar,
which is rightly pliant, and you do not labor
much.

June 15, 1853. P. M. To Trillium Woods.
Clover now in its prime. What more luxuriant than a clover field. The poorest soil that
is covered with it looks incomparably fertile.
This is perhaps the most characteristic feature
of June, resounding with the hum of insects,
such a blush on the fields. The rude health of
the sorrel cheek has given place to the blush
of clover. Painters are wont, in their pictures
of Paradise, to strew the field too thickly with
flowers. There should be moderation in all
things. Though we love flowers we do not
want them so thick under our feet that we
cannot walk without treading on them. But
a clover field in bloom is some excuse for
them. . . .

Here are many wild roses northeast of Trillium Woods. We are liable to underrate this
flower, on account of its commonness. Is it not

the queen of our flowers? How ample and high-colored its petals, glancing half concealed from its own green bowers. There is a certain noble and delicate civility about it, not wildness. It is properly the type of the rosaceæ, or flowers, among others, of most wholesome fruits. It is at home in the garden, as readily cultivated as apples. It is the pride of June. In summing up its attractions I should mention its rich color, size, and form, the rare beauty of its bud, its fine fragrance and the beauty of the entire shrub, not to mention the almost innumerable varieties it runs into. I bring home the buds ready to expand, put them into a pitcher of water, and the next morning they open, and fill my chamber with fragrance. This found in the wilderness must have reminded the Pilgrim of home.

For a week past I have heard the cool, watery note of the goldfinch, from time to time, as it twittered past.

June 15, 1854. I think the birds sing somewhat feebler now-a-days. The note of the bobolink begins to sound somewhat rare.

June 15, 1858. That coarse grass in the Island Meadow which grows in full circles, as in the Great Meadows, is wool grass. Some is now fairly in bloom. Many plants have a similar habit of growth. The *Osmunda rega-*

lis growing in very handsome hollow circles, or
sometimes only crescents, or arcs of circles, is
now generally of a peculiarly tender green, but
some has begun to go to seed and look brown;
hollow circles one or two feet to a rod in diameter. These two are more obvious when, as
now, all the rest of the meadow is covered with
water.

June 16, 1852. 4.30 A. M. A low fog on
the meadows. The scattered cloud wisps in the
sky, like a squadron thrown into disorder, at the
approach of the sun. The sun now gilds an
eastern cloud, giving it a broad, bright, coppery-
golden edge, fiery bright, notwithstanding which
the protuberances of the cloud cast dark shadows ray-like up into the day. The earth looks
like a debauchee after the sultry night. Birds
sing at this hour as in the spring. The white
lily is budded. Paddle down from the ash tree
to the swimming-place. The farther shore is
crowded with polygonum and pontederia leaves.
There seems to have intervened no night. The
heat of the day is unabated. You perspire before sunrise. The bull-frogs boom still. No
toads now. The river appears covered with an
almost imperceptible blue film. The sun is not
yet over the bank. What wealth in a stagnant
river! There is music in every sound in the
morning atmosphere. As I look up over the

bay I see the reflection of the meadow, woods, and Hosmer Hill, at a distance, the tops of the trees cut off by a slight ripple. Even the pine groves on the near bank are distinctly reflected. Owing to the reflections of the distant woods and hills you seem to be paddling into a vast hollow country, doubly novel and interesting. Thus the *voyageur* is lured onward to fresh pastures. The melting heat begins again as soon as the sun gets up. The bull-frog lies on the very surface of the pads, showing his great yellow throat (color of the yellow breeches of the old school), and protuberant eyes, his whole back out, revealing a vast expanse of belly, his eyes like ranunculus, or yellow lily buds, winking from time to time, and showing his large, dark-bordered tympanum, imperturbable looking. His yellow throat swells up like a small moon at a distance over the pads when he croaks.

The floating pond-weed, *Potamogeton natans*, with the oblong oval leaf floating on the surface, now in bloom. The yellow water ranunculus still yellows the river in the middle where shallow, in beds many rods long. It is one of the capillary leaved plants.

By and by the Bidens (marigold) will stand in the river as now the ranunculus. The spring yellows are faint, cool, innocent as the saffron morning compared with the blaze of noon. The autumnal, methinks, are the fruit of the dog days, heats of manhood or age, not youth. The former are pure, transparent, crystalline, viz., the willow catkins and the early cinquefoils. This ranunculus, too, standing two or three inches above the water, is of a light yellow, especially at a distance. This I think is the rule with respect to spring flowers, though there are exceptions.

9 P. M. Down railroad. Heat lightning in the distance; a sultry night. The sound of a flute from some villager. How rare among men so fit a thing as the sound of a flute at evening! — Have not the fire-flies in the meadow relation to the stars above, *étincelant.* When the darkness comes we see stars beneath also. — The sonorous note of the bull-frog is heard a mile off in the river, the loudest sound this evening. Ever and anon the sound of his trombone comes over the meadows and fields.

Do not the stars, too, show their light for love, like the fire-flies? There are northern lights, shooting high up, withal.

June 16, 1853. 4 A. M. To Nashawtuck, by boat. Before 4 A. M. or sunrise, the sound of chip-birds, robins, blue-birds, etc., is incessant. It is a crowing on the roost, I fancy, as the cock crows before he goes abroad. They do not sing deliberately as at evening, but greet the morning

with an incessant twitter. Even the crickets
seem to join the concert. Yet I think it is not
the same every morning, though it may be fair.
An hour or two later there is comparative silence. The awaking of the birds, a tumultuous
twittering.

At sunrise a slight mist curls along the surface of the water. When the sun falls on this,
it looks like a red dust.

As seen from the top of the hill, the sun just
above the horizon, red and shorn of beams, is
somewhat pear-shaped, owing to some irregular-
ity in the refraction of the lower strata of the
air, produced, as it were, by the dragging of the
lower part, and then it becomes a broad ellipse,
the lower half a dun red, owing to the greater
grossness of the air there.

The distant river is like molten silver at this
hour. It reflects merely the light, not the blue.

What shall I name that small cloud that attends the sun's rising, that hangs over the por-
tals of the day, like an embroidered banner, and
heralds his coming, though sometimes it proves
a portcullis which falls and cuts off the new day
in its birth.

Found four tortoises' nests on the high bank
just robbed, and the eggs devoured, one not
emptied of its yolk. Others had been robbed
some days. Apparently about three eggs to

each. Presently I saw a skunk making off with an undulating motion, a white streak above and a parallel and broader black one below; undoubtedly the robber.

A sweet brier, apparently yesterday.

Coming along I heard a singular sound as of a bird in distress amid the bushes, and turned to relieve it. Next thought of a squirrel in an apple-tree barking at me. Then found that it came from a hole in the ground under my feet, a loud sound between a grunting and a wheezing, yet not unlike the sound a red squirrel sometimes makes, though louder. Looking down the hole, I saw the tail and hind quarters of a wood-chuck which seemed to be contending with another farther in. Reaching down carefully I took hold of the tail, and though I had to pull very hard indeed, I drew him out between the rocks, a bouncing, great fat fellow, and tossed him a little way down the hill. As soon as he recovered from his bewilderment he made for the hole again, but I barring the way, he ran elsewhere.

P. M. To Baker Farm by boat.

Was that a smaller bittern or a meadow-hen that we started from out the button-bushes? What places for the mud-hen beneath the stems of the button-bushes along the shore, all shaggy with rootlets, as if all the weeds the river pro-

tected, all the ranunculus at least, had drifted
and lodged against them. Their stems are so
nearly horizontal near the mud and water that
you can clamber along on them over the water
many rods. It is one of the wildest features in
our scenery. There is scarcely any firm footing
on the ground except where a musk-rat has made
a heap of clam shells. Picture the river at a
low stage of the water, the pads, shriveled in the
sun, hanging from the dark brown stems of the
button-bushes which are all shaggy with masses
of dark rootlets, an impenetrable thicket, and a
stake-driver or *Ardea minor* sluggishly winging
his way up the stream.

The breams' nests, like large, deep milk pans,
are left high and dry on the shore. They are
not only deepened within, but have raised edges.
In some places they are as close together as they
can be, with each a great bream in it whose
waving fins and tail are tipped with a sort of
phosphorescent luminousness.

We sailed all the way back from Baker Farm,
though the wind blew very nearly at right angles
with the river much of the way. By sitting on
one side of the boat we made its edge serve for
a keel, so that it would mind the helm. The
dog swam for long distances behind us. Each
time we passed under the lee of a wood, we were
becalmed, and then met with contrary and flawy

winds till we got fairly beyond its influence.
But you can always sail either up or down the
river, for the wind inclines to blow along the
channel, especially where the banks are high.
We taste at each cool spring with which we are
acquainted in the bank, making haste to reach it
before the dog, who otherwise is sure to be found
cooling himself in it. We sometimes use him
to sit in the stern and trim the boat while we
both row, for he is heavy, and otherwise we sink
the bow too much in the water. But he has a
habit of standing too near the rower, and at each
stroke receiving a fillip from the rower's fists;
so at last he tumbles himself overboard and takes
a riparian excursion. We are amused to see how
judiciously he selects his points for crossing the
river from time to time, in order to avoid long
circuits made necessary on land by bays and
meadows, and keep as near us as possible.

Found at Bittern Cliff the *Potentilla arguta,*
crowded cinquefoil, our only white one, stem and
leaves somewhat like the Norvegica, but more
woolly ; a yellowish white.

June 16, 1854. 5 A. M. Up railroad. As the
sun went down last night round and red in a
damp, misty atmosphere, so now it rises in the
same manner, though there is no dense fog.

Observed yesterday the erigeron with a purple
tinge. I cannot tell whether this which seems in

other respects the same with the white is the strigosum or the annuum.

Nymphœa odorata.   Again I scent the white lily, and a season I had waited for has arrived. How indispensable all these experiences to make up the summer.   It is the emblem of purity, and its scent suggests it.   Growing in stagnant and muddy water, it bursts up so pure and fair to the eye and so sweet to the scent, as if to show us what purity and sweetness reside in and can be extracted from the slime and muck of earth. It is the resurrection of virtue.   It is these sights and sounds and fragrances that convince us of our immortality.   No man believes against all evidence.   Our external senses consent with our internal.   This fragrance assures me that though all other men fall, one shall stand fast, though a pestilence sweep over the earth, it shall at least spare one man.   The Genius of Nature is unimpaired.   Her flowers are as fair and as fragrant as ever.

As for birds, I think that their choir begins to be decidedly less full and loud. . . . The bobolink, full strains, but farther between.

The *Rosa nitida* grows along the edge of the ditches, the half open flowers showing the deepest rosy tints, so glowing that they make an evening or twilight of the surrounding afternoon, seeming to stand in the shade or twilight.

Already the bright petals of yesterday's flowers
are thickly strewn along on the black sand at the
bottom of the ditch.

The *Rosa nitida*, the earlier (?), with its narrow, shiny leaves and prickly stem, and its mod-
erate-sized rose-pink petals.

The *Rosa lucida*, with its broader and duller
leaves, but larger and perhaps deeper-colored
and more purple petals, perhaps yet higher
scented, and its great yellow centre of stamens.

The smaller, lighter, but perhaps more delicately tinted *Rosa rubiginosa*. One and all
drop their petals the second day. I bring home
the buds of the three ready to expand at night,
and the next day they perfume my chamber.
Add to these the white lily just begun, also the
swamp pink, and the great orchis, and mountain
laurel, now in prime, and perhaps we must say
that the fairest flowers are now to be found, or
say a few days later. The arethusa is disappearing.

It is eight days since I plucked the great orchis. One is perfectly fresh still in my pitcher.
It may be plucked when the spike is only half
opened, and will open completely and keep perfectly fresh in a pitcher more than a week. Do
I not live in a garden, in Paradise? I can go
out each morning before breakfast, — I do, —
and gather these flowers with which to perfume
my chamber where I read and write all day.

The note of the cherry-bird is fine and ringing, but peculiar and very noticeable. With its crest it is a resolute and combative looking bird.

Meadow-sweet to-morrow.

June 16, 1855.   See young and weak striped squirrels now-a-days with slender tails, asleep on horizontal boughs above their holes, or moving feebly about.   Might catch them.

June 16, 1858.   How agreeable and wholesome the fragrance of the low blackberry blossoms, reminding one of all the rosaceous, fruit-bearing plants, so near and dear to our humanity. It is one of the most deliciously fragrant flowers, reminding of wholesome fruits.

June 16, 1860. . . . It appears to me that the following phenomena occur simultaneously, say June 12, viz. : Heat about 85° at 2 P. M.   True summer.

Hylodes cease to peep.

Purring frogs (*Rana palustris*) cease.

Lightning bugs first seen.

Bull-frogs trump generally.

Afternoon showers almost regular.

Turtles fairly and generally begin to lay.

June 17, 1840.   Our lives will not attain to be spherical by lying on one or the other side forever, but only so far as we resign ourselves to the law of gravity in us, will our axis become coincident with the celestial axis, and by revolving incessantly through all circles, shall we acquire a perfect sphericity. . . .

Even the motto " business before friends " admits of a high interpretation. No interval of time can avail to defer friendship. The concerns of time must be attended to in time. I need not make haste to explore the whole secret of a star. If it were vanished quite out of the firmament so that no telescope could longer discover it, I should not despair of knowing it entirely one day.

We meet our friend with a certain awe, as if he had just lighted on the earth, and yet as if we had some title to be acquainted with him by our old familiarity with sun and moon.

June 17, 1852. 4 A. M. To Cliffs. No fog this morning. At early dawn, the windows being open, I hear a steady, breathing, cricket-like sound from the chip-bird (?) ushering in the day. Perhaps these mornings are the most memorable in the year, after a sultry night and before a sultry day, when especially the morning is the most glorious season of the day, when its coolness is most refreshing and you enjoy the glory of the summer, gilded or silvered with dews, without the torrid summer's sun or the obscuring haze. The sound of the crickets at dawn after these first sultry nights seems like the dreaming

11

of the earth still continued into the day-light.
I love that early twilight hour when the crickets
still creak right on with such dewy faith and
promise, as if it were still night, expressing the
innocence of morning, when the creak of the
cricket is fresh and bedewed.   While it has that
ambrosial sound, no crime can be committed.   It
buries Greece and Rome past resurrection.   The
earth song of the cricket!   Before Christianity
was, it is.   Health! health! health! is the burden of its song.   It is, of course, that man re-
freshed with sleep is thus innocent and healthy
and hopeful.   When we hear that sound of the
crickets in the sod, the world is not so much
with us.

I hear the universal cock-crowing with sur-
prise and pleasure, as if I never heard it before.
What a tough fellow!   How native to the earth!
Neither wet nor dry, cold nor warm kills him.

The prudent farmer improves the early morning to do some of his work before the heat becomes too oppressive, while he can use his oxen.
As yet no whetting of the scythe. . . . Ah, the
refreshing coolness of the morning, full of all
kinds of fragrance! — What is that little oliva-
ceous, yellowish bird, whitish beneath, that followed me cheeping under the bushes ?   The birds
sing well this morning, well as ever.   The brown
thrasher drowns the rest.   The lark, and in the

woods, the red-eye, veery, chewink, oven-bird, wood-thrush.

The cistus is well open now, with its broad cup-like flower, one of the most delicate yellow flowers, with large spring-yellow petals, and its stamens laid one way. It is hard to get home fresh; caducous and inclined to droop. The yellow Bethlehem-star is of a deeper yellow than the cistus, a very neat flower, grass-like.

P. M. On the river, by Hubbard's Meadow. Looking at a clump of trees and bushes on the meadow, which is commonly flooded in the spring, I saw a middling-sized rock concealed by the leaves, lying in the midst, and perceived that this had obtained a place, had made good the locality for the maples and shrubs which had found a foothold about it. Here the weeds and tender plants were detained and protected. The bowlder dropped once on a meadow makes at length a clump of trees there, and is concealed by the beneficiaries it had protected.

June 17, 1853. The pogonias, adder's tongue arethusas I see now-a-days, are getting to be numerous ; they are far too pale to compete with the *Arethusa bulbosa*, and then their snake-like odor is much against them.

There have been three ultra reformers, lecturers on slavery, temperance, the church, etc., in and about our house and Mrs. B——'s, the last

three or four days. Though one of them was a
stranger to the others, you would have thought
them old and familiar cronies. They happened
here together by accident. They addressed each
other constantly by their Christian names, and
rubbed you continually with the greasy cheek of
their kindness. I was awfully pestered with the
benignity of one of them, feared I should get
greased all over with it past restoration, tried to
keep some starch in my clothes. He wrote a
book called " A Kiss for a Blow," and he behaved as if I had given him a blow, was bent on
giving me the kiss when there was neither quar-
rel nor agreement between us. I wanted that he
should straighten his back, smooth out those
ogling wrinkles of benignity about his eyes, and
with a healthy reserve pronounce something in a
downright manner. . . . He addressed me as
" Henry " within one minute from the time I
first laid eyes on him ; and when I spoke, he
said with drawling, sultry sympathy, " Henry, I
know all you would say, I understand you perfectly, you need not explain anything to me,"
and to another, " I am going to dive into Henry's
inmost depths." I said, " I trust you will not
strike your head against the bottom." He could
tell in a dark room, with his eyes blinded, and
in perfect stillness, if there was one there whom
he loved. One of the most attractive things

about the flowers is their beautiful reserve. The truly beautiful and noble puts its lover, as it were, at an infinite distance, while it attracts him more strongly than ever. . . . What a relief to have heard the ring of one healthy, reserved tone.

The dense fields of blue-eyed grass now blue the meadows, as if, in this fair season of the year, the clouds that envelope the earth were dispersing, and blue patches begin to appear answering to the blue sky. The eyes pass from these blue patches into the surrounding green as from the patches of clear sky into the clouds.

One of the night-hawk's eggs is hatched. The young is unlike any that I have seen, exactly like a pinch of rabbit's fur, or down of that color, dropped on the ground, not two inches long, with a dimpling, somewhat regular arrangement of minute feathers in the middle, destined to become the wings and tail. Yet it even half opened its eye, and peeped, if I mistake not. Was ever bird more completely protected, both by the color of its eggs, and of its own body that sits on them, and of the young bird just hatched? Accordingly the eggs and young are rarely discovered. There was one egg still, and by the side of it this little pinch of down flattened out and not observed at first.

A foot down the hill had rolled half the egg

it came out of. There was no callowness as in
the young of most birds. It seemed a singular
place for a bird to begin its life, this little pinch
of down, and lie still on the exact spot where
the egg lay, a flat exposed shelf on the side of a
bare hill, with nothing but the whole heavens,
the broad universe above, to brood it when its
mother was away.

The huckleberry apple is sometimes a red
shoot, with tender and thick red leaves and
branchlets, in all three inches long. It is, as it
were, a monstrous precocity, and what should
have waited to become fruit is a merely bloated
or puffed up flower, a child with a great dropsi-
cal head, and prematurely bright, in a huckleberry apple. The really sweet and palateable
.huckleberry is not matured before July, and
runs the risk of drying up in drouth, and never
attaining its proper size.

There are some fine large clusters of lambkill
close to the shore of Walden, under the Peak,
fronting the south. They are early, too, and
large, apparently, both on account of the warmth
and the vicinity of the water. These flowers
are in perfect cylinders, sometimes six inches
long by two wide, and three such raying out or
upward from one centre, that is, three branches
clustered together. Examined close by, I think
this handsomer than the mountain laurel. The

color is richer, but it does not show so well at a
little distance, and the corymbs are somewhat
concealed by the green shoot and leaves rising
above them, and also by the dry remains of last
year's flowers.

The mountain laurel by Walden in its prime.
It is a splendid flower, and more red than that
in Mason's pasture. Its dry, dead-looking, brittle stems lean, as it were, over other bushes or
each other, bearing at the ends great dense corymbs five inches in diameter, of rose or pink (?)
tinged flowers, without an interstice between
them, overlapping each other, each of more than
an inch in diameter. A single flower would
be esteemed very beautiful. It is a highlander
wandered down into the plain.

June 17, 1854. 5 A. M. To Hill. A cold
fog. These mornings those who walk in grass
are thoroughly wet above mid-leg. All the earth
is dripping wet. I am surprised to feel how
warm the water is by contrast with the cold,
foggy air. . . . The dewy cobwebs are very
thick this morning, little napkins of the fairies
spread on the grass. . . .

From the Hill I am reminded of more youthful mornings, seeing the dark forms of the trees
eastward in the low grounds, partly within and
against the shining white fog, the sun just risen
over it. The mist fast rolls away eastward from

them, their tops at last streaking it and dividing it into vales, all beyond a submerged and unknown country, as if they grew on the sea-shore. Why does the fog go off always towards the sun, seen in the east when it has disappeared in the west? The waves of the foggy ocean divide and flow back for us Israelites of a day to march through.

Saw the sun reflected up from the Assabet to the hill-top through the dispersing fog, giving to the water a peculiarly rippled, pale golden hue, "gilding pale streams with heavenly alchemy."

P. M. To Walden and Cliffs. . . . It is dry, hazy June weather. We are more of the earth, farther from heaven these days. We live in a grosser element, getting deeper into the mists of earth. Even the birds sing with less vigor and vivacity. The season of hope and promise is past. Already the season of small fruits has arrived. The Indian marked the midsummer as the season when berries were ripe. We are a little saddened because we begin to see the interval between our hopes and their fulfillment. The prospect of the heavens is taken away, and we are presented only with a few small berries.

Before sundown I reached Fair Haven Hill and gathered strawberries. I find beds of large and lusty strawberry plants in sproutlands, but they appear to run to leaves and bear very little fruit, having spent themselves in leaves by the time the dry weather arrives. It is those still earlier and more stinted plants which grow on dry uplands that bear the early fruit, formed before the droughts. But the meadows produce both leaves and fruit.

I begin to see the flowering fern at a distance in the river meadows.

The sun goes down red again, like a high-colored flower of summer; as the white and yellow flowers of spring are giving place to the rose, and will soon to the red lily, etc., so the yellow sun of spring has become a red sun of June drought, round and red like a midsummer flower, production of torrid heats.

June 18, 1840. I am startled when I consider how little I am *actually* concerned about the things I write in my journal.

A fair land, indeed, do books spread open to us, from the Genesis down, — but, alas! men do not take them up kindly into their own being, and breathe into them a fresh beauty, knowing that the grimmest of them belongs to such warm sunshine and still moonlight as the present.

June 18, 1852. The hornet's nest is built with many thin layers of his paper, with an interval of about one eighth of an inch between them, so that his wall is one or two inches thick.

This probably for warmth, dryness, and light-
ness. So the carpenter has learned to sometimes build double walls.

7 P. M. To Cliffs. . . . Pyrolas are begin-
ning to blossom. The four-leaved loosestrife.
The longest days in the year have now come.
The sun goes down now (this moment) behind
Watatic, from the Cliffs. St. John's-wort is
beginning to blossom.

I hear a man playing a clarionet far off.
Apollo tending the herds of Admetus. How
cultivated, how sweet and glorious is music!
Men have brought this art to great perfection,
the art of modulating sound, by long practice,
since the world began. What superiority over
the rude harmony of savages! There is something glorious and flower-like in it. What a
contrast this evening melody with the occupa-
tions of the day. It is perhaps the most admirable accomplishment of man.

June 18, 1853. 4 A. M. By boat to Nashawtuck, to Azalea or Pinxter Spring. . . . Almost all birds appear to join the early morning
chorus before sunrise on the roost, the matin
hymn. I hear now the robin, the chip-bird, the
blackbird, the martin, etc., but I see none flying, or at least only one wing in the air not yet
illumined by the sun. As I was going up the
hill, I was surprised to see rising above the June

grass, near a walnut, a whitish object, like a
stone with a white top, or a skunk erect, for it
was black below. It was an enormous toadstool,
or fungus, a sharply conical parasol in the form
of a sugar loaf, slightly turned up at the edges,
which were rent half an inch for every inch or
two. The whole length was sixteen inches.
The pileus, or cap, was six inches long by seven
in width at the rim, though it appeared longer
than wide. . . . The stem was about one inch
in diameter and naked. The top of the cap
was quite white within and without, not smooth,
but with a stringy kind of scales turned upward
at the edge. These declined downward into a
coarse hoariness, as if the compact white fibres
had been burst by the spreading gills. It looked
much like an old felt hat pushed up into a cone,
its rim all ragged, with some meal shaken upon
it. It was almost big enough for a child's head.
It was so delicate and fragile that its whole cap
trembled at the least touch, and as I could not
lay it down without injuring it, I was obliged to
carry it home all the way in my hand, erect,
while I paddled my boat with one hand. It was
a wonder how its soft cone ever broke through
the earth. Such growths ally our age to those
earlier periods which geology reveals. I wondered if it had not some relation to the skunk,
though not in odor, yet in its color and the gen-

eral impression it made. It suggests a vegeta-
tive force which may almost make man tremble
for his dominion. It carries me back to the era
of the formation of the coal measures, the age
of the Saurus and the Pliosaurus, and when
bull-frogs were as big as bulls. Its stem had
something massy about it, like an oak, large
in proportion to the weight it had to support
(though not perhaps to the size of the cap), like
the vast hollow columns under some piazzas,
whose caps have hardly weight enough to hold
their tops together. It made you think of pictures of parasols of Chinese mandarins, or it
might have been used by the great fossil bull-
frog in his walks. What part does it play in
the economy of the world? . . . I have just been
out (7.30 A. M.) to show my fungus. . . . It is
so fragile I was obliged to walk at a funereal
pace for fear of jarring it. It is so delicately
balanced that it falls to one side on the least
inclination. It is rapidly curling up on the
edge, and the rents increasing, until it is completely fringed, and is an inch wider there. It
is melting in the sun and light, black drops and
streams falling on my hand, and fragments of
the black-fringed rim falling on the sidewalk.
Evidently such a plant can only be seen in perfection in the early morning. It is a creature
of the night, like the great moth. . . . It is

to be remarked that this grew not in low and damp soil, but high up on the open side of a dry hill . . . in the midst of, and rising above, the thin June grass. The last night was warm, the earth was very dry, and there was a slight sprinkling of rain.

I think the blossom of the sweetbrier, eglantine (now in prime), is more delicate and interesting than that of the common wild roses, though smaller and paler, and without their spicy fragrance. But its fragrance is in its leaves all summer, and the form of the bush is handsomer, curving over from a considerable height in wreaths sprinkled with numerous flowers. They open out flat soon after sunrise. Flowers whitish in middle, then pinkish rose, inclining to purple toward the edges.

How far from our minds now the early blossoms of the spring, the willow catkins, for example.

I put the parasol fungus in the cellar to preserve it, but it went on rapidly melting and wasting away from the edges upward, spreading as it dissolved, till it was shaped like a dishcover. By night, though left in the cellar all the day, there was not more than two of the six inches of the height of the cap left, and the barrel-head beneath it and its own stem looked as if a large bottle of ink had been broken

there. It defiled all it touched. The next
morning the hollow stem was left perfectly
bare, and only the hoary apex of the cone,
spreading about two inches in diameter, lay on
the ground beneath. Probably one night produced it, and in one day, with all our pains, it
wasted away. Is it not a giant mildew or mould?
In the warm, muggy night the surface of the
earth is mildewed. The mould which is the
flower of humid darkness and ignorance. The
pyramids and other monuments of Egypt are a
vast mildew or toad-stool which have met with
no light of day sufficient to waste them away.
Slavery is such a mould and superstition which
are most rank in the warm and humid portions
of the globe. Luxor sprang up one night out
of the slime of the Nile. The humblest, puniest
weed that can endure the sun is thus superior to
the largest fungus, as is the peasant's cabin to
those foul temples. . . . All things flower, both
vices and virtues, but one is essentially foul, another fair. In hell, toad-stools should be represented as overshadowing men. The priest is the
fungus of the graveyard, of the tomb. In the
animal world there are toads and lizards.

P. M. To Island by boat.

The first white lily to-day perhaps. It is the
only *bud* I have seen. The river has gone down
and left it nearly dry. On the Island, where a

month ago plants were so fresh and early, it is
now parched and crisp under my feet. I feel
the heat reflected from the ground and perceive
the dry scent of grass and leaves. So universally on dry and rocky hills, where the spring
was earliest, the autumn has already commenced. . . .

At the Flower Exhibition saw the rhododendron plucked yesterday in Fitzwilliam, N. H.
It was the earliest to be found there, and only
one bud was fully open. They say it is in perfection there the 4th of July, nearer Monadnock
than the town.

The unexpected display of flowers culled from
the gardens of the village suggests how many
virtues also are cultivated by the villagers more
than meet the eye.

Saw to-night ———'s horse, which works on the
sawing-machine at the depot, now let out to
graze along the road. At each step he lifts his
hind legs convulsively from the ground, as if the
whole earth were a treadmill continually slipping
away from under him while he climbed its con-
vex surface. It was painful to witness, but it
was symbolical of the moral condition of his
master and of all artisans in contradistinction
from artists, all who are engaged in any routine,
for to them also the whole earth is a treadmill,
and the routine results instantly in a similar

painful deformity. The horse may bear the
mark of his servitude in the muscles of his legs,
the man on his brow.

8.30 P. M. To Cliffs. Moon not quite full.
There is no wind. The greenish fires of lightning bugs are already seen in the meadow. I
almost lay my hand on one amid the leaves as I
get over the fence at the brook. I hear the
whippoorwills on different sides. White flowers
alone show much at night, as white clover and
white weed. The day has gone by with its wind
like the wind of a cannon ball, and now far in
the west it blows. By that dun-colored sky you
may track it. There is no motion nor sound in
the woods (Hubbard's Grove) along which I am
walking. The trees stand like great screens
against the sky. The distant village sounds are
the barking of dogs, that animal with which man
has allied himself, and the rattling of wagons,
for the farmers have gone into town a shopping
this Saturday night. The dog is the tamed wolf,
as the villager is the tamed savage. Near at
hand the crickets are heard in the grass chirping
from everlasting to everlasting. The humming
of a dor-bug drowns all the noise of the village,
so roomy is the universe. The moon comes out
of the mackerel cloud, and the traveler rejoices.
How can a man write the same thoughts by the
light of the moon, resting his book on a rail by

the side of a remote potato field, that he does by the light of the sun at his study table. The light is but a luminousness. My pencil seems to move through a creamy, mystic medium. The moonlight is rich and somewhat opaque, like cream, but the daylight is thin and blue, like skimmed milk. I am less conscious than in the presence of the sun, my instincts have more influence.

The farmer has improved the dry weather to burn his meadow. I love the smell of that burning, as a man may his pipe. It reminds me of a new country offering sites for the hearths of men. It is cheering as the scent of the peat fire of the first settler.

At Potter's sand bank, the sand, though cold on the surface, begins to be warm two inches beneath, and the warmth reaches at least six inches deeper. The tortoise buries her eggs just deep enough to secure this greatest constant warmth.

I passed into and along the bottom of a lake of cold and dewy evening air. Anon, as I rise higher, here comes a puff of warm air, trivially warm, a straggler from the sun's retinue, now buffeted about by the vanguard night breezes.

Before me, southward toward the moon, on higher land than I, but springy, I saw a low film of fog, like a veil, reflecting the moonlight, though none on lower ground which was not

12

springy, and up the river beyond, a battalion of
fog rising white in the moonlight in ghost-like
wisps, or like a flock of scared covenanters in a
recess amid the hills. . . .

It is worth while to walk thus in the night
after a warm or sultry day, to enjoy the fresh,
up-country, brake-like, spring-like scent in low
grounds. At night the surface of the earth is a
cellar, a refrigerator, no doubt wholesomer than
those made with ice by day. Got home at 11.

June 18, 1854. P. M. To Climbing Fern.
The meadows, like this Nut Meadow, are now
full of the latter grasses just beginning to flower,
and the graceful columns of the rue (*thalictrum*)
not yet generally in flower, and the large tree
or shrub-like Archangelica with its great umbels now fairly in bloom along the edge of the
brook. . . .

I discover that Dugan found the eggs of my
snapping turtle of June 7th, apparently the same
day. It is perhaps five or six rods from the
brook, in the sand near its edge. The surface
had been disturbed over a foot and a half in diameter, and was slightly concave. The nest commenced five inches beneath, and at its neck was
two and a half inches across, and from this
nearly four inches deep, and swelled out below
to four inches in width, shaped like a short,
rounded bottle with a broad mouth, and the sur-

rounding sand was quite firm. I took out forty-two eggs closely packed, and Dugan says he had previously taken one. They are dirty, white and spherical, a little more than one and a sixteenth of an inch in diameter, soft-shelled so that my finger left a permanent dimple in them. It was now ten days since they had been laid, and a little more than half of each was darker colored (probably the lower half) and the other, white and dry-looking. I opened one, but could detect no organization with the unarmed eye. The halves of the shell, as soon as emptied, curled up as we see them where the skunks have sucked them. They must all have been laid at one time. If it were not for the skunks and probably other animals, we should be overrun with them. Who can tell how many tortoise eggs are buried in this small desert.

Often certain words or syllables which have suggested themselves remind one better of a bird's strain than the most elaborate and closest imitation.

June 18, 1855. To Hemlocks. . . . At 3 P. M., as I walked up the bank by the Hemlocks, I saw a painted tortoise just beginning its hole. Then another a dozen rods from the river on the bare, barren field near some pitch pines, where the earth was covered with cladonias, cinquefoil, sorrel, etc. Its hole was about two thirds done.

I stooped down over it, and to my surprise, after a slight pause, it proceeded in its work directly under and within eighteen inches of my face. I retained a constrained position for three quarters of an hour or more, for fear of alarming it. It rested on its fore-legs, the front part of its shell about an inch higher than the rear, and this position was not changed, essentially, to the last. The hole was oval, broadest behind, about an inch wide and one and three quarters long, and the dirt already removed was quite wet or moistened. It made the hole and removed the dirt with its hind legs only, not using its tail or shell, which last, of course, could not enter the hole, though there was some dirt on it. It first scratched two or three times with one hind foot, then took up a pinch of the loose sand and deposited it directly behind that leg, pushing it backward to its full length, and then deliberately opening it and letting the dirt fall. Then the same with the other hind foot. This it did rapidly, using each leg alternately with perfect regularity, standing on the other one the while, and thus tilting up its shell each time, now to this side, then to that. There was half a minute or a minute between each change. The hole was made as deep as the feet could reach, or about two inches. It was very neat about its work, not scattering the dirt about more than was neces-

sary. The completing of the hole occupied perhaps five minutes. It then, without any pause,
drew its head completely into its shell, raised the
rear a little, and protruded and dropped a wet,
flesh-colored egg into the hole, one end foremost.
Then it put out its head again a little slowly,
and placed the egg one side with one hind foot.
After a delay of about two minutes it again drew
in its head and dropped another, and so on to the
fifth, drawing in its head each time, and pausing
somewhat longer between the last. The eggs
were placed in the hole without any particular
care, only well down flat, and each out of the
way of the next. I could plainly see them from
above.

After ten minutes or more, without pause or
turning, it began to scrape the moist earth into
the hole with its hind legs, and, when it had half
filled it, carefully pressed the earth down with
the edges of its hind feet, dancing on these alternately for some time, as on its knees, tilting
from side to side, pressing by the whole weight
of the rear of its shell. When it had drawn in
thus all the earth that had been moistened, it
stretched its hind legs further back and to each
side, and drew in the dry and lichen-clad crust,
and then danced upon and pressed that down,
still not moving the rear of its shell more than
one inch to right or left all the while, or chang-

ing the position of the forward part at all. The thoroughness with which the covering was done was remarkable. It persevered in drawing in and dancing on the dry surface which had never been disturbed, long after you thought it had done its duty, but it never moved its fore-feet, nor once looked round, nor saw the eggs it had laid. There were frequent pauses throughout the whole, when it rested, or ran out its head and looked about circumspectly at any noise or motion. These pauses were especially long during the covering of its eggs, which occupied more than half an hour. Perhaps it was hard work.

When it had done, it immediately started for the river at a pretty rapid rate (the suddenness with which it made these transitions was amusing), pausing from time to time, and I judged it would reach it in fifteen minutes. It was not easy to detect that the ground had been disturbed there. An Indian could not have made his cache more skillfully. In a few minutes all traces of it would be lost to the eye.

The object of moistening the earth was perhaps to enable it to take it up in its hands (?), and also to prevent its falling back into the hole. Perhaps it also helped to make the ground more compact and harder when it was pressed down. [September 10. I can find no trace of the tor-

toise eggs of June 18th, though there is no trace
of their having been disturbed by skunks. They
must have been hatched earlier.]

June 18, 1859. P. M. Sail up river. Rain
again, and we take shelter under a bridge, and
again under our boat, and again under a pine-
tree. It is worth while to sit or lie through a
shower thus under a bridge, or under a boat on
the bank, because the rain is a much more interesting and remarkable phenomenon under these
circumstances. The surface of the stream betrays every drop from the first to the last, and
all the variations of the storm, so much more
expressive is the water than the comparatively
brutish face of earth. We no doubt often walk
between drops of rain falling thinly, without
knowing it, though if on the water we should
have been advertised of it. At last the whole
surface is nicked with the abounding drops, as
if it rose in little cones to accompany or meet
the drops, till it looks like the back of some
spiny fruit or animal, and yet the differently
colored currents, light and dark, are seen through
it all. Then, when it clears up, how gradually
the surface of the water becomes more placid
and bright, the dimples becoming fewer and
finer till the prolonged reflections of trees are
seen in it, and the water is lit up with a joy in
sympathy with our own, while the earth is comparatively dead.

I saw swarms of little gnats, light-winged, dancing over the water in the midst of the rain, though you would say any drop might end one's days.

June 19, 1852.   8.30 A. M.   To Flag Hill, on which Stow, Acton, and Boxboro corner, with C——.   A fine, clear June morning, comfortable and breezy, no dust, a journey day. . . . The traveler now has the creak of the cricket to encourage him on all country routes, out of the fresh sod, still fresh as in the dawn, not interrupting his thoughts.   Very cheering and refreshing to hear, so late in the day, this morning sound.   The white-weed colors some meadows as completely as the frosting does a cake.   The waving June grass shows watered colors like grain.   No mower's scythe is heard.   The farmers are hoeing their corn and potatoes. . . . The clover is now in its glory, whole fields are *rosed* with it, mixed with sorrel, and looking deeper than it is.   It makes fields look luxuriant which are really thinly clad.   The air is full of its fragrance.   I cannot find the Linnæa at Loring's, perhaps because the woods are cut down.   Perhaps I am too late.   The robins sing more than usual, may be because of the coolness.   Buttercups and geraniums cover the meadows, the latter appearing to float on the grass, of various tints.   It has lasted long, this rather tender flower. . . . The

light of June is not golden but silvery, not torrid, but somewhat temperate. I see it reflected
from the bent grass and the under - sides of
leaves. Also I perceive faint, silvery, gleaming ripples where there is a rapid in the river
(from railroad bridge at D——'s) without sun
on it.

The mullein out with a disagreeable scent, and
the dogsbane with a quite handsome, bell-shaped
flower, beautifully striped with red (rose red ?)
within.

Facts collected by a poet are set down at last
as winged seeds of truth, *samaræ*, tinged with
his expectation. O may my words be verdurous
and sempiternal as the hills. Facts fall from the
poetic observer as ripe seeds.

The river has a June look; dark, smooth,
reflecting surfaces in shade. The sight of the
water is refreshing, suggesting coolness. The
shadows in and under elms and other trees have
not been so rich hitherto. It is grateful to look
forward half a mile into some dark, umbrageous
elm or ash.

The grape in bloom, an agreeable perfume to
many; not so to me. This is not the meadow
fragrance then which I have perceived.

May be the huckleberry bird best expresses
the season, or the red-eye. What subtile differences between one season and another.

The veiny-leaved hawk-weed out. A large swelling pasture hill with hickories left for shade, and cattle now under them. The bark is rubbed smooth and red with their hides. Pleasant to go over the hills, for there most air is stirring, but you must look out for bulls in the pastures. Saw one here reclining in the shade amid the cows. His short sanguineous horns betrayed him, and we gave him a wide berth, for they are not to be reasoned with. On our right is Acton, on our left is Stow, and forward, Boxboro. Thus King Richard sailed the Ægean, and passed kingdoms on his right and left. We are on one of the breezy hills that make the western horizon from Concord, from which we see our familiar Concord hills much changed and reduced in height and breadth. We are in a country very different from Concord, of swelling hills and long vales on the bounds of these three towns, more up-countryish. It requires considerable skill in crossing a country to avoid the houses and too cultivated parts, somewhat of the engineer's or gunner's skill so to pass a house (if you must go near it through high grass), pass the enemy's lines where houses are thick, as to make a hill or wood screen you, to shut every window with an apple-tree, for that route which most avoids the houses is not only the one in which you will be least molested, but it is by far the most agreeable. It is rare that you cannot avoid a grain-field or piece of English mowing by skirting a corn-field or nursery near by, but if you must go through high grass, then step lightly and in each other's tracks.

We soon fell into a dry swamp filled with high bushes and trees, and beneath, tall ferns, one with a large pinnate leaf five or six feet high and one foot broad, making a dense undergrowth in tufts at bottom, spreading every way. There were two species of this size, one more compound than the other. These we opened with our hands, making a path through, completely in the cool shade. I steered by the sun, though it was so high now at noon that I observed which way my short shadow fell before I entered the swamp (for in it we could see nothing of the country around), and then by keeping it on a particular side of me, I steered surely, standing still sometimes till the sun came out of a cloud, to be sure of our course. Came out at length on a side hill very near the South Acton line or Stow. . . .

The orchis keeps well. One put in my hat this morning and carried all day will last fresh a day or two at home. These are peculiar days when you find the purple orchis and the arethusa, too, in the meadows.

The fields a walker loves best to strike into

are bare, extended, rolling, bordered by copses,
with brooks and meadows in sight, sandy beneath the thin sod where now blackberries and
pinks grow, erst rye or oats, perchance these and
stony pastures where is no high grass, nor grain,
nor cultivated ground, nor houses near.

Flag Hill is about eight miles by the road
from Concord. We went much farther both
going and returning. But by a how much nobler road! Suppose you were to drive to Boxboro, what then? You pass a few teams with
their dust, drive past many farmers' barn-yards,
see where Squire Tuttle lives and barrels his apples, bait your horse at White's tavern, and so
return with your hands smelling of greasy leather
and horse hair, and the squeak of a chaise body
in your ears, with no new flower nor agreeable
experience. But going as we did, before you
got to Boxboro line, you often went much farther, many times ascended New Hampshire hills,
taking the noble road from hill to hill across
swamps and valleys, not regarding political
courses and boundaries, many times far west
in your thoughts. It is a journey of a day and
a picture of human life.

June 19, 1853. P. M. To Flint's Pond. I
see large patches of blue-eyed grass in the
meadow across the river from my window. The
pine woods at Thrush Alley emit that hot, dry

scent, reminding me even of days when I used to go a blackberrying. . . . The wood-thrush sings as usual far in the wood. A blue jay and a tanager come dashing into the pine under which I stand. The first flies directly away screaming with suspicion or disgust, but the latter, more innocent, remains. The cuckoo is heard, too, in the depths of the wood. Heard my night warbler on a solitary white pine in the Heywood clearing by the Peak. Discovered it at last looking like a small piece of black bark curving partly over the limb. No fork to its tail. It appeared black beneath; was very shy, not bigger than a yellow bird and more slender. . . .

The strain of the bobolink now sounds a little rare. It never again fills the air as in the first week after its arrival.

June 19, 1854. P. M. Up Assabet. A thunder shower in the north. Will it strike us? How impressive this artillery of the heavens! It rises higher and higher. At length the thunder seems to roll quite across the sky and all round the horizon, even where there are no clouds, and I row homeward in haste. How by magic the skirts of the cloud are gathered about us, and it shoots forward over our head, and the rain comes at a time and place which baffles all our calculations. Just before it the swamp white oak in Merrick's pasture was a very beautiful sight, with its rich shade of green, its top, as it were, incrusted with light. Suddenly comes the gust, and the big drops slanting from the north. The birds fly as if rudderless, and the trees bow and are wrenched. It comes against the windows like hail, and is blown over the roofs like steam or smoke. The lightning runs down the large elm at Holbrook's and shatters the house near by. Soon the sun shines in silver puddles in the streets.

Men may talk about measures till all is blue and smells of brimstone, and then go home and sit down and expect their measures to do their duty for them. The only measure is integrity and manhood.

June 19, 1859. To Heywood Meadow and Well Meadow. A flying squirrel's nest . . . in a covered hollow in a small old stump . . . covered with fallen leaves and a portion of the stump. Nest apparently of dry grass. Saw three young run out after the mother, and up a slender oak. The young half grown, very tender looking and weak-tailed. Yet one climbed quite to the top of an oak twenty-five feet high, though feebly. Their claws must be very sharp and early developed. The mother rested quite near on a small projecting stub, big as a pipe stem, curled crosswise on it. They have a more rounded head and snout than our other squirrels. The young in danger of being picked off by hawks.

Scare up young partridges the size of chickens; just hatched, yet they fly. The old one in the woods near makes a chuckling sound just like a red squirrel's bark, also mewing.

June 19, 1860. Let an oak be hewed and put into the frame of a house where it is sheltered, and it will last several centuries. Even as a sill it may last one hundred and fifty years. But let it be simply cut down and lie, though in an open pasture, and it will probably be thoroughly rotten in twenty-five years. There is the oak cut down at Clam Shell some twenty years ago, the butt left on the ground. It has about two thirds wasted away, and is hardly fit for fuel.

I follow a distinct fox path amid the grass and bushes for some forty rods, beyond Brittan's Hollow, leading from the great fox hole. It branches on reaching the peach orchard. No doubt by these routes they oftenest go and return. As broad as a cart wheel, and at last best seen when you do not look too hard for it.

June 20, 1840. Perfect sincerity and transparency make a great part of beauty, as in dew drops, lakes, and diamonds. A spring is a cynosure in the fields. All Muscovy glitters in the minute particles of mica at its bottom, and the ripples cast their shadows flickeringly on the white sand as the clouds which flit across the landscape.

Something like the woodland sounds will be heard to echo through the leaves of a good book. Sometimes I hear the fresh, emphatic note of the oven-bird, and am tempted to turn many pages; sometimes the hurried chuckling sound of the squirrel, when he dives into the wall.

If we only see clearly enough how mean our lives are, they will be splendid enough. Let us remember not to strive upwards too long, but sometimes drop plumb down the other way. From the deepest pit we may see the stars. Let us have presence of mind enough to sink when we can't swim. At any rate, a carcass had better lie on the bottom than float an offense to all nostrils. It will not be falling, for we shall ride wide of the earth's gravity as a star, and always be drawn upward still (*semper cadendo nunquam cadit*), and so, by yielding to universal gravity, at length become fixed stars.

Praise begins when things are seen partially, or when we begin to feel a thing needs our assistance.

When the heavens are obscured to us, and nothing noble or heroic appears, but we are oppressed by imperfection and shortcoming on all hands, we are apt to suck our thumbs and decry our fates, as if nothing were to be done in cloudy weather. If you cannot travel the upper road, then go by the lower; you will find that they equally lead to heaven. Sometimes I feel so cheap that I am inspired, and could write a poem about it, but straightway I cannot, for I am no longer mean. Let me know that I am ailing and I am well. We should not always beat off the impression of trivialness, but make haste to welcome and cherish it. Water the weed till it blossoms ; with cultivation it will bear fruit. There are two ways to victory, to strive bravely, or to yield. How much pains the last will save, we have not yet learned.

June 20, 1852. 7 P. M. To Hubbard bathing-place. The blue-eyed grass is shut up. When does it open? Some blue flags are quite a red purple, dark wine color. Identified the *Iris prismatica*, Boston iris, with linear leaves and round stem.

The stake driver is at it in his favorite meadow. I followed the sound, and at last got within two rods, it seeming always to recede, and drawing you, like a will-o'-the-wisp, farther away into the meadows. When thus near, I heard some lower sounds at the beginning like striking on a stump or a stake, a dry, hard sound, and then followed the gurgling, pumping notes fit to come from a meadow. This was just within the

blueberry and other bushes, and when the bird
flew up alarmed, I went to the place, but could
see no water, which makes me doubt if water is
necessary to it in making the sound. Perhaps it
thrusts its bill so deep as to reach water where
it is dry on the surface. It sounds more like
wood chopping or pumping because you seem to
hear the echo of the stroke or the reverse motion
of the pump handle. After the warm weather
has come, both morning and evening you hear
the bittern pumping in the fens. It does not
sound loud near at hand, and it is remarkable
that it should be heard so far. Perhaps it is
pitched on a favorable key. Is it not a call to
its mate? Methinks that in the resemblance of
this note to rural sounds, to sounds made by farmers, the security of the bird is designed.

Dry fields have now a reddish tinge from the
seeds of the grass. Lying with my window
open these warm, even sultry nights, I hear the
sonorously musical trump of the bull-frogs from
time to time from some distant shore of the
river, as if the world were given up to them. . . .
When I wake thus at midnight, and hear this
sonorous trump from far in the horizon, I need
not go to Dante for an idea of the infernal regions. . . . I do not know for a time in what world
I am. It affects my morals, and all questions
take a new aspect from this sound. It is the

snoring music of nature at night. How allied to
the pad in place and color is this creature! His
greenish back is the leaf, and his yellow throat,
the flower, even in form, with his sesquipedality
of belly. Through the summer he lies on the
pads or with his head out, and in the winter buries himself at their roots (?). The bull paddock!
His eyes like the buds of the *Nuphar Kalmiana.*
I fancy his skin would stand water, without
shrinking, forever. Gloves made of it for rainy
weather, for trout fishers !

Frogs appear slow to make up their minds,
but then they act precipitately. As long as they
are here, they are here, and express no intention
of removing. But the idea of removing fills
them instantaneously, as Nature, abhorring, fills
a vacuum. Now they are fixed and imperturbable like the sphinx, and now they go off with
short, squatty leaps over the spatterdock on the
irruption of the least idea.

June 20, 1853. . . . Meadow-sweet out probably yesterday. It is an agreeable, unpretending
flower. . . . The bosky bank shows bright roses
from its green recesses. . . . Found two lilies
open in the very shallow inlet of the meadow.
Exquisitely beautiful, and unlike anything we
have, is the first white lily just expanded in some
shallow lagoon where the water is leaving it,
perfectly fresh and pure before the insects have

discovered it. How admirable its purity! How innocently sweet its fragrance! How significant that the rich black mud of our dead stream produces the water lily! Out of that fertile slime springs this spotless purity. It is remarkable that those flowers which are most emblematic of purity should grow in the mud. There is also the exquisite beauty of the small sagittaria which I find out, may be a day or two. Three transparent crystalline white petals with a yellow eye, and as many small purplish calyx leaves, four or five inches above the same mud. Coming home at twelve I see that the white lilies are nearly shut.

8 P. M. Up North River to Nashawtuck.

The moon full. Perhaps there is no more beautiful scene than that on the North River seen from the rock this side the hemlocks. As we look up stream we see a crescent-shaped lake completely embowered in the forest. There is nothing to be seen but the smooth black mirror of the water on which there is now the slightest discernible bluish mist a foot high, and thickset alders and willows and the green woods without an interstice, sloping steeply upward from its very surface, like the sides of a bowl. The river is here for half a mile completely shut in by the forest.

Saw a little skunk coming up the river bank in the woods at the white oak, a funny little fel-

low, about six inches long and nearly as broad.
It faced me and actually compelled me to retreat
before it for five minutes. Perhaps I was between it and its hole. Its broad black tail, tipped
with white, was erect like a kitten's. It had
what looked like a broad white band drawn tight
across its forehead or top-head, from which two
lines of white ran down one on each side of its
back, and there was a narrow white line down
its snout. It raised its back, sometimes ran a
few feet forward, sometimes backward, and repeatedly turned its tail to me, prepared to dis-
charge its fluid, like the old ones. Such was its
instinct, and all the while it kept up a fine
grunting like a little pig or a squirrel. It reminded me that the red squirrel, the woodchuck,
and the skunk all make a similar sound.

The leafy columned elms planted by the river
at foot of P——'s field are exceedingly beautiful,
the moon being behind them. . . . Their trunks
look like columns of a portico wreathed with
evergreens on the evening of an illumination for
some great festival. They are the more rich because in this creamy light you cannot distinguish
the trunk from the verdure that drapes it.

June 21, 1840. A man is never inspired unless his body is also. It, too, spurns a tame and
commonplace life. They are fatally mistaken
who think while they strive with their minds

that they may suffer their bodies to stagnate in luxury or sloth. The body is the first proselyte the soul makes. Our life is but the soul made known by its fruits, the body. The whole duty of man may be expressed in one line. Make to yourself a perfect body.

June 21, 1852. 7 P. M. To Cliffs *via* Hubbard bathing-place. Cherry birds I have not seen, though I think I have heard them before, their fine seringo note, like a vibrating spring in the air. They are a handsome bird with their crest and chestnut breasts. There is no keeping the run of their comings and goings, but they will be ready for the cherries when they shall be ripe.

The adder's-tongue arethusa smells exactly like a snake. How singular that in Nature, too, beauty and offensiveness should be thus combined. In flowers as well as persons we demand a beauty pure and fragrant which perfumes the air. The flower which is showy but has no odor, or an offensive one, expresses the character of too many mortals.

Nature has looked uncommonly bare and dry to me for a day or two. With our senses applied to the surrounding world we are reading our physical and corresponding moral revolutions. Nature was shallow all at once. I did not know what had attracted me all my life. I was therefore encouraged when, going through a field this evening, I was unexpectedly struck with the beauty of an apple-tree. The perception of beauty is a moral test.

I see the tephrosia out through the dusk, a handsome flower. What rich crops this dry hillside has yielded! First I saw the *Viola pedata* here. Then the lupines, and then the snapdragon covered it, and now that the lupines are done, and their pods are left, the tephrosia has taken their place. This small, dry hillside is thus a natural garden. I omit other flowers which grow here, and name only those which, to some extent, cover or possess it. No eighth of an acre in a cultivated garden could be better clothed or with a more pleasing variety from month to month, and while one flower is in bloom you little suspect that which is to succeed and perchance eclipse it. It is a warmly placed, dry hillside beneath a wall, very thinly clad with grass, a natural flower-garden. Of this succession I hardly know which to admire most. It would be pleasant to write the history of such a hillside for one year. First and last you have the colors of the rainbow and more, and the various fragrances which it has not. The blackberry, rose, and dogsbane, also, are now in bloom here.

I hear the sound of distant thunder, though

no cloud is obvious, muttering like the roar of artillery. . . . Thunder and lightning are remarkable accompaniments to our life, as if to remind us that there always is or should be a kind of battle raging. They are signal guns to us.

June 21, 1853. 4.30 A. M. Up river for lilies. . . .

The few lilies begin to open about five.

The morning-glory still fresh at 3 P. M. A fine, large, delicate bell, with waved border, some pure white, some reddened. The buds open perfectly in a vase. I find them open when I wake at 4 A. M. . . .

For the last two or three days it has taken me all the forenoon to wake up.

June 21, 1854. P. M. To Walden, etc. Mitchella in Deep Cut Woods probably a day or two. Its scent is agreeable and refreshing, between the may-flower and rum-cherry bark, or like peach-stone meats. . . .

When I see the dense, shady masses of weeds about water, already an unexplorable maze, I am struck with the contrast between this and the spring when I wandered about in search of the first faint greenness along the borders of the brooks. Then an inch or two of green was something remarkable and obvious afar. Now there is a dense mass of weeds along the water-

side, where the muskrats bask, and overhead a
canopy of leaves conceals the birds and shuts
out the sun. It is hard to realize that the
seeds of all this growth were buried in that
bare, frozen earth. . . .

In the little meadow pool or bog in Hubbard's
shore I see two old pouts tending their countless
young close to the shore. The former are slate-
colored, the latter are about half an inch long,
and very black, forming a dark mass from eight
to twelve inches in diameter. The old one constantly circles around them, over, and under,
and through, as if anxiously endeavoring to keep
them together, from time to time moving off
five or six feet to reconnoitre. The whole mass
of the young, and there must be a thousand of
them at least, is incessantly moving, pushing
forward and stretching out. They are often in
the form of a great pout, apparently keeping
together by their own instinct chiefly, now on
the bottom, now rising to the top. The old, at
any rate, do not appear to be very successful in
their apparent efforts to communicate with and
direct them. Alone they might be mistaken
for pollywogs. At length they break into four
parts.

The Indians say this fish hatches its young
in a hole in the mud, and that they accompany
her for some time afterwards. Yet in Ware's

Smellie it is said that fishes take no care of their young. I think also that I see the young breams in schools hovering over their nests while the old ones are still protecting them.

Rambled up the grassy hollows in the sprout-lands north (?) of Goose Pond. I felt a pleasing sense of strangeness and distance. Here in the midst of extensive sproutlands are numerous open hollows, more or less connected, where, for some reason, perhaps frosts, the wood does not spring up, and I was glad of it, filled with a fine, wiry grass, with the panicled andromeda, which loves dry places, now in blossom round the edges, and small black cherries and sand cherries struggling down into them. The wood-chuck loves such places, and now wabbles off with a peculiar loud squeak like the sharp bark of a red squirrel, then stands erect at the entrance of his hole, ready to dive into it as soon as you approach. As wild and strange a place as you might find in the unexplored west or east. The quarter of a mile of sproutlands which separates it from the highway seems as complete a barrier as a thousand miles of earth. Your horizon is there all your own. . . .

Again I am attracted by the deep scarlet of the wild moss rose, half open in the grass, all glowing with rosy light.

June 21, 1856. A very hot day, as was

yesterday, 99° at 3 P. M. . . . Saw the night-
hawks fly low and touch the water like swallows,
at Walden.

June 21, 1860. Having noticed the pine
pollen washed up on the shore of three or four
ponds in the woods lately, at Ripple Lake, a
dozen rods from the nearest pine, also having
seen the pollen carried off visibly half a dozen
rods from a pitch pine which I had jarred, and
rising all the while when there was very little
wind, it occurred to me that the air must be full
of this fine dust at this season, that it must at
times be carried to great distances, and that its
presence might be detected remote from pines
by examining the edges of pretty large bodies
of water where it would be collected on one side
by winds and waves from a large area. So I
thought over all the small ponds in the township
in order to select one or more most remote from
the woods or pines, whose shores I might examine and thus test my theory. I could think
of none more favorable than this little pond,
only four rods in diameter, . . . in John
Brown's pasture, which has but few pads in it.
It is a small round pond at the bottom of a
hollow in the midst of a perfectly bare, dry
pasture. The nearest wood of any kind is just
thirty-nine rods distant northward, and across a
road from the edge of a pond. Any other wood

in other directions is five or six times as far. I
knew it was a bad time to try my experiment
just after such heavy rains and when the pines
are effete, — a little too late. The wind was now
blowing quite strong from the northeast, whereas
all the pollen I had seen hitherto had been collected on the northeast sides of ponds by a
southwest wind. I approached the pond from
the northeast, and looking over it, and carefully
along the shore there, could detect no pollen.
I then proceeded to walk round it, but still
could detect none. I then said to myself, if
there was any here before the rain and northeast
wind, it must have been on the northeast side,
and then have been washed over quite to or on
the shore. I looked there carefully, stooping
down, and was gratified to find after all a distinct yellow line of pollen dust, about half an
inch wide, or washing off to two or three times
that width, quite on the edge, and some dead
twigs which I took up from the wet shore were
completely coated with it as with sulphur. This
yellow line reached half a rod along the southwest side, and I then detected a little of the
dust slightly graying the surface for two or three
feet out there. When I thought I had failed,
I was much pleased to detect after all this distinct yellow line revealing unmistakably the
presence of pines in the neighborhood, and thus

confirming my theory. As chemists detect the presence of ozone in the atmosphere by exposing to it a delicately prepared paper, so the lakes detect for us thus the presence of the pine pollen in the atmosphere. They are our pollenometers. How much of this invisible dust must be floating in the atmosphere, and be inhaled and drunk by us at this season! Who knows but the pollen of some plants may be unwholesome to inhale, and produce the diseases of the season, and but it may be the source of some of the peculiar fragrances in the atmosphere which we cannot otherwise account for.

Of course a large pond will collect the most, and you will find most at the bottom of very deep bays into which the wind blows. I do not believe there is any part of this town into which the pollen of the pine may not fall. The time to examine the ponds this year was, I should say, from the 15th to the 20th of this month. I find that the pines are now effete, especially the pitch-pine. The sterile flowers are turned reddish. The flower of the white pine is lighter colored, and all but a very little indeed is effete. In the white pine there is a dense cluster of twenty or thirty little flowers about the base of this year's shoot. I did not expect to find any pollen, the pond was so small and distant from any wood, but thought I would examine.

June 22, 1839. I have within the last few days come into contact with a pure, uncompromising spirit that is somewhere wandering in the atmosphere, but settles not positively anywhere. Some persons carry about them the air and conviction of virtue, though they themselves are unconscious of it, and are even backward to appreciate it in others. Such it is impossible not to love. Still is their loveliness, as it were, independent of them, so that you seem not to lose it when they are absent, for when they are near, it is like an invisible presence which attends you.

That virtue we appreciate is as much ours as another's. We see so much only as we possess.

June 22, 1840. When we are shocked at vice we express a lingering sympathy with it. Have no affinity for what is shocking.

Do not present a gleaming edge to ward off harm, for that will oftenest attract the lightning, but rather be the all-pervading ether which the lightning does not strike, but purify. Then will the rudeness or profanity of your companion be like a flash across the face of your sky, lighting up and revealing its serene depths. Earth cannot shock the heavens; but its dull vapor and foul smoke make a bright cloud-spot in the ether, and anon the sun, like a cunning artificer, will cut and paint it, and set it for a jewel in the breast of the sky.

June 22, 1851. The birch is the surveyor's tree. It makes the best stake to look at through the sights of a compass, except when there is snow on the ground. Its white bark was not made in vain. In surveying wood-lots I have frequent occasion to say this is what it was made for.

We are enabled to criticise others only when we are different from, and, in a given particular, superior to, them ourselves. By our aloofness from men and their affairs we are enabled to overlook and criticise them. There are but few men who stand on the hills by the roadside. I am sure only when I have risen above my common sense, when I do not take the foolish view of things which is commonly taken, when I do not live for the low ends for which men commonly live. Wisdom is not common. To what purpose have I senses if I am thus absorbed in affairs. My pulse must beat with Nature. After a hard day's work without a thought, turning my very brain into a mere tool, only in the quiet of evening do I so far recover my senses as to hear the cricket which in fact has been chirping all day. In my better hours I am conscious of the influx of a serene and unquestionable wisdom which partly unfits — and, if I yielded to it

more rememberingly, would wholly unfit — me
for what is called the active business of life, for
that furnishes nothing on which the eye of reason can rest. What is that other kind of life
to which I am continually allured? which alone
I love? Is it a life for this world? Can a man
feed and clothe himself gloriously who keeps only
the truth steadily before him? who calls in no
evil to his aid? Are there duties which necessa-
rily interfere with the serene perception of truth?
Are our serene moments mere foretastes of heavenly joys gratuitously vouchsafed to us as a con-
solation? or simply a transient realization of
what might be the whole tenor of our lives? —
There is the calmness of the lake when there is
not a breath of wind; there is the calmness of a
stagnant ditch. So is it with us. Sometimes
we are clarified and calmed healthily, . . . not by
an opiate, but by some unconscious obedience to
the all-just laws, so that we become like a still
lake of purest crystal, and, without an effort, our
depths are revealed to ourselves. All the world
goes by us and is reflected in our deeps. Such
clarity! obtained by such pure means, by simple living, by honest purpose. We live and rejoice. I awoke to a music which no one about
me heard. Whom shall I thank for it? The
luxury of wisdom! the luxury of virtue! Are
there any intemperate in these things? I feel

my Maker blessing me. To the sane man the world is a musical instrument. The very touch affords an exquisite pleasure. . . . It is hot noon. . . . I am threading an open pitch and white pine wood, easily traversed where the pine needles redden all the ground, which is as smooth as a carpet. Still the blackberries love to creep over this floor, for it is not many years since it was a blackberry field. I hear around me, but never in sight, the many wood-thrushes whetting their steel-like notes. Such keen singers! It takes a fiery heat, the dry pine needles adding to the furnace of the sun, to temper their strain. After what a moderate pause they deliver themselves again, saying ever a new thing, avoiding repetition, methinks answering one another. While most other birds take their siesta, the wood-thrush discharges his song. It is delivered like a piece of jingling steel.

The domestic ox has his horns tipped with brass. This and his shoes are the badges of servitude which he wears, as if he would soon get to jacket and trowsers. I am singularly affected when I look over a herd of reclining oxen in their pasture, and find that every one has these brazen balls on his horns. They are partly humanized so. It is not pure brute. There is art added. . . . The bull has a ring in his nose.

14

The *Lysimachia quadrifolia* exhibits its small yellow blossoms now in the wood path.

The *Utricularia vulgaris* or bladder-wort, a yellow pea-like flower, has blossomed in stagnant pools.

June 22, 1852. 8 P. M. Up the Union turnpike. We have had a succession of thunder showers to-day, and at sunset, a rainbow. How moral the world is made! This bow is not utilitarian. Men, I think, are great in proportion as they are moral. After the rain he sets his bow in the heavens! The world is not destitute of beauty. Ask the skeptic who inquires " *Cui bono?* " why the rainbow was made. While men cultivate flowers below, God cultivates flowers above, he takes charge of the pastures in the heavens. Is not the rainbow a faint vision of God's face? How glorious should be the life of man passed under this arch!

Near the river thus late I hear the peet-weet with white barred wings. The scent of the Balm of Gilead leaves fills the road after the rain. There are the amber skies of evening, the colored skies of both morning and evening. Nature adorns these seasons.

Unquestionable truth is sweet, though it were the announcement of our dissolution.

The fire-flies in the meadows are very numerous, as if they had replenished their lights from the lightning. The far-retreated thunder-clouds low in the south-east horizon and in the north, emitting low flashes which reveal their forms, appear to lift their wings like fire-flies, or it is a steady glare like the glow-worm. Wherever they go, they make a meadow.

June 22, 1853. I do not remember a warmer night than the last. In my attic under the roof, with all windows and doors open, there was still not a puff of the usual coolness of the night. It seemed as if the heat which the roof had absorbed during the day were being brought down upon me. It was far more intolerable than by day. All windows being open I heard the sounds made by pigs and horses in the neighborhood, and of children who were partially suffocated by the heat. It seemed as if it would be something to tell of, the experience of that night, as of the Black Hole of Calcutta in a degree, if one survived it.

The sun down, and I am crossing Fair Haven Hill, sky overcast, landscape dark and still. I see the smooth river in the north reflecting two shades of light, one from the water, another from the surface of the pads which broadly border it on both sides, and the very irregular waving or winding edge of the pads, especially perceptible in this light, makes a very agreeable border, the edge of the film which seeks to bridge over and

inclose the river wholly.   These pads are to the
smooth water between like a calyx to its flower.
The river at such an hour, seen half a mile away,
perfectly smooth and lighter than the sky, reflecting the clouds, is a paradisaical scene. What
are the rivers around Damascus to this river sleeping around Concord? Are not the Musketaquid
and the Assabet, rivers of Concord, fairer than
the rivers of the plain?   And then the rich
warble of the blackbird may occasionally be
heard. As I come over the hill, I hear the wood-
thrush singing his evening lay. This is the only
bird whose note affects me like music, affects the
flow and tenor of my thought, my fancy, and
imagination.   It lifts and exhilarates me. . . .
It is a medicative draught to my soul, an elixir
to my eyes, and a fountain of youth to all my
senses. It changes all hours to an eternal morning.   It banishes all trivialness.   It reinstates
me in my dominion, makes me the lord of creation.   This bird is chief musician of my court.
He sings in a time, a heroic age with which no
event in the village can be contemporary.   How
can they be contemporary when only the latter
is temporary at all.   So there is something in
the music of the cow-bell sweeter and more nu-
tritious than the milk which the farmers drink.
The thrush's song is a *ranz des vâches* to me.
I long for wildness, a nature which I cannot put

my foot through, woods where the wood-thrush forever sings, where the hours are early morning ones, and there is dew on the grass, and the day is forever unproved, where I might have a fertile unknown for a soil about me. I would go after the cows, I would watch the flocks of Admetus there forever, only for my board and clothes, a New Hampshire everlasting and unfallen. All that was ripest and fairest in the wilderness and the wild man is preserved and transmitted to us in the strain of the wood-thrush. It is the mediator between barbarism and civilization. It is unrepentant as Greece.

The strawberries may perhaps be considered a fruit of the spring, for they have depended chiefly on the freshness and moisture of spring, and on high lands are already dried up; a soft fruit, a sort of manna which falls in June, and in the meadows they lurk at the shady roots of the grass. Now the blueberry, a somewhat firmer fruit, is beginning. Nuts, the firmest, will be the last.

Is not June the month in which all trees and shrubs do the greatest part of their growing? Will the shoots add much to their length in July?

June 22, 1856. R. W. E. imitates the wood-thrush by " *He willy willy — ha willy willy — O willy O.*"

The song sparrow is said to be imitated in New Bedford thus : " *Maids, maids, maids — hang on your tea kettle — ettle, ettle, ettle, ettle.*"

June 22, 1860. . . . R—— tells me that he saw, in a mud-hole near the river in Sudbury, about a fortnight ago, a pout protecting her ova. They were in a ball about as big as an apple, under which she swam, all exposed, not at all hatched, I think he said on a stick.

Hear the peculiar peep of young golden robins on the elms this morning.

June 23, 1840. We Yankees are not so far from right, who answer one question by asking another. Yes and No are lies. A true answer will not aim to establish anything, but rather to set all well afloat. All answers are in the future, and day answereth to day. Do we think we can anticipate them ? In Latin, to respond is to pledge one's self before the gods to do faithfully and honorably, as a man should, in any case. This is good.

How can the language of the poet be more expressive than Nature ? He is content that what he has already read in simple characters or indifferently in all be translated into the same again.

He is the true artist whose life is his material. Every stroke of the chisel must enter his own flesh and bones, and not grate dully on marble.

What is any man's discourse to me, if I am not sensible of something in it as steady and cheery as the creak of the crickets? In it the woods must be relieved against the sky. Men tire me when I am not constantly greeted and cheered in their discourse as it were by the flux of sparkling streams.

I cannot see the bottom of the sky, because I cannot see to the bottom of myself. It is the symbol of my own infinity. My eye penetrates as far into the ether as that depth is inward from which my contemporary thought springs.

Not by constraint or severity shall you have access to true wisdom, but by abandonment and childlike mirthfulness. If you would know aught, be gay before it.

June 23, 1851. It is a pleasant sound to me, the squeaking and booming of the night-hawks flying over high, open fields in the woods. They fly like butterflies, not to avoid birds of prey, but apparently to secure their own insect prey. . . . Often you must look a long while before you can detect the mote in the sky from which the note proceeds.

The common cinquefoil, *Potentilla simplex*, greets me with its simple and unobtrusive yellow flower in the grass. The *Potentilla argentea*, hoary cinquefoil, also is now in blossom. *Poten-*

tilla sarmentosa, running cinquefoil, we had common enough in the spring.

June 23, 1852. 5 A. M. To Laurel Glen. The bobolink still sings, though not as in May. . . .

The pretty little *Mitchella repens*, with its twin flowers, spots the ground under the pines, its downy-petaled, cross-shaped flowers, and its purplish buds.

The grass is not nearly so wet after thunder showers in the night as after an ordinary dew. Apparently the rain falls so swiftly and hard that it does not rest on the leaves, and then there is no more moisture to be deposited in dew.

The mountain laurel in bloom in cool and shady woods reminds one of the vigor of Nature. It is perhaps a first-rate flower, considering its size and its evergreen leaves. The flower, curiously folded in a ten-angled, pyramidal form, is remarkable. A profusion of flowers with an innocent fragrance. It reminds me of shady mountain-sides where it forms the underwood.

I hear my old Walden owl. Its first note is almost like the somewhat peevish scream or squeal of a child shrugging its shoulders. Then succeed two more moderate and musical ones. — The wood-thrush sings at all hours. I associate it with the cool morning, the sultry noon, and the serene evening. At this hour it suggests a cool vigor!

p. m. To the mountain laurel in Mason's pasture. It is what I call a *washing* day, such as we sometimes have when buttercups first appear in the spring, an agreeably cool, clear, and breezy day, when all things appear as if washed bright, and shine, and at this season especially the sound of the wind rustling the leaves is like the rippling of a stream. You see the light-colored under-side of the still fresh foliage, and a sheeny light is reflected from the bent grass in the meadow. Haze and sultriness are far off. The air is cleared and cooled by yesterday's thunder-storms. The river, too, has a fine, cool, silvery sparkle or sheen on it. You can see far into the horizon, and you hear the sound of the crickets with such feelings as in the cool morning.

These are very agreeable pastures to me, no house in sight, no cultivation. I sit under a large white oak upon its swelling instep, which makes an admirable seat, and look forth over these pleasant rocky and bushy pastures, where for the most part there are not even cattle grazing, but patches of huckleberry bushes, birches, pitch-pines, barberry bushes, creeping juniper in great circles, its edges curving upward, wild roses spotting the green with red, numerous tufts of indigo weed, and above all, great gray boulders lying about, far and near, with some barberry bush perchance growing half way up them, and, between all, the short sod of the pasture here and there appears.

The beauty and fragrance of the wild rose are wholly agreeable and wholesome, and wear well. I do not wonder much that men have given the preference to this family of flowers notwithstanding their thorns. It is hardy and more complete in its parts than most flowers, its color, buds, fragrance, leaves, the whole bush, frequently its stem in particular, and finally its red or scarlet hips. Here is the sweet briar in blossom, which to a fragrant flower adds more fragrant leaves. . . .

As I walk through these old deserted wild orchards, half pasture, half huckleberry field, the air is filled with fragrance from I know not what source.

I sit on one of these boulders and look south to Ponkawtasset. Looking west, whence the wind comes, you do not see the under-sides of the leaves, but looking east, every bough shows its under-side. Those of the maples are particularly white. All leaves tremble like aspen leaves.

Two or three large boulders, fifteen or twenty feet square, make a good foreground in the land-

scape, for the gray color of the rock contrasts
well with the green of the surrounding and more
distant hills and woods and fields. They serve
instead of cottages for a wild landscape, as
perches or *points d'appui* for the eye.

The red color of cattle also is agreeable in a
landscape, or let them be what color they may,
red, black, white, mouse-color, or spotted, all
which I have seen this afternoon. The cows
which, confined to the barn or barnyard all winter, were covered with filth, after roaming in
flowery pastures possess now clean and shining
coats, and the cowy odor is without alloy. . . .

It seems natural that rocks which have lain
under the heavens so long should be gray, as it
were an intermediate color between the heavens
and the earth. The air is the thin paint in
which they have been dipped and brushed with
the wind. Water, which is more fluid and like
the sky in its nature, is still more like it in color.
Time will make the most discordant materials
harmonize. . . .

This grassy road now dives into the wood, as
if it were entering a cellar or bulkhead, the
shadow is so deep. . . . And now I scent the
pines. I plucked a blue geranium near the
Kibbe place, which appeared to me remarkably
fragrant, like lilies and strawberries combined.
. . . The sweet fragrance of the swamp pink

fills all the swamps, and when I look down, I
see commonly the leaf of the gold-thread. . . .
June 23, 1853. . . . P. M. To White Pond.
. . . After bathing, I paddled to the middle in
the leaky boat. The heart-leaf, which grows
thinly here, is an interesting plant, sometimes
floating at the end of a solitary, almost invisible,
thread-like stem, more than six feet long, and
again many purplish stems intertwined into loose
ropes, or like large skeins of silk, abruptly
spreading at top, of course, into a perfectly
flat shield, a foot or more in diameter, of
small heart-shaped leaves, which rise or fall on
their stems as the water is higher or lower.
This perfectly horizontal disposition of the
leaves in a single plane is an interesting and
peculiar feature in water plants of this kind.
Leaves and flowers made to float on the dividing line between two elements. . . .

In the warm noons now-a-days I see the spotted, small, yellow eyes of the four-leaved loosestrife looking at me from under the birches and
pines springing up in sandy, upland fields. . . .

The other day I saw what I took to be a scarecrow in a cultivated field, and noting how un-
naturally it was stuffed out here and there, and
how ungainly its arms and legs were, I thought
to myself, " Well, it is thus they make these
things, they do not stand much about it," but

looking round again, after I had gone by, I
saw my scarecrow walking off with a real live
man in it.

I was just roused from my writing by the
engine's whistle, and, looking out, saw shooting through the town two enormous pine sticks,
stripped of their bark, just from the northwest,
and going to Portsmouth Navy Yard, they say.
. . . Not a tree grows now in Concord to compare with them. They suggest what a country
we have to back us up that way. A hundred
years ago or more perchance the wind wafted
a little winged seed out of its cone to some
favorable spot, and this is the result. In ten
minutes they were through the township, and
perhaps not half a dozen Concord eyes rested
on them during their transit.

June 23, 1854. . . . Disturbed three different broods of partridges in my walk this P. M.
in different places. In one, they were as big as
chickens ten days old, and went flying in various
directions a rod or two into the hillside.

In another, the young were two and a half
inches long only, not long hatched, making a
fine peep. Held one in my hand, where it
squatted without winking. . . . Thus we are
now in the very midst of them. The young
broods are being led forth. The old bird will
return mewing, and walk past within ten feet.

June 23, 1856.   To New Bedford with R———.
. . . Baywings sang morning and evening about
R———'s house, often resting on a bean-pole,
and dropping down and running and singing on
the bare ground amid the potatoes.   Their note
somewhat like — " *Come, here-here, there-there,*
— [then three rapid notes] *quick-quick-quick,* —
or I 'm gone."

June 24, 1840.   When I read Cudworth I
find I can tolerate all, atomists, pneumatologists,
atheists, and theists, Plato, Aristotle, Leucippus,
Democritus, and Pythagoras.   It is the attitude
of these men, more than any communication,
which charms me.   It is so rare to find a man
musing.   But between them and their commen-
tators there is an endless dispute.   If it come
to that, that you compare notes, then you are
all wrong.   As it is, each takes me up into the
serene heavens, and paints earth and sky.   Any
sincere thought is irresistible.   It lifts us to the
zenith, whither the smallest bubble rises as surely
as the largest.

Dr. Cudworth does not consider that the belief
in a deity is as great a heresy as exists.   Epi-
curus held that the gods were " of human form,
yet were so thin and subtile as that, comparatively with our terrestrial bodies, they might be
called incorporeal; they having not so much
carnem as *quasi-carnem,* nor *sanguinem* as

quasi-sanguinem, a certain kind of aerial or ethereal flesh and blood." This, which Cudworth pronounces "romantical," is plainly as good doctrine as his own, as if any sincere thought were not the best sort of truth.

There is no doubt but the highest morality in the books is rhymed or measured, is in form, as well as substance, poetry. Such is the scripture of all nations. If I were to compile a volume to contain the condensed wisdom of mankind, I should quote no rhythmless line.

Not all the wit of a college can avail to make one harmonious line. It never *happens.* It may get so as to jingle. But a jingle is akin to a jar — jars regularly recurring.

So delicious is plain speech to my ears, as if I were to be more delighted by the whistling of the shot than frightened by the flying of the splinters. I am content, I fear, to be quite battered down and made a ruin of. I outgeneral myself when I direct my enemy to my vulnerable points.

Sympathy with what is sound makes sport of what is unsound. The loftiest utterance of love is perhaps sublimely satirical.

Cliffs. Evening. Though the sun set a quarter of an hour ago, his rays are still visible, darting half way to the zenith. That glowing morrow in the west flashes on me like a faint presentiment of morning when I am falling asleep. A dull mist comes rolling from the west, as if it were the dust which day has raised. A column of smoke is rising from the woods yonder to uphold heaven's roof till the light comes again. The landscape, by its patient resting there, teaches me that all good remains with him that waiteth, and that I shall sooner overtake the dawn by remaining here than by hurrying over the hills of the west.

Morning and evening are as like as brother and sister. The sparrow and thrush sing, and the frogs peep, for both.

The woods breathe louder and louder behind me. With what hurry-scurry night takes place! The wagon rattling over yonder bridge is the messenger which day sends back to night, but the despatches are sealed. In its rattle, the village seems to say, "This one sound and I have done."

Red, then, is day's color; at least, it is the color of his heel. He is " stepping westward." We only notice him when he comes and goes.

With noble perseverance the dog bays the stars yonder. I, too, like thee, walk alone in this strange, familiar night, my voice, like thine, beating against its friendly concave, and barking. I hear only my own voice; 10 o'clock.

June 24, 1852. P. M. To White Pond. —

The drifting, white downy clouds are to the landsman what sails on the sea are to him who dwells by the shore, objects of a large, diffusive interest. When the laborer lies on the grass or in the shade for rest, they do not too much tax or weary his attention. They are unobtrusive. I have not heard that white clouds, like white houses, made any one's eyes ache. They are the flitting sails in that ocean whose bounds no man has visited. They are like all great themes, always at hand to be considered, or they float over us unregarded. Far away they float in the serene sky, the most inoffensive of objects, or near and low they smite us with their lightnings and deafen us with their thunder. We know no Ternate or Tidore grand enough whither we can imagine them bound. There are many mares'-tails to-day, if that is the name. What could a man learn by watching the clouds? These objects which go over our heads unobserved are vast and indefinite. Those clouds which have the most distinct and interesting outlines are commonly below the zenith, somewhat low in the heavens, seen on one side. They are among the most glorious objects in Nature. A sky without clouds is a meadow without flowers, a sea without sails. Some days we have the mackerel fleet. But our devilishly industrious laborers rarely lie in the shade. How much better if

15

they were to take their nooning like the Italians, relax and expand and never do any work in the middle of the day, — enjoy a little sabbath then.

I still perceive that wonderful fragrance from the meadow (?) on the Corner causeway, intense as ever. It is one of those effects whose cause it is best not to know perchance.

White Pond very handsome to-day. The shore alive with pollywogs of large size, which ripple the water on our approach. There is a fine sparkle on the water, though not equal to the fall one quite. The water is very high, so that you cannot walk round it, but it is the more pleasant while you are swimming to see how the trees actually rise out of it on all sides. It bathes their feet. The dog worried a wood-chuck half-grown, which did not turn its back and run into its hole, but backed into it, and faced him and us, gritting its teeth and prepared to die. Even this little fellow was able to defend himself against the dog with his sharp teeth. That fierce gritting of their teeth is a remarkable habit with these animals.

The *Linnæa borealis* just going out of bloom. I should have found it long ago. Its leaves densely cover the ground.

June 24, 1853. . . . It is surprising that so many birds find hair enough to line their nests with. If I wish for a horse-hair for my compass sights, I must go to the stable ; but the hair-bird, with her sharp eyes, goes to the road.

June 24, 1856. [New Bedford.] To Sassa-cowen Pond and to Long Pond. Lunched by the spring on the Brady Farm in Freetown, and there it occurred to me how to get clear water from a spring when the surface is covered with dust or insects. Thrust your dipper down deep in the middle of the spring, and lift it up quickly, straight and square. This will heap up the wa-ter in the middle so that the scum will run off.

June 24, 1857. . . . Went to Farmer's Swamp to look for the screech-owl's nest which he had found. . . . I found it at last near the top of a mid-dling-sized white pine, about thirty feet from the ground. As I stood by the tree, the old bird dashed by within a couple of rods, uttering a peculiar mewing sound which she kept up amid the bushes, a blackbird in close pursuit of her. I found the nest empty on one side of the main stem, but close to it, resting on some limbs. It was made of twigs rather less than an eighth of an inch thick, and was almost flat above, only an inch lower in the middle than at the edge, about sixteen inches in diameter and six or eight inches thick. With the twigs in the midst and beneath was mixed sphagnum and sedge from the swamp beneath, and the lining or flooring was coarse strips of grape-vine bark. The whole

pretty firmly matted together. How common
and important a material is grape-vine bark for
birds' nests! Nature wastes nothing. There
were white droppings of the young on the nest,
and one large pellet of fur and small bones two
and a half inches long. In the meanwhile the
old bird was uttering that hoarse, worried note
from time to time, somewhat like a partridge's,
flying past from side to side, and alighting amid
the trees or bushes. When I had descended, I
detected one young one, two thirds grown,
perched on a branch of the next tree about fifteen feet from the ground, which was all the
while staring at me with its great yellow eyes.
It was gray, with gray horns and a dark beak.
As I walked past near it, it turned its head
steadily, always facing me, without moving its
body, till it looked directly the opposite way over
its back, but never offered to fly. Just then, I
thought surely that I heard a puppy faintly
barking at me four or five rods distant amid the
bushes, having tracked me into the swamp, *what-
what, what-what-what.* It was exactly such a
noise as the barking of a very small dog or perhaps a fox. But it was the old owl, for I presently saw her making it. . . . She was generally
reddish brown or partridge-colored, the breast
mottled with dark brown and fawn color . . .
and had plain fawn-colored thighs.

June 24, 1860. . . . Saw young blue-birds fully grown yesterday, but with a feeble note and dull colors.

June 25, 1840. Let me see no other conflict but with prosperity. If my path run on before me level and smooth, it is all a mirage. In reality it is steep and arduous as a chamois pass. I will not let the years roll over me like a Juggernaut car.

We will warm us at each other's fire. Friendship is not such a cold refining process as a double sieve, but a glowing furnace in which all impurities are consumed. Men have learned to touch before they scrutinize, to shake hands and not to stare.

June 25, 1852. Just as the sun was rising this morning under clouds, I saw a rainbow in the western horizon, the lower parts quite bright.

> " Rainbow in the morning
> Sailors take warning,
> Rainbow at night
> Sailors' delight."

A few moments after, it rained heavily and continued to do so for half an hour, and it has continued cloudy as well as cool most of the day.

I observe that young birds are usually of a duller color and more speckled than old ones, as if for their protection in their tender state. They have not yet the markings and the beauty

which distinguish their species, and which betray
it often, but by their color are merged in the
variety of colors of the season.

To Cliffs. 4 P. M. It is cool and cloudy weather
in which the crickets still heard remind you of
the fall, a clearer ring to their creak. Also the
prunella, cool in the grass, and the Johnswort
make you think it late in the year. *Maruta
cotula* or Mayweed. Why so named? Just
begins, with its strong-scented leaf. It has taken
up its position by the roadside close to the ruts
— in bad taste. . . .

The bobolink and golden robin are occasionally heard now-a-days.

The *Convolvulus sepium*, bind-weed. Morning glory is the best now. It always refreshes
me to see it. . . . " In the morning and cloudy
weather," says Gray. I associate it with holiest
morning hours. It may preside over my morning walks and thoughts. There is a flower for
every mood of the mind.

Methinks roses oftenest display their bright
colors which invariably attract all eyes and betray them, against a dark ground, as the dark
green or the shady recesses of other bushes and
copses, where they show to best advantage.
Their enemies do not spare the open flower for
an hour. Hence, if for no other reason, their
buds are most beautiful. Their promise of per-

fect and dazzling beauty, when their buds are just beginning to expand, beauty which they can hardly contain, as in most youths, commonly surpasses the fulfillment of their expanded flowers. The color shows fairest and brightest in the bud. The expanded flower has no higher or deeper tint than the swelling bud exposed. This raised a dangerous expectation. The season when wild roses are in bloom should have some preëminence, I think.

Linaria vulgaris, butter-and-eggs, toad-flax, on Fair Haven. Was seen the 19th. It is rather rich colored, with a not disagreeable scent. It is called a troublesome weed. Flowers must not be too profuse and obtrusive, else they acquire the reputation of weeds. It grows almost like a cotton-grass so above and distinct from its leaves, in wandering patches higher and higher up the side of the hill.

One man lies in his words and gets a bad reputation, another in his manners, and enjoys a good one.

The air is clear as if a cool, dewy brush had swept the meadows of all haze. A liquid coolness invests them, as if their midnight aspect were suddenly revealed to midday. The mountain outline is remarkably distinct and the intermediate earth appears more than usually scooped out like a vast saucer sloping upward to its sharp

mountain rim. The mountains are washed in
air. The sunshine now seen far away on fields
and hills in the northwest looks cool and wholesome like the yellow grass in the meadows. I
am too late for the white-pine flowers. The cones
are half an inch long and green, and the male
flowers effete. The sun now comes out bright,
though westering, and shines on Fair Haven,
which, rippled by the wind, is of an unusual
clay-muddy color. . . . There are little recesses
a rod or two square in bosky woods which have
not grown fast, where a fine wiry grass invites to
lie down in the shade, under the shrub-oaks on
the edge of the well-meadow-head field.

8.30 P. M. To Conantum. Moon half full.
Fields dusky. The evening star and one other
bright one near the moon. It is a cool, but pretty
still night. Methinks I am less thoughtful than
I was last year at this time. The flute I now
hear from the Depot field does not find such caverns to echo and resound in within me, no such
answering depths. Our minds should echo at
least as many times as a mammoth cave to every
musical sound. It should awaken reflections
in us.

Now his day's work is done, the laborer plays
his flute, only possible at this hour. Contrasted
with his work, what an accomplishment ! Some
drink and gamble. He plays some well-known

march. But the music is not in the tune ; it is
in the sound. It does not proceed from the
trading nor the political world. He practices
this ancient art. . . .

I hear the bull-frog's trump from far. Now
I turn down the Corner road. At this quiet
hour the evening wind is heard to moan in the
hollows of your face, mysterious, spirit-like, conversing with you. . . . The whippoorwill sings.
I hear a laborer going home coarsely singing to
himself. Though he has scarcely had a thought
all day, killing weeds, at this hour he sings or
talks to himself. His humble, earthly content-
ment gets expression. It is kindred in its origin
with the notes or music of many creatures. A
more fit and natural expression of his mood this
humming than conversation is wont to be. — The
fire-flies appear to be flying, though they may be
stationary on the grass stems, for their perch
and the nearness of the ground are obscured by
the darkness, and now you see one here and then
another there, as if it were one in motion. Their
light is singularly bright and glowing to proceed
from a living creature. Nature loves variety in
all things, and so she adds glow-worms to fire-
flies, though I have not noticed any this year. —
The great story of the night is the moon's adventures with the clouds. What innumerable
encounters she has had with them! When I

enter on the moonlit causeway where the light
is reflected from the glistening alder leaves, and
their deep, dark, liquid shade beneath strictly
bounds the firm, damp road and narrows it, it
seems like autumn. The rows of willows completely fence the way, and appear to converge in
perspective as I had not noticed by day. — The
bull-frogs are of various tones. Some horse in
a distant pasture whinnies. Dogs bark. There
is that dull dumping sound of frogs, as if a bubble containing the lifeless, sultry air of day
burst on the surface, a belching sound. When
two or more bull-frogs trump together, it is a ten-
pound-ten note. — In Conant's meadow I hear
the gurgling of unwearied water, the trill of a
toad, and go through the cool, primordial, liquid
air that has settled there. As I sit on the
great door step, the loose clapboards on the old
house rattle in the wind weirdly, and I seem to
hear some wild mice running about on the floor,
sometimes a loud crack from some weary timber
trying to change its position. How distant day
and its associations! The night wind comes cold
and whispering, murmuring weirdly from distant
mountain tops. No need to climb the Andes
or Himalayas; for brows of lowest hills are
highest mountain tops in cool, moonlight nights.
Is it a cuckoo's chuckling note I heard? Occasionally there is something enormous and mon-

strous in the size and distance of objects. A
rock is it, or an elephant asleep? Are these
trees on an upland or a lowland, or do they skirt
a sea beach? When I get there, shall I look off
on the sea? — The white weed is the only obvious flower. I see the tops of the rye wave, and
grain fields are more interesting than by day.
The water is dull-colored, hardly more light than
a rye field.

You may not suspect that the milk of the
cocoanut, which is imported from the other side
of the world, is mixed. So pure do some truths
come to us, I trust.

What a mean and wretched creature is man.
By and by some Dr. Morton may be filling your
cranium with white mustard-seed to learn its internal capacity. Of all ways invented to come
at a knowledge of a living man, this seems to me
the worst, as it is the most belated. You would
learn more by once paring the nails of the living subject. There is nothing out of which the
spirit has more completely departed, and in
which it has left fewer significant traces.

June 25, 1853. P. M. To Assabet bathing-
place. Found an unusual quantity of Amelanchier berries. I think of the two common kinds,
one a taller bush twice as high as my head, with
thinner and lighter colored leaves, and larger,
or at least somewhat softer, fruit, the other, a

shorter bush, with more rigid and darker leaves,
and dark, blue berries, with often a sort of wool-
iness on them. Both these are now in their
prime. These are the first berries after strawberries, or the first and, I think, the sweetest
bush berries, somewhat like high blueberries, but
not so hard. Much eaten by insects, worms,
etc., as big as the largest blueberries or peas.
These are the "service berries" which the Indians of the north and the Canadians use "*la
poire*" of the latter. They, by a little, precede
the early blueberry (though H—— brought two
quarts of the last, day before yesterday), being
now in their prime, while blueberries are but just
beginning. I never saw nearly so many before.
It is a very agreeable surprise. I hear the cherry-birds and others about me, no doubt attracted
by this fruit. It is owing to some peculiarity of
the season that they bear fruit. I have picked
a quart of them for a pudding. I felt all the
while I was picking them, in the low, light, waving, shrubby wood they make, as if I were in a
foreign country. Several old farmers say, "Well,
though I have lived seventy years, I never saw
nor heard of them." I think them a delicious
berry. No doubt they require only to be more
abundant every year to be appreciated.

I think it must be the purple finch with the
crimson head and shoulders which I see and

hear singing so sweetly and variedly in the garden once or twice to-day. It sits on a bean pole or fence pick. It has a little of the martin warble and of the canary bird.

June 25, 1854. A green bittern apparently, awkwardly alighting on the trees, and uttering its hoarse *zarry* note, *zskeow* — *xskeow* — *xskeow.*

Through June the song of the birds is gradually growing fainter.

June 25, 1858. P. M. To Conantum. — Sitting on the Conantum House sill still left, I see two and perhaps three young striped squirrels, two thirds grown, within fifteen or twenty feet, one or more on the wall, another on the ground. Their tails are rather imperfect as well as their bodies. They are running about, yet rather feebly, nibbling the grass, etc., or sitting upright, looking very cunning. The broad, white line above and below the eye make it look very long as well as large, and the black and white stripe on its sides, curved as it sits, are very conspicuous and pretty. Who striped the squirrel's side? Several times I saw two approach each other, and playfully, and as it were affectionately, put their paws and noses to each other's faces. This was done very deliberately. There was no rudeness nor excessive activity in the sport. At length the old one appears, larger and much more bluish. She is shy, and with a sharp cluck or chip calls the others gradually to her, and draws them off along the wall, they from time to time frisking ahead of her, then she ahead of them. The hawks must get many of these inexperienced creatures.

June 26, 1840. The best poetry has never been written, for when it might have been, the poet forgot it, and when it was too late, remembered it.

The highest condition of art is artlessness.

Truth is always paradoxical.

He will get to the goal first who stands stillest.

By sufferance you may escape suffering.

He who resists not at all will never surrender.

When a dog runs at you, whistle for him.

Say "Not so," and you will outcircle the philosophers.

Stand outside the wall, and no harm can reach you; the danger is that you be walled in with it.

June 26, 1851. — Visited a menagerie this afternoon. I am always surprised to see the same spots and stripes on wild beasts from Africa and Asia, and also from South America, on the Brazilian tiger and the African leopard, and their general similarity. All these wild animals, lions, tigers, chetas, leopards, etc., have one hue, tawny commonly, and spotted or striped, what you may call pard color, a color and marking which I had not associated with America. These are wild animals (beasts). What constitutes the difference between a wild beast and a tame one? How much more human the one than the other! Growling, scratching, roaring, with whatever beauty and gracefulness, still untamable, this royal Bengal tiger or the leopard. They have the character and the importance of another order of men. The majestic lion, the king of beasts, he must retain his title.

I was struck by the gem-like, changeable, greenish reflections from the eyes of the grizzly bear, so glassy that you never saw the surface of the eye. They are quite demonic. Its claws, though extremely large and long, look weak and made for digging or pawing the earth and leaves. It is unavoidable, the idea of transmigration; not merely a fancy of the poets, but an instinct of the race.

June 26, 1852. I have not put darkness, duskiness enough into my night and moonlight walks. Every sentence should contain some twilight or night. At least the light in it should be the yellow or creamy light of the moon, or the fine beams of stars, and not the white light of day. The peculiar dusky serenity of the sentences must not allow the reader to forget that it is evening or night, without my saying that it is dark.   Otherwise he will, of course, presume a daylight atmosphere.

The earliest water surfaces, as I remember, as soon as the ice is melted, present as fair and matured scenes, as soft and warm, reflecting the sky through the clear atmosphere, as in midsummer, far in advance of the earth.   The earliest promise of the summer, is it not in the smooth reflecting surface of woodland lakes in which the ice is just melted?   Those liquid eyes of Nature, blue, or black, or even hazel, deep or shallow, clear or turbid, green next the shore, the color of their iris.

P. M.   By boat up the Assabet.

The *Nymphæa odorata*, sweet water lily, pond lily, in bloom.   A superb flower, our lotus, queen of the waters.   Now is the solstice in still waters.   How sweet, innocent, wholesome its fragrance, how pure its white petals, though its root is in the mud.   It must answer in my mind for what the orientals say of the lotus flower. Probably the first a day or two since.   To-morrow, then, will be the first Sabbath when the young men, having bathed, will walk slowly and soberly to church, in their best clothes, each with a lily in his hand or bosom, with as long a stem as he could get.   At least I used to see

them go by and come into church, when I used
to go myself, smelling a pond lily, so that the
flower is to some extent associated with bathing
on Sabbath mornings and going to church, its
odor contrasting with and atoning for that of
the sermon. We have roses on the land and
lilies on the water. Both land and water have
done their best, now just after the longest day.
Nature says, You behold the utmost I can do.
And the young women carry their finest roses
on the other hand. Roses and lilies. The flo-
ral days. The red rose, with the intense color
of many suns concentrated, spreads its tender
petals perfectly fair, its flower not to be overlooked, modest, yet queenly, on the edges of
shady copses and meadows, against its green
leaves, surrounded by blushing buds, of perfect
form, not only beautiful, but rightfully com-
manding attention, unspoiled by the admiration
of gazers. And the water lily floats on the surface of slow waters, amid rounded shields of
leaves, bucklers red beneath, which simulate a
green field, perfuming the air. Each instantly
the prey of the spoiler, the rose-bug and water
insects. How transitory the perfect beauty of
the rose and the lily. The highest, intensest
color belongs to the land; the purest, perchance,
to the water. The lily is perhaps the only flower
which all are eager to pluck. It may be partly

16

because of its inaccessibility to most. The farmers' sons will frequently collect every bud that shows itself above the surface within half a mile. They are so infested by insects, and it is so rare you get a perfect one which has opened itself (though these only are perfect), that the buds are commonly plucked and opened by hand. I have a faint recollection of pleasure derived from smoking dried lily stems, before I was a man. I had commonly a supply of these. I have never smoked anything more noxious. I used to amuse myself with making the yellow, drooping stamens rise and fall by blowing through the pores of the long stem.

I see the nests of the bream, each with its occupant, scooped out in the sunny water, and partly shaded by the leaves of the *limnanthemum* or floating heart now in blossom and the *Potamogeton natans*, or pondweed. — Under the cool, glossy green leaves of small swamp white oaks, and leaning against their scaly bark near the water, you see the wild roses five or six feet high looking forth from the shade, but almost every bush and copse near the river or in low land which you approach these days, emits the noisome odor of the carrion-flower, so that you would think that all the dead dogs had drifted to that shore. All things, both beautiful and ugly, agreeable and offensive, are expressed in

flowers, all kinds and degrees of beauty, and all
kinds of foulness. For what purpose has Nature
made a flower to fill the low lands with the odor
of carrion. Just so much beauty and virtue as
there is in the world, and just so much ugliness
and vice, you see expressed in flowers. Each
human being has his flower which expresses his
character. In them nothing is concealed, but
everything published. Many a villager whose
garden bounds on the river, when he approaches
the willows and cornels by the river's edge,
thinks that some carrion has lodged on his shore,
when it is only the carrion-flower he smells. . . .

All shadows or shadowlets on the sandy bottom of the river are interesting. All are circular, almost lenticular, for they appear to have
thickness. Even the shadows of grass blades
are broken into several separate circles of shade.
Such is the fabulous or Protean character of the
water light. A skater insect casts seven flat or lenticular shades, four smaller in front, two larger behind, and the smallest of all in the centre. From
the shadow on the bottom you cannot guess the
form on the surface. Everything is transmuted
by the water. The shadow, however small, is
black within, edged with a sunny halo, corresponding to the day's twilight, and a certain liquidness
is imparted to the whole by the incessant motion
from the undulation of the surface. The oblong

leaves of the *Potamogeton hybridus* (?) now in
seed, make a circular shadow also, somewhat
coin-like, a halo produced by the thick atmosphere which the water is. These bright, sparkling brook and river bottoms are the true gold
washings, where the stream has washed the pebbly earth so long.

It is pleasant to walk in sproutlands now in
June; there is so much light reflected from the
underside of the new foliage. The rich meadows, too, reflect much of the bluish light from
the bent grass. We land on the south side opposite Barrett's. — There are some interesting,
retired natural meadows here, concealed by the
woods near the river bank, which are never cut,
long, narrow, and winding, full of a kind of stiff,
dry, cut grass and tender meadow-sweet and occasional cranberry patches now in bloom, with a
high border, almost as high as the meadows are
wide, of maples, birches, swamp white oaks, alders, etc. The flashing, silvery light from the under-sides of the maple leaves, high, rippling, washing towers far and near, — this cool, refreshing,
breezy, flashing light is very memorable. When
you think you have reached the end of such a
winding meadow, you pass between two alders
where the copses meet, and emerge into another
meadow beyond. I suppose that these meadows
are as nearly in their primitive state as any that

we see. So this country looked, in one of its aspects, a thousand years ago. What difference to the meadow-sweet, or the swamp white oak, or to the silver flashing maple leaves a thousand years ago or to-day! . . . The prevalence of the meadow-sweet at least distinguishes these meadows from the ordinary ones.

Forded the river with our clothes on our heads. The rounded heaps of stones, whether made by the suckers or lamprey-eels, are among the curiosities of the river. From the sand-bank we looked at the arched bridge while a traveler, in a simple carriage with a single pair of wheels, went over it. It interested me because the stratum of earth beneath him was so thin that he appeared quite in the air. While he sat with his elbows on his knees entertaining all earthly thoughts, or thoughtless, we looked directly beneath him through much air to a fair and distant landscape beyond. C—— says that is what men go to Italy to see. I love to see the firm earth mingled with the sky, like the spray of the sea tossed up. Is there not always, wherever an arch is constructed, a latent reference to its beauty. The arch supports itself like the stars, by gravity. " *Semper cadendo nunquam cadit.*" By always falling it never falls.

June 26, 1853. At Cliffs. The air warmer, but wonderfully clear after the hail-storm. I do not remember when I have seen it more clear. The mountains and horizon outlines on all sides are distinct and near. Nobscot has lost all its blue, is only a more distant hill-pasture, and the northwest mountains are too terrestrial a blue and too firmly defined to be mistaken for clouds. Billerica is as near as Bedford commonly. I see new spires far in the south, and on every side the horizon is extended many miles. It expands me to look so much farther over the rolling surface of the earth. Where I had seen or fancied only a hazy forest outline, I see successive swelling hills and remote towns. So often to the luxurious and hazy summer in our minds, when, like Fletcher's " Martyrs in Heaven," we,

> " estranged from all misery
> As far as Heaven and Earth discoasted lie,
> Swelter in quiet waves of immortality,"

some great chagrin succeeds, some chilling cloud comes over. But when it is gone, we are surprised to find that it has cleared the air, summer returns without its haze, we see infinitely farther into the horizon on every side, and the boundaries of the world are enlarged.

A beautiful sunset about half-past seven ; just clouds enough in the west (we are on Fair Haven hill) ; they arrange themselves about the western gate. And now the sun sinks out of sight just on the north side of Watatic, and the

mountains north and south are at once a dark
indigo blue, for they had been darkening an
hour or more. Two small clouds are left on the
horizon between Watatic and Monadnock, their
sierra edges all on fire. Three minutes after the
sun is gone, there is a bright and memorable
afterglow in his path, and a brighter and more
glorious light falls on the clouds above the por-
tal. His car borne farther round brings us into
the angle of excidence. Those little sierra clouds
look like two castles on fire, and I see the fire
through the windows. The low western horizon
glows now, five or six minutes after sunset, with
a delicate salmon color tinged with rose, deepest
where the sun disappeared, and fading off upward. North and south are deep blue cloud
islands in it. When I invert my head those delicate salmon-colored clouds look like a celestial
Sahara, sloping gently upward, a plane inclined
upward, to be traveled by caravans bound heav-
enward, with blue oases in it.

June 26, 1856. [New Bedford.] Rode to
Sconticut Neck or Point, in Fair Haven, five or
six miles. . . . Heard of and sought out the hut
of Martha Simons, the only pure-blooded Indian
left about New Bedford. She lives alone on the
narrowest part of the Neck, near the shore, in
sight of New Bedford. Her hut stands some
twenty-five rods from the road on a small tract

of Indian land, now wholly hers. It was formerly exchanged by a white man for some better
land, then occupied by Indians at Westport,
which he wanted. So said a Quaker minister,
her neighbor. The squaw was not at home when
we first called. It was a little hut, not so big as
mine. No garden, only some lettuce amid the
thin grass in front, and a great pile of clam and
quahog shells one side. Ere long she came from
the seaside and we called again. We knocked
and walked in, and she asked us to sit down.
She had half an acre of the real tawny Indian
face, broad with high cheek bones, black eyes,
and straight hair, originally black, but now a
little gray, parted in the middle. Her hands
were several shades darker than her face. She
had a peculiarly vacant expression, perhaps characteristic of the Indian, and answered our questions listlessly, without being interested or impli-
cated, mostly in monosyllables, as if hardly
present there. To judge from her physiognomy,
she might have been King Philip's own daugh-
ter. Yet she could not speak a word of Indian,
and knew nothing of her race, said she had lived
with the whites, gone out to service to them
when seven years old. Had lived part of her
life at Squaw Betty's Neck, Assawampsett Pond.
. . . She said she was sixty years old, but was
probably nearer seventy. She sat with her

elbows on her knees and her face in her hands,
and that peculiar vacant stare, perhaps looking
out the window between us, not repelling us in
the least, but perfectly indifferent to our presence. She was born on that spot. Her grandfather also lived on the same spot, though not in
the same house. He was the last of her race
who could speak Indian. She had heard him
pray in Indian, but could only understand "Je-
sus Christ." Her only companion was a miser-
able tortoise-shell kitten, which took no notice
of us. She had a stone chimney, a small cook-
ing stove without fore-legs, and set up on bricks
within it, and a bed covered with dirty bed-
clothes. Said she hired out her field as pasture ;
better for her than to cultivate it. . . . The question she answered with most interest was, "What
do you call that plant ? " and I reached her the
aletris from my hat. She took it, looked at it
a moment, and said, " That 's husk-root. It 's
good to put into bitters for a weak stomach."
The last year's light-colored and withered leaves
surround the present green star like a husk.
This must be the origin of the name. Its root
is described as intensely bitter. I ought to have
had my hat full of plants.

June 27, 1856. [New Bedford.] P. M. Went
with R—— and his boys in the steamer Eagle's
Wing, with a crowd and band of music, to the

northeast end of Naushon . . . some fifteen
miles from New Bedford. About two hours
going. Saw all the Elizabeth Isles, going and
coming. They are mostly bare, except the east
end of Naushon. This island is some seven
miles long by one to two wide. I had some two
and a half hours there. I was surprised to find
such a noble, primitive wood, chiefly beech, such
as the English poets celebrate, and oak (black
oak, I think), large and spreading, like pasture
oaks with us, though in a wood. The ground
under the beeches was covered with the withered
leaves, and peculiarly free from vegetation. On
the edge of a swamp I saw great tupelos running
up particularly tall, without lower branches, two
or three feet in diameter, with a rough, light-
colored bark. Saw a common wild grape-vine
running over a beech which was apparently flattened out by it, which vine measured at six feet
from the ground twenty-three inches in circum-
ference. It was larger below where it had already forked. At five feet from the ground it
divided into three great branches. It did not
rise directly, but with a great half spiral sweep.
. . . No sight could be more primeval. It was
partly or chiefly dead. This was in the midst
of the woods by a path side. Just beyond we
started up two deer.

June 27, 1840. . . . A dull, cloudy day; no

sun shining. The clink of the smith's hammer sounds feebly over the roofs, and the wind is sighing gently as if dreaming of cheerfuller days. The farmer is ploughing in yonder field, craftsmen are busy in the shops, the trader stands behind the counter, and all works go steadily forward. But I will have nothing to do, will tell Fortune that I play no game with her, and she may reach me in my Asia of serenity and indolence, if she can.

For an impenetrable shield stand inside yourself.

He was no artist, but an artisan, who first made shields of brass.

Unless we meet religiously, we profane one another. What was the consecrated ground around the temple we have used as no better than a domestic court. Our friend's is as holy a shrine as any God's, to be approached with sacred love and awe. Veneration is the measure of love. Our friend answers ambiguously, and sometimes before the question is propounded, like the oracle of Delphi. He forbears to ask explanation, but doubts and surmises darkly with full faith, as we silently ponder our fates. In no presence are we so susceptible to shame. Our hour is a sabbath; our abode, a temple; our gifts, peace offerings; our conversation, a communion; our silence, a prayer. In profanity we

are absent; in holiness, near; in sin, estranged;
in innocence, reconciled.

June 27, 1852.   P. M.   To Bear Hill, Lincoln.
The epilobium, spiked willow herb, shows its
pale purple spikes (pinkish?).   I will set it
down to the 20th.   *Epilobium angustifolium,*
one of the most conspicuous flowers at this
season, on dry, open hillsides in the woods,
sproutlands. . . .   I still perceive that ambrosial sweetness from the meadows in some places.
Give me the strong, rank scent of ferns in the
spring for vigor, just blossoming late in the
spring.   A healthy and refined nature would
always derive pleasure from the landscape.   As
long as the bodily vigor lasts, man sympathizes
with Nature.

Looking from Bear Hill I am struck by the
yellowish green of meadows, almost like an
ingrained sunlight.   Perhaps they have that
appearance, because the fields generally incline
now to a reddish-brown green.   The freshness
of the year in most fields is already past.   The
tops of the early grass are white, killed by the
worms.

It is somewhat hazy, yet I can just distinguish
Monadnock.   It is a good way to describe the
density of a haze to say how distant a mountain
can be distinguished through it, or how near a
hill is obscured by it.

Saw a very large white-ash tree, three and a
half feet in diameter, . . . which was struck by
lightning the 22d. The lightning apparently
struck the top of the tree and scorched the bark
and leaves for ten or fifteen feet downward, then
began to strip off the bark and enter the wood,
making a ragged, narrow furrow or crack, till
reaching one of the upper limbs it apparently
divided, descending on both sides and entering
deeper and deeper into the wood. At the first
general branching it had got full possession of
the tree in its centre, and tossed off the main
limbs, butt foremost, making holes in the ground
where they struck, and so it went down in the
midst of the trunk to the earth, where it apparently exploded, rending the trunk into six seg-
ments, whose tops, ten or twenty feet long, were
rayed out on every side at an angle of about
30° from a perpendicular, leaving the ground
bare directly under where the tree had stood,
though they were still fastened to the earth by
their roots. The lightning appeared to have
gone off through the roots, furrowing them as
it had furrowed the branches, and through the
earth, making a furrow like a plow, four or five
rods in one direction, and in another passing
through the cellar of the neighboring house,
about thirty feet distant, scorching the tin
milk-pans, and throwing dirt into the milk,

and coming out the back side of the house in a furrow, splitting some planks there. The main body of the tree was completely stripped of bark, which was cast in every direction, two hundred feet, and large pieces of the inside of the tree were hurled, with tremendous force, in various directions, — one into the side of a shed, smashing it, another burying itself in a wood-pile. The heart of the tree lay by itself. Probably a piece as large as a man's leg could not have been sawed out of the trunk, which would not have had a crack in it, and much of it was very finely splintered. The windows in the house were broken and the inhabitants knocked down by the concussion. All this was accomplished in an instant by a kind of fire out of the heavens called lightning or a thunderbolt, accompanied by a crashing sound. For what purpose? The ancients called it Jove's bolt, with which he punished the guilty, and we moderns understand it no better. There was displayed a Titanic force, some of that force which made and can unmake the world. The brute forces are not yet wholly tamed. Is this of the character of a wild beast? or is it guided by intelligence and mercy? If we trust our natural impressions, it is a manifestation of brutish force, or vengeance more or less tempered with justice. Yet it is our consciousness

of sin probably which suggests the idea of vengeance, and to a righteous man it would be
merely sublime without being awful. This is
one of those cases in which a man hesitates to
refer his safety to his prudence, as the putting
up of a lightning-rod. There is no lightning-
rod by which the sinner can avert the avenging
Nemesis. Though I should put up a rod, if its
utility were satisfactorily demonstrated to me,
yet, so mixed are we, I should feel myself safe
or in danger quite independently of the senseless
rod. There is a degree of faith and righteous-
ness in putting up a rod as well as in trusting
without one, though the latter, which is the rarer,
I feel to be the more effectual rod of the two.
It only suggests that impunity in respect to all
forms of death or disease, whether sickness or
casualty, is only to be attained by moral integrity. It is the faith with which we take
medicine that cures us. Otherwise we may be
cured into greater disease. In a violent tempest
we both fear and trust. We are ashamed of
our fear, for we know that a righteous man
would not suspect danger, nor incur any. Wherever a man feels fear, there is an avenger. The
savage's and the civilized man's instincts are
right. Science affirms too much. Science as-
sumes to show *why* the lightning strikes a tree,
but it does not show us the moral *why* any better

than our instincts did. It is full of presumption. Why should trees be struck? It is not enough to say, Because they are in the way. Science answers, "*Non scio*, I am ignorant." All the phenomena of Nature need to be seen from the point of view of wonder and awe, like lightning; and, on the other hand, the lightning itself needs to be regarded with serenity, as are the most innocent and familiar phenomena. There runs through the righteous man's spinal column a rod with burnished points to heaven, which conducts safely away into the earth the flashing wrath of Nemesis so that it merely clarifies the air. This moment the confidence of the righteous man erects a sure conductor within him; the next, perchance, a timid staple diverts the fluid to his vitals. If a mortal be struck with a thunderbolt *cœlo sereno*, it is naturally felt to be more awful and vengeful. Men are probably nearer to the essential truth in their superstitions than in their science. Some places are thought to be particularly exposed to lightning, some oaks on hill tops, for instance.

I meet the partridge with her brood in the woods, a perfect little hen. She spreads her tail into a fan and beats the ground with her wings fearlessly, within a few feet of me, to attract my attention while her young disperse.

But they keep up a faint, wiry kind of peep
which betrays them, while she mews and squeaks
as if giving them directions. — Chestnut trees
are budded. — I picked a handful or two of
blueberries. These and huckleberries deserve to
be celebrated, such simple, wholesome, universal fruits, food for the gods and for aboriginal
men. They are so abundant that they concern
our race much. Tournefort called some of this
genus at least, *Vitis-Idœa*, which apparently
means the vine of Mount Ida. I cannot imagine
any country without this kind of berry. Berry
of berries, on which men live like birds, still
covering our hills as when the red men lived
here. Are they not the principal wild fruit?

June 27, 1853. 4.30 A. M. To Island by
river. . . . Saw a little pickerel with a minnow
in its mouth. It was a beautiful little silver-
colored minnow, two inches long, with a broad
stripe down the middle. The pickerel held it
crosswise near the tail, as he had seized it, and
as I looked down on him, he worked the minnow along in his mouth toward the head, and
then swallowed it head foremost. Was this instinct?

June 27, 1859. . . . P. M. To Walden. . . .
I find an *Attacus Luna* half hidden under a
skunk cabbage leaf, with its back to the ground
and motionless, on the edge of a swamp. The

17

underside is a particularly pale, hoary green. It is somewhat greener above, with a slightly purplish brown border on the front edge of its front wings, and a brown, yellowish, and whitish eye-spot in the middle of each wing. It is very sluggish, and allows me to turn it over and cover it up with another leaf, sleeping till the night comes. It has more relation to the moon by its pale, hoary green color, and its sluggishness by day, than by the form of its tail.

June 28, 1840. The profane never hear music ; the holy ever hear it. It is God's voice, the divine breath audible. Where it is heard, there is a Sabbath. It is omnipotent. All things obey it, as they obey virtue. It is the herald of virtue. It passes by sorrow, for grief hangs its harp on the willows.

June 28, 1854. Tall anemone. Pontederia to-morrow.

June 28, 1857. . . . I hear on all hands these days, from the elms and other trees, the twittering peep of young golden robins which have recently left their nests, and apparently indicate their locality to their parents by thus incessantly peeping all day long.

June 28, 1860. . . . I meet to-day with a wood-tortoise which is eating the leaves of the early potentillas, and soon after another . . . deliberately eating sorrel. It was evidently quite an old one, its back being worn quite smooth, and its motions peculiarly sluggish. It continued to eat when I was within a few feet, holding its head high and biting down at it, each time bringing away a piece of the leaf. It made you think of an old and sick tortoise eating some salutary herb to cure itself with, and reminded me of the stories of the ancients, who, I *think*, made the tortoises thus cure themselves with dittany or origanum when bitten by a venomous snake. It impressed me as if it must know the virtues of herbs well, and could select the one best suited to the condition of its body. When I came nearer, it at once drew in its head. Its back was smooth and yellowish, a venerable tortoise. When I moved off, it at once withdrew into the woods.

June 29, 1840. Of all phenomena my own race are the most mysterious and undiscoverable. For how many years have I striven to meet one, even on common, manly ground, and have not succeeded !

June 29, 1851. There is a great deal of white clover this year. In many fields where there has been no clover seed sown, for many years at least, it is more abundant than the red, and the heads are nearly as large. Also pastures which are close cropped, and where I think there was little or no clover last year, are spotted white

with an humbler growth. And everywhere by
roadsides, garden borders, etc., even where the
sward is trodden hard, the small white heads on
short stems are sprinkled. As this is the season
for the swarming of bees, and this clover is very
attractive to them, it is probably the more difficult to secure them; at any rate it is more important, now that they can make honey so fast.
It is an interesting inquiry why this year is so
favorable to the growth of clover.

Swamp pink I see for the first time this season.

How different is day from day! Yesterday
the air was filled with a thick, fog-like haze, so
that the sun did not once shine with ardor, and
everything was so tempered under this thin veil
that it was a luxury merely to be out doors.
You were the less out for it. The shadows of
the apple trees even early in the afternoon were
remarkably distinct. The landscape wore a
classical smoothness. Every object was as in
picture with a glass over it. I saw some hills
on this side the river looking from Conantum,
on which the grass being of a yellow tinge,
though the sun did not shine out on them, they
had the appearance of being shone upon peculiarly. It was merely an unusual yellow tint of
the grass. The mere surface of the water was
an object for the eye to linger on.

I thought that one peculiarity of my "Week" was its *hypæthral* character, to use an epithet applied to those Egyptian temples which are open to the heavens above, *under the ether.* I thought that it had little of the atmosphere of the house about it, but might have been written wholly, as in fact it was to a great extent, out of doors. It was only at a late period in writing it, as it happened, that I used any phrases implying that I lived in a house or led a domestic life. I trust it does not smell so much of the study and library, even of the poet's attic, as of the fields and woods, that it is a hypæthral or unroofed book, lying open under the ether, and permeated by it, open to all weathers, not easy to be kept on a shelf.

At a distance in the meadow I hear still, at long intervals, the hurried commencement of the bobolink's strain, the bird just dashing into song, which is as suddenly checked, as it were, by the warder of the seasons, and the strain is left incomplete forever. [P. S.] I have since heard some complete strains.

The voice of the crickets, heard at noon from deep in the grass, allies day to night. It is unaffected by sun and moon. It is a midnight sound heard at noon, a midday sound heard at midnight.

I observed some mulleins growing on the western slope of the sandy railroad embankment, in as warm a place as can easily be found, where the heat was reflected oppressively from the sand at three o'clock P. M. this hot day. Yet the green and living leaves felt rather cool than otherwise to the hand, but the dead ones at the root were quite warm. The living plant thus preserves a cool temperature in the hottest exposure, as if it kept a cellar below from which cooling liquors were drawn up.

How awful is the least unquestionable meanness, when we cannot deny that we have been guilty of it. There seem to be no bounds to our unworthiness.

June 29, 1852. P. M. On the North River. . . . The *Rana halecina?* shad-frog is our handsomest; bronze, striped with brown spots edged and intermixed with bright green. . . . The frogs and tortoises striped and spotted for concealment. The painted tortoise's throat held up above the pads, streaked with yellowish, makes it the less obvious. The mud turtle is the color of the mud; the wood frog and the hylodes, of the dead leaves; the bull-frog, of the pads; the toad, of the earth, etc.; the tree-toad, of the bark.

In my experience nothing is so opposed to poetry, not crime, as business. It is a negation of life.

The wind exposes the red under-sides of the white lily pads. This is one of the aspects of the river now. The bud-bearing stem of this plant is a little larger, but otherwise like the leaf stem, and coming like it from the long, large root. It is interesting to pull up the lily roots with flowers and leaves attached, and see how it sends its buds upward to the light and air to expand and flower in another element. How interesting the bud's progress from the water to the air! So many of these stems are leaf-bearing, and so many, flower-bearing. Then consider how defended these plants against drought, at the bottom of the water, at most their leaves and flowers floating on its surface. How much mud and water are required to support their vitality! It is pleasant to remember those quiet Sabbath mornings by remote stagnant rivers and ponds where pure white water lilies just expanded, not yet infested by insects, float on the waveless water and perfume the atmosphere. Nature never appears more serene and innocent and fragrant. A hundred white lilies open to the sun rest on the surface smooth as oil amid their pads, while devil's needles are glancing over them. It requires some skill so to pull a lily as to get a long stem.

The great yellow lily, the spatterdock, expresses well the fertility of the river.

One flower on a spike of the *Pontederia cordata* just ready to expand.

Children bring you the early blueberry to sell now. It is considerably earlier on the tops of hills which have been recently cut off than in the plains or in vales. The girl that has Indian blood in her veins and picks berries for a living will find them out as soon as they turn.

The *Anemone virginiana*, tall anemone, looking like a white buttercup, on Egg Rock, cannot have been long in bloom.

I see the columbine lingering still.

June 29, 1859. I see two chestnut-sided warblers hopping and chipping a long time, as if they had a nest within six feet of me. No doubt they are breeding near. Yellow crown with a fine, dark, longitudinal line, reddish chestnut sides, black triangle on side of head. White beneath.

June 30, 1840. I sailed from Fair Haven last evening as gently and steadily as the clouds sail through the atmosphere. The wind came blowing blithely from the southwest fields, and stepped into the folds of our sails like a winged horse, pulling with a strong and steady impulse. The sail bends gently to the breeze as swells some generous impulse of the heart, and anon flutters and flaps with a kind of human suspense. I could watch the motions of a sail forever, they

are so rich and full of meaning. I watch the
play of its pulse as if it were my own blood beating there. The varying temperature of different
atmospheres is graduated on its scale. It is a
free, buoyant creature, the bauble of the heavens
and the earth. A gay pastime the air plays with
it. If it swells and tugs, it is because the sun
lays his windy finger on it. The breeze it plays
with has been out doors so long, so thin is it, and
yet so full of life, so noiseless when it labors
hardest, so noisy and impatient when least ser-
viceable. So am I blown by God's breath, so
flutter and flap, and fill gently out with the
breeze.

In this fresh evening, each blade and leaf
looks as if it had been dipped in an icy liquid
greenness. Let eyes that ache come here and
look, the sight will be a sovereign eye-water, or
else wait and bathe them in the dark.

We go forth into the fields, and there the
wind blows freshly onward, and still on, and we
must make new efforts not to be left behind.
What does the dogged wind intend, that like a
wilful cur it will not let me to turn aside to rest
or content? Must it always reprove and provoke
me, and never welcome me as an equal?

The truth shall prevail and falsehood discover
itself as long as the wind blows on the hills.

A man's life should be a stately march to a

sweet but unheard music, and when to his fellows it shall seem irregular and inharmonious, he will only be stepping to a livelier measure, or his nicer ear hurry him into a thousand symphonies and concordant variations. There will be no halt ever, but at most a marching on his post, or such a pause as is richer than any sound, when the melody runs into such depth and wildness as to be no longer heard, but implicitly consented to with the whole life and being. He will take a false step never, even in the most arduous times, for the music will not fail to swell into greater sweetness and volume, and itself rule the movement it inspired.

Value and effort are as much coincident as weight and a tendency to fall. In a very wide but true sense, effort is the deed itself, and it is only when these sensible stuffs intervene, that our attention is distracted from the deed to the accident. It is never the deed men praise, but some marble or canvas which are only a staging to the real work.

June 30, 1851. Haying has commenced. I see the farmers in distant fields cocking their hay now at six o'clock. The day has been so oppressively warm, that some workmen have lain by at noon, and the haymakers are mowing now at early twilight. The blue flag, *Iris versicolor,* enlivens the meadow, and the lark sings there at

sundown afar off. It is a note which belongs to
a New England summer evening. Though so late
I hear the summer hum of a bee in the grass, as
I am on my way to the river . . . to bathe.
After hoeing in a dusty garden all this warm
afternoon, so warm that the baker says he never
knew the like, and expects to find his horses
dead in the stable when he gets home, it is very
grateful to wend one's way at evening to some
pure and cool stream, and bathe there. . . .

What I suppose is the *Aster miser*, small-flow-
ered aster, like a small many-headed white-weed,
has now for a week been in bloom, a humble
weed, but one of the earliest of the asters.

I first observed about ten days ago that the
fresh shoots of the fir-balsam, *Abies balsamifera*,
found under the tree wilted, or plucked and kept
in the pocket or in the house a few days, emit
the fragrance of strawberries, only it is somewhat more aromatic and spicy. It was to me a
very remarkable fragrance to be emitted by a
pine, a very rich, delicious, aromatic, spicy fragrance, which, if the fresh and living shoots
emitted, they would be still more to be sought
after.

June 30, 1852. Nature must be viewed hu-
manly to be viewed at all, that is, her scenes
must be associated with humane affections, such
as are associated with one's native place, for in-

stance. She is most significant to a lover. If I have no friend, what is Nature to me? She ceases to be morally significant. . . .

Is not this period more than any other distinguished for flowers when roses, swamp pinks, morning glories, arethusas, orchises, blue-flags, epilobiums, mountain laurel, and white lilies are all in blossom at once.

June 30, 1860. Try the temperature of the springs and pond. At 2.15 P. M., the atmosphere north of house is 83° above zero.

The same afternoon, the water of the boiling spring, 45°.

Our well, after pumping, 49°.

Brister's spring, 49°.

Walden Pond at bottom, in four feet of water, 71°.

River at one rod from shore, 77°.

(2 P. M., July 1, the air is 77° and the river 75°.)

I see that the temperature of the boiling spring, on the 6th of March, 1846, was also 45°, and I suspect it varies very little throughout the year.

In sand, both by day and night, you find the heat to be permanently greatest some three inches below the surface. It is so to-day, and this is about the depth at which the tortoises place their eggs, where the temperature is highest permanently and changes least between night and day.

Generally speaking, the fields are not imbrowned yet, but the freshness of the year is preserved. As I stand on the side of Fair Haven Hill, the verdure generally appears at its height, the air clear, and the water sparkling after the rain of yesterday. It is a world of glossy leaves, and grassy fields and meads. The foliage of deciduous trees is now so nearly as dark as evergreens that I am not struck by the contrast. I think that the shadows under the edge of woods are less noticed now because the woods themselves are darker; so, too, with the darkness and shadows of elms.

Seen through this clear, sparkling, breezy air, the fields, woods, and meadows are very brilliant and fair. The leaves are now hard and glossy (the oldest), yet still comparatively fresh, and I do not see a single acre of grass that has been cut. The river meadows on each side the stream, looking toward the light, have an elysian beauty. . . . They are by far the most bright and sunny looking spots, such is the color of the sedges which grow there, while the pastures and hillsides are dark green, and the grain fields glaucous green. It is remarkable that the meadows which are the lowest part should have the lightest, sunniest, yellowest look.

I hear scarcely any toads of late, except a few
at evening. See in the garden, on the side of a
corn-hill, the hole in which one sits by day. It
is round, and about the width of his body across,
extending one side underneath about the length
of my little finger. It is shaped in the main
like a turtle's nest, but not so broad beneath,
and not quite so deep. There sits the toad in
the shade and concealed completely under the
ground, with its head toward the entrance, waiting for evening.

July 1, 1840. To be a man is to do a man's
work. Always our resource is to endeavor. We
may well say, Success to our endeavors. Effort
is the prerogative of virtue.

The true laborer is recompensed by his labor
not by his employer. Industry is its own wages.
Let us not suffer our hands to lose one jot of their
handiness by looking behind to a mere recom-
pense, knowing that our true endeavor cannot be
thwarted, nor we be cheated of our earnings unless by not earning them. Some symbol of value
may shape itself to the senses in wood or marble
or verse, but this is fluctuating as the laborer's
hire, which may or may not be withheld. Perhaps the hugest and most effective deed may
have no sensible result at all on earth, but paint
itself in the heavens in new stars and constella-
tions. Its very material lies out of Nature.

When in rare moments we strive wholly with
one consent, which we call a yearning, we may
not hope that our work will stand in any artist's
gallery.

July 1, 1852. 9.30 A. M. To Sherman's
Bridge by land and water. One object, to see
the white lilies in bloom. The *Trifolium arvense,*
or rabbit's foot clover, is just beginning to show
its color. . . . The mulleins generally now begin
to show their pure yellow in roadside fields, and
the white cymes of the elder are conspicuous on
the edges of the copses. I perceive the meadow
fragrance still. . . . Roses are in their prime
now, growing amid huckleberry bushes, ferns,
and sweet ferns, especially about some dry pond
hole, some paler, some more red. It would seem
they must have bloomed in vain while only wild
men roamed, yet now they adorn only the pasture of these cows. — How well - behaved are
cows ! When they approach me reclining in the
shade, from curiosity, or to receive a wisp of
grass, or to share the shade, or to lick the dog
held up, like a calf, though just now they ran at
him to toss him, they do not obtrude ; their company is acceptable, for they can endure the longest pause. They have not to be entertained.
They occupy the most eligible lots in the town.
I love to see some pure white about them. It
suggests the more neatness.

Borrowed his boat of B——, the wheelwright, at the Corner bridge. He was quite ready to lend it, and took pains to shave down the handle of a paddle for me, conversing the while on the subject of spiritual knocking which he asked if I had looked into. Our conversation made him the slower. An obliging man who understands that I am abroad viewing the works of Nature and not loafing, though he makes the pursuit a semi-religious one, as are all more serious ones to most men. All that is not sporting in the field, as hunting and fishing, is of a religious or else love-cracked character.

The white lilies were in all their splendor, fully open, sometimes their lower petals lying flat on the surface. The largest appeared to grow in the shallower water, where some stood five or six inches out of water, and were five inches in diameter. Two which I examined had twenty-nine petals each. . . . Perhaps there was not one open which had not an insect in it, and most had some hundreds of small gnats. We shook them out, however, without much trouble, instead of drowning them out, which makes the petals close. The freshly opened lilies were a pearly white, and though the water amid the pads was quite unrippled, the passing air gave a slight oscillating, boatlike motion to and fro to the flowers, like boats held fast by their cables.

Some of the lilies had a beautiful rosaceous tinge, most conspicuous in the half-opened flower, extending through the calyx to the second row of petals, or those parts of the petals between the calyx leaves which were most exposed to the light. It seemed to be owing to the same coloring principle which is seen in the under-sides of the pads as well as in the calyx leaves. Yet the rosaceous ones are chiefly interesting to me for variety, and I am contented that lilies should be white, and leave these higher colors to the land. I wished to breathe the atmosphere of lilies, and get the full impression which they are fitted to make. The form of this flower is very perfect, the petals are so distinctly arranged at equal intervals and at all angles from nearly a vertical to horizontal about the centre. Buds that were half expanded were interesting, showing the regularly notched outline of the points of the petals above the erect green calyx leaves. Some of the bays we entered contained a quarter of an acre, through which we with difficulty forced our boat. First there is the low, smooth, green surface of the pads, some of the Kalmianas purplish, then the higher level of the pickerel weed just beginning to blossom, and rising a little higher in the rear, often extensive fields of pipes (*Equisetum*) making a very level appearance. Mingled with the white lilies were the large yellow ones, and

18

the smaller, and here at least much more common, *Nuphar lutea* (var. *Kalmiana*), and the floating heart also still in blossom, and the *Brasenia peltata*, water target or shield, not yet in bloom, the petiole attached to its leaf, like a boy's string to his sucking leather. The rich violet purple of the pontederias was the more striking as the blossoms were still rare. Nature will soon be very lavish of this blue along the river sides. It is a rich spike of blue flowers with yellowish spots. Over all these flowers hover devil's needles in their zigzag flight. On the edge of the meadow I see blushing roses and cornels (probably the panicled). The woods ring with the veery this cloudy day, and I also hear the red-eye, oven-bird, Maryland yellow-throat, etc. — After eating our luncheon . . . we observed that every white lily in the river was shut, and they remained so all the afternoon (though it was no more sunny nor cloudy than the forenoon), except some which I had plucked before noon and cast into the river. These had not power to close their petals. It would be interesting to observe how instantaneously these lilies close at noon. I only noticed that though there were myriads fully open before I ate my luncheon at noon, after it, I could not find one open anywhere for the rest of the day. . . .

Counted twenty-one fishes' nests by the shal-

low shore just beyond Sherman's bridge, within
less than half a rod, edge to edge, with each a
bream poised in it. In some cases the fish had
just cleared away the mud or frog spittle, exposing the yellow sand or pebbles (sixteen to twen-
ty-four inches in diameter).

July 1, 1854. P. M. To Cliffs. . . . From
the hill I perceive that the air is beautifully
clear after the rain of yesterday, and not hot ;
fine grained. The landscape is fine as behind
a glass, the horizon edge distinct. The distant
vales toward the northwest mountains lie up
open and clear and elysian, like so many
Tempes. The shadows of trees are dark and
distinct. On the river I see the two broad borders of pads reflecting the light, the dividing
line between them and the water, their irregular
edge, perfectly distinct. The clouds are separate glowing masses or blocks floating in the
sky, not threatening rain. I see from this hill
their great shadows pass slowly here and there
over the top of the green forest.

July 1, 1859. P. M. To 2d Division Brook.
. . . White water ranunculus in fresh bloom,
at least a week, . . . in the shade of the bank,
a clear day. Its leaves and stems waving in the
brook are interesting, much cut and green.

July 2, 1840. I am not taken up, like Moses,
upon a mountain, to learn the law, but lifted up

in my seat here in the warm sunshine and genial light.

Neither men nor things have any true mode of invitation but to be inviting. They who are ready to go are already invited.

Can that be a task which all things abet, and to postpone which is to strive against Nature?

July 2, 1851. It is a fresh, cool summer morning. From the road here, at N. Barrett's, at 8.30 A. M., the Great Meadows have a slight bluish, misty tinge in part, elsewhere a sort of hoary sheen, like a fine downiness, inconceivably fine and silvery far away, the light reflected from the grass blades, a sea of grass hoary with light, the counterpart of the frost in spring. As yet no mower has profaned it, scarcely a footstep since the waters left; miles of waving grass adorning the surface of the earth.

Last night, a sultry night which compelled one to leave all windows open. I heard two travelers talking aloud, was roused out of my sleep by their loud, day-like and somewhat unearthly discourse, at perchance one o'clock; from the country, whiling away the night with loud discourse. I heard the words Theodore Parker and Wendell Phillips loudly spoken, and so did half a dozen of my neighbors who also were awakened. Such is fame. It affected me like Dante talking of the men of this world in the infernal regions. If the travelers had called my own name, I should equally have thought it an unearthly personage which it would have taken me some hours into daylight to realize. O traveler, have not you got any further than that? My genius hinted before I fairly awoke, "Improve your time." What is the night that a traveler's voice should sound so hollow in it? that a man, speaking aloud in it, speaking in the regions under the earth, should utter the words Theodore Parker?

A traveler! I love his title. A traveler is to be reverenced as such. His profession is the best symbol of our life. Going from —— toward ——; it is the history of every one of us. I am interested in those that travel in the night.

It takes but little distance to make the hills and even the meadows look blue to-day. That principle which gives the air an azure color is more abundant.

To-day the milk-weed is blossoming. Some of the raspberries are ripe, the most innocent and simple of fruits, the purest and most ethereal. Cherries, too, are ripe.

Many large trees, especially elms, about a house, are a sure indication of old family distinction and worth. . . . Any evidence of care bestowed on these trees receives the traveler's respect as for a nobler husbandry than the raising of corn and potatoes.

July 2, 1852. . . . Last night, as I lay awake, I dreamed of the muddy and weedy river on which I had been paddling, and I seemed to derive some vigor from my day's experience, like the lilies which have their roots at the bottom.

I plucked a white lily bud just ready to expand, and after keeping it in water for two days (till July 3d), as I set about opening it, touching the lapped points of its petals, they sprang open and rapidly expanded in my hand into a perfect blossom with the petals as perfectly disposed at equal intervals as on their native lake, and in this case, of course, untouched by an insect. I cut its stem short and placed it in a broad dish of water, where it sailed about under the breath of the beholder with a slight undulatory motion. The breeze of his half-suppressed admiration it was that filled its sail, a kind of popular aura that may be trusted, methinks. It was a rose-tinted one. Men will travel to the Nile to see the lotus flower, who have never seen in their glory the lotuses of their native streams.

The spikes of the pale lobelia, some blue, some white, passing insensibly from one to the other, and especially hard to distinguish in the twilight, are quite handsome now in moist ground, rising above the grass. The prunella has various tints in various lights, now blue, now lilac. As the twilight deepens into night, its color changes. It always suggests freshness and coolness from the places where it grows. I see the downy heads of the senecio gone to seed, thistle-like, but small. The gnaphaliums and this are among the earliest to present this appearance. . . .

At the bathing-place there is a hummock which was floated on to the meadow some springs ago, now densely covered with the handsome red-stemmed wild rose, — a full but irregular clump, showing no bare stems below, but a dense mass of shining leaves, and small, red stems above in their midst, and on every side countless roses ; now in the twilight more than usually beautiful they appear, hardly closed, of a very deep rich color, as if the rays of the departed sun still shone through them ; a more spiritual rose at this hour, beautifully blushing ; and then the unspeakable beauty and promise of those fair swollen buds that spot the mass and will blossom to-morrow, and the more distant promise of the handsomely formed green ones which yet show no red ; for few things are handsomer than a rose-bud in any stage. These are mingled with a few pure white elder blossoms and some rosaceous or pinkish meadow-sweet. I am confident that there can be nothing so beautiful in any culti-vated garden with all its varieties as this wild swamp. . . .

Nature is reported not by him who goes forth consciously as an observer, but in the fullness of life. To such a one she rushes to make her report. To the full heart she is all but a figure of speech. This is my year of observation, and I fancy that my friends are also more devoted to outward observation than ever before, as if it were an epidemic.

I cross the brook by Hubbard's little bridge. Now nothing but the cool, invigorating scent which is perceived at night in these low meadowy places where the alders and ferns grow can restore my spirits. . . .

At this season I think we do not regard the larger features of the landscape as in the spring, but are absorbed in details. Then, when the meadows were flooded, I looked far over them to the distant woods and the outlines of the hills which were more distinct. I should not have so much to say of extensive water or landscapes at this season. One is a little bewildered by the variety of objects. There must be a certain meagreness of details and nakedness, for wide views.

Nine o'clock. The full moon rising (or full last night) is revealed first by some slight clouds above the eastern horizon looking white, the first indication that she is about to rise, the traces of day not yet gone in the west. There, similar

clouds seen against a lighter sky look dark and
heavy. Now a lower cloud in the east reflects a
more yellowish light. The moon, far over the
round globe, traveling this way, sends her light
forward to yonder cloud from which the news of
her coming is reflected to us. The moon's aurora! it is without redness . . . like the dawn
of philosophy and its noon, too. At her dawn-
ing no cocks crow. How few creatures to hail
her rising, only some belated travelers that may
be abroad this night. What graduated infor-
mation of her coming! More and more yellow
glows the low cloud with concentrating light, and
now the moon's edge suddenly appears above a
low bank of cloud not seen before, and she seems
to come forward apace without introduction,
after all. The steadiness with which she rises
with undisturbed serenity, like a queen who has
learned to walk before her court, is glorious, and
she soon reaches the open sea of the heavens.
She seems to advance (so perchance flows the
blood in the veins of the beholder) by graceful, sallying essays, trailing her garment up the
sky.

July 2, 1854. 4 A. M. To Hill. Hear the
chip-bird and robin very lively at dawn. From
the hill, as the sun rises, I see a fine river-fog
wreathing the trees, elms and maples, by the
shore. . . . It is clear summer now. The cocks

crow hoarsely, ushering in the long-drawn, summer-day.

P. M. An abundance of red lilies in an upland dry meadow, from one to two feet high, upright-flowered, more or less dark shade of red, freckled and sometimes wrinkle-edged petals. Must have been out some days. This has come with the intense summer heat, a torrid July heat. . . . The spring now seems far behind, yet I do not remember the interval; I feel as if some broad, invisible, Lethean gulf lay between this and spring.

July 2, 1855. Young bobolinks are now fluttering over the meadow, but I have not been able to find a nest, so concealed are they in the meadow grass.

At 2 P. M. Thermometer north side of house, 93°.

Air over river at Hubbard's bathing-place, 88°.

Water six feet from shore and one foot deep, 84½°.

Water near surface in middle when up to neck, 83½°.

Water at bottom in same place, pulling [thermometer] up quickly, 83½°.

Yet the air on the wet body, there being a strong southwest wind, feels colder than the water.

July 2, 1857. *Calla palustris*, with its con-
volute point, like the cultivated, at the south end
of Gowing's swamp. Having found this in one
place, I now find it in another. Many an object
is not seen, though it falls within the range of
our visual ray, because it does not come within
the range of our intellectual ray. So in the
largest sense we find only the world we look for.

July 2, 1860. Yesterday I detected the smallest grass that I know, apparently *Festuca tenella?*
It seemed to be out of bloom. In a dry path,
two to four inches high, like a moss.

July 2, 1858. A. M. Start for the White
Mountains in a private carriage with E——
H——. Spent the noon close by the old Dun-
stable graveyard, by a small stream north of it.
. . . . Walked to and along the river, and bathed
in it. . . . What a relief and expansion of my
thoughts when I came out from that inland position by the graveyard to this broad river's shore.
This vista was incredible there. Suddenly I see
a broad reach of blue beneath, with its curves
and headlands, liberating me from the more terrene earth. What a difference it makes whether
I spend my four hours nooning between the hills
by yonder roadside, or on the brink of this fair
river, within a quarter of a mile of that! Here
the earth is fluid to my thought, the sky is reflected from beneath, and around yonder cape is

the highway to other continents. This current allies me with the world. Be careful to sit in an elevating and inspiring place. There my thoughts were confined and trivial, and I hid myself from the gaze of travelers. Here they are expanded and elevated, and I am charmed by the beautiful river reach. It is equal to a different season and country, and creates a different mood. . . . This channel conducts our thoughts as well as our bodies to classic and famous ports, and allies us to all that is fair and great. I like to remember that at the end of half a day's walk I can stand on the bank of the Merrimack. It is just wide enough to interrupt the land, and leads my eye and thought down its channel to the sea. A river is superior to a lake in its liberating influence. It has motion and indefinite length. A river touching the back of a town is like a wing, unused it may be as yet, but ready to waft it over the world. With its rapid current, it is a slightly fluttering wing. . . .

The wood-thrush sings almost wherever I go, eternally recommending the world morning and evening for us. Again it seems habitable and more than habitable to us.

July 4, 1858. . . . It is far more independent to travel on foot, you have to sacrifice so much to the horse. You cannot choose the most agree-

able places in which to spend the noon, com-
manding the finest views, because commonly
there is no water there, or you cannot get there
with your horse. New Hampshire being a more
hilly and newer State than Massachusetts, it is
very difficult to find a suitable place to camp in
near the road, affording water, a good prospect,
and retirement. Several times we rode on, as
much as ten miles, with a tired horse, looking
in vain for such a place, and then almost invariably camped in some low and unpleasant spot.
There are very few, scarcely any, lanes, or even
paths and bars along the road. As we are beyond the range of the chestnut, the few bars that
might be taken down are long and heavy planks
or slabs intended to confine sheep, and there is
no passable road behind. Besides, when you
have chosen your place, one must stay behind to
watch your effects, while the other looks about.
I frequently envied the independence of the
walker who can spend the midday hours and
take his lunch in the most agreeable spot on his
route. The only alternative is to spend your
noon at some trivial inn, pestered by flies and
tavern loungers.

Camped within a mile south of Senter Harbor,
in a birch wood on the right, near the lake.
Heard in the night a loon, screech-owl, and
cuckoo ; and our horse, tied to a slender birch

close by, restlessly pawing the ground all night, and whinnying to us whenever we showed ourselves, asking for something more than meal to fill his belly with.

July 5, 1858. Go on through Senter Harbor, and ascend Red Hill in Moultonboro. Dr. Jackson says it is so called from the *Uva ursi* on it turning red in the fall. On the top we boil a dipper of tea for our dinner, spend some hours, having carried up water for the last half mile. Enjoyed the famous view of Winnepiseogee and its islands south-easterly, and Squam Lake on the west, but I was as much attracted at this hour by the wild mountain view on the northward. Chocorua and the Sandwich Mountains a dozen miles off seemed the boundary of cultivation on that side, as indeed they are. They are, as it were, the impassable southern barrier of the mountain region, themselves lofty and bare, and filling the whole northerly horizon, with the broad valley of Sandwich between you and them. Over their ridges, in one or two places, you detect a narrow blue edging or a peak of the loftier White Mountains, strictly so called. . . . Chocorua (which the inhabitants pronounce Shecorway, or Corway) is in some respects the wildest and most imposing of all the White Mountain peaks. . . . Descended and rode along the west and northwest side of Ossi-

pee Mountain. Sandwich, in a large, level space
surrounded by mountains, lay on our left. Here
first in Moultonboro I heard the *tea-lee* of the
white-throated sparrow. We were all the afternoon riding along under Ossipee Mountain,
which would not be left behind, unexpectedly
large, still lowering over our path. Have new
and memorable views of Chocorua as we get
round it eastward. Stop at Tamworth village
for the night. We are now near the edge of
a wild and unsettleable mountain region lying
northwest, apparently including parts of Albany
and Waterville. The landlord said that bears
were plenty in it, that there was a little interval
on Swift River that might be occupied, and that
was all.

July 6, 1858. 5.30 A. M. Keep on through
North Tamworth, and breakfast by shore of one
of the Ossipee Lakes. Chocorua north-northwest. Here I see loons. . . . Chocorua is as
interesting a peak as any to remember. You
may be jogging along steadily for a day before
you get round it and leave it behind, first seeing
it on the north, then northwest, then west, and
at last southwesterly, ever stern, rugged, [appar-
ently] inaccessible, and omnipresent. . . . The
scenery in Conway and onward to North Conway
is surprisingly grand. You are steadily advancing into an amphitheatre of mountains. I do

not know exactly how long we had seen one of
the highest peaks before us in the extreme northwest, with snow on its side just below the summit, when a boy, a little beyond Conway, called
it Mount Washington. If it were that, the snow
must have been in Tuckerman's Ravine, which,
methinks, is rather too low. Perhaps it was that
we afterwards saw on Mount Adams. . . . The
road, which is for the most part level, winds
along the Saco through groves of maples, etc.,
on the intervals, with little of rugged New
Hampshire under your feet, often a soft and
sandy road. The scenery is remarkable for this
contrast of level interval having soft and shady
groves with mountain grandeur and ruggedness.
Often from the midst of level maple groves
which remind you only of classic lowlands, you
look out through a vista of the most rugged scenery of New England. It is quite unlike New
Hampshire generally, quite unexpected by me,
and suggests a superior culture. . . . After leaving North Conway, the higher White Mountains
were less seen, if at all. They had not appeared
in pinnacles as sometimes described, but broad
and massive. Only one of the higher summits,
called by the boy Mount Washington, was conspicuous. . . . At Bartlett Corner we turned up
the Ellis River and took our nooning on its bank,
by the bridge just this side of Jackson Centre,

in a rock-maple grove. . . . There are but few
narrow intervals on the road, two or three only
after passing Jackson, and each is improved by
a settler. . . . Hear the night-warbler all along
thus far. Saw the bones of a bear at the house
[of one Wentworth, afterwards their attendant]
and camped rather late, on right-hand side of
road just beyond, a little more than four miles
from Jackson. . . . Heard at evening the wood-
thrush, veery, white-throated sparrow, etc. . . .
Wentworth said he was much troubled by the
bears. They killed his sheep and calves, and
destroyed his corn when in the milk, close by
his house. He has trapped and killed many of
them, and brought home and reared the young.

July 7, 1858. Having engaged the services
of Wentworth to carry up some of our baggage,
and to keep our camp, we rode onward to the
Glen House, eight miles further, sending back
our horse and wagon to his house. He has lived
here thirty years, and is a native. . . . Began
the ascent of the mountain road at 11.30 A. M.
Near the foot of the ledge and limit of trees,
only their dead trunks standing, probably fir and
spruce, a merry collier and his assistant, who had
been making coal for the summit, and were preparing to leave the next morning, made us welcome to their shanty, where we spent the night,
and entertained us with their talk. We here
19

boiled some of our beef tongues, a very strong wind pouring in gusts down the funnel, and scattering the fire about through the cracked stove. This man . . . had imported goats on to the mountain, and milked them to supply us with milk for our coffee. . . . The wind blowing down the funnel set fire to a pile of dirty bed-quilts while I was out, and came near burning up the building. There were many barrels of spoiled beef in the cellar, and the collier said that a person coming down the mountain, some time ago, looked into the cellar and saw five wild cats (*loups cerviers*) there. He had heard two fighting like cats near by a few nights before.

July 8, 1858. Though a fair day, the sun did not rise clear. I started before my companions, wishing to secure a clear view from the summit, while they accompanied the collier, who, with his assistant, was conducting his goats up to the summit for the first time. He led the old one, and the rest followed.

I reached the summit about half an hour before my party, and enjoyed a good view, though it was hazy. By the time the rest arrived, a cloud invested us all, a cool, driving mist, which wet one considerably. As I looked downward over the rocky surface I saw tinges of blue sky and a light as of breaking away close to the rocky edge of the mountain, far

below me, instead of above, showing that there
was the edge of the cloud. It was surprising
to look down thus under the cloud, at an angle
of thirty or forty degrees, for the only evidences
of a clear sky and breaking away. There was
a ring of light encircling the summit thus close
to the rocks under the thick cloud, and the
evidences of a blue sky in that direction were
just as strong as ordinarily when you look upward. . . .

I observed that the enduring snow-drifts were
such as had lodged under the southeast cliffs,
having been blown over the summit by the
northwest wind. They lie up under such cliffs,
and at the head of the ravines on the southeast
slopes. . . .

About 8.15 A. M., being still in a dense fog,
we started direct for Tuckerman's Ravine, I having taken the bearing of it before the fog, but
Spaulding [one of "the landlords of the Tip-
Top and Summit Houses"], also went some ten
rods with us, and pointed toward the head of
the Ravine, which was about S. 15° W. . . .
The landlords were rather anxious about us. I
looked at my compass every four or five rods,
and then walked toward some rock in our
course, but frequently, after taking three or four
steps, though the fog was no more dense, I would
lose the rock I steered for. The fog was very

bewildering. You would think the rock you steered for was some large boulder twenty rods off, or perchance it looked like the brow of a distant spur, but a dozen steps would take you to it, and it would suddenly have sunk into the ground. Discovering this illusion, I said to my companions, "You see that boulder of a peculiar form, slanting over another. Well, that is in our course. How large do you think it is? and how far?" To my surprise, one answered, three rods, but the other said nine. I guessed four, and we all thought it about eight feet high. We could not see beyond it, and it looked like the highest point of a ridge before us. At the end of twenty-one paces, or three and a half rods, I stepped upon it less than two feet high, and I could not have distinguished it from the hundred similar ones around it, if I had not kept my eye on it all the while. It is unsafe for one to ramble over these mountains at any time, unless he is prepared to move with as much certainty as if he were solving a geometrical problem. A cloud may at any moment settle around him, and unless he has a compass and knows which way to go, he will be lost at once. One lost on the summit of these mountains should remember that if he will travel due east or west eight or nine miles, or commonly much less, he will strike a public road; or whatever direction he might

take, the average distance would not be more
than eight miles, and the extreme distance
twenty. Follow some watercourse running
easterly or westerly. If the weather were
severe on the summit, so as to prevent searching for the summit houses or the path, I should
at once take a westward course from the southern
part of the range, and an eastward one from the
northern part. To travel then with security, a
person must know his bearings at every step, be
it fair weather or foul. An ordinary rock in a
fog, being in the apparent horizon, is exaggerated to perhaps ten times its size and distance.
You will think you have gone further than you
have, to get to it. Descending straight by compass through the cloud toward the head of Tuckerman's Ravine, we found it an easy descent
over, for the most part, bare rocks, not very
large, with at length moist, springy places, green
with sedge, etc., between little sloping shelves of
green meadow, where the hellebore grew within
half a mile of the top, and the *Oldenlandia cœru-
lea* was abundantly out, very large and fresh,
surpassing ours in the spring. . . . We crossed
a narrow portion of the snow, but found it unexpectedly hard and dangerous to traverse. I
tore up my nails in efforts to save myself from
sliding down its steep surface. The snow field
now formed an irregular crescent on the steep

slope at the head of the ravine, some sixty rods wide horizontally, or from north to south, and twenty-five rods wide from upper to lower side. It may have been a half dozen feet thick in some places, but it diminished sensibly in the rain while we were there; said to be all gone commonly by the end of August. The surface was hard, difficult to work your heels into, a perfectly regular steep slope, steeper than an ordinary roof from top to bottom. A considerable stream, a source of the Saco, was flowing out from beneath it, where it had worn a low arch a rod or more wide. Here were the phenomena of winter and earliest spring contrasted with summer. On the edge of and beneath the overarching snow, many plants were just pushing up as in spring. The great plaited elliptical buds of the hellebore had just pushed up there, even under the edge of the snow, and also bluets. Also, close to the edge of the snow, the bare, upright twigs of a willow, with small, silvery buds, not yet expanded, of a satiny lustre, one to two feet high (apparently *Salix repens*), but not, as I noticed, procumbent, while a rod off, on each side, where it had been melted some time, it was going to seed, and fully leaved out. Saw also what was apparently the *Salix phylicifolia*. The surface of the snow was dirty, being covered with cinder-like rubbish of vegetation which had blown on to it. Yet from the camp it looked quite white and pure. For thirty or forty rods, at least, down the stream, you could see the print where the snow-field had recently melted. It was a dirty brown flattened stubble, not yet at all greened, covered with a blackish, shining dirt, the dust of the snow-crust. Looking closely I saw that it was composed, in great part, of golden-rods (if not asters), now quite flattened, with other plants. I should have said that from the edge of the ravine, having reached the lower edge of the cloud, we came out into the sun again, much to our satisfaction, and discovered a little lake called Hermit Lake, about a mile off, at the bottom of the ravine, just within the limit of the trees. For this we steered, in order to camp by it, for the sake of the protection of the wood. But following down the edge of the stream, the source of Ellis River, which was quite a brook within a stone's throw of its head, we soon found it very bad walking in the scrubby fir and spruce, and therefore, when we had gone about two thirds of the way to the lake, decided to camp in the midst of the dwarf firs, clearing away a space with our hatchet. Having cleared a space with some difficulty where the trees were seven or eight feet high, Wentworth kindled a fire on the lee side, without, against my advice, removing the moss, which was especially dry on

the rocks, and directly ignited and set fire to
the fir leaves, spreading off with great violence
and crackling over the mountain, and making
us jump for our baggage. Fortunately, it did
not burn a foot toward us, for we could not have
run in that thicket. It spread particularly fast
in the procumbent creeping spruce, scarcely a
foot deep, and made a few acres of deers' horns,
thus leaving our mark on the mountain side.
We thought at first it would run for miles, and
Wentworth said it would do no harm, — the
more there was burned the better; but such was
the direction of the wind that it soon reached
the brow of a ridge east of us, and then burned
very slowly down its east side. Yet Willey
says, p. 23 [of his "Incidents of White Mountain History"], speaking of the dead trees,
"bucks' horns," "Fire could not have caused
the death of these trees; for fire will not spread
here in consequence of the humidity of the whole
region at this elevation," and he attributes their
death to the cold of 1816. Yet fire did spread
above the limit of trees in this ravine. — Finally,
we kept on, leaving the fire raging, down to the
first little lake, walking in the stream, jumping
from rock to rock with it. It may have fallen a
thousand feet, within a mile below the snow.
We camped on a slightly rising ground between
that first little lake and the stream, in a dense

fir and spruce wood, thirty feet high, though it was but the limit of trees there. On our way we found the *Arnica mollis* (recently begun to bloom), a very fragrant yellow-rayed flower by the side of the brook, also half way up the ravine. The *Alnus viridis* was a prevailing shrub all along this stream, seven or eight feet high near our camp. Near the snow it was dwarfish, and still in flower, but in fruit only below ; had a glossy, roundish, wrinkled, green, sticky leaf. Also a little *Ranunculus abortivus* by the brook, in bloom. . . . Our camp was opposite a great slide on the south, apparently a quarter of a mile wide, with the stream between us and it, and I resolved, if a great storm should occur, that we would flee to higher ground northeast. The little pond by our side was perfectly clear and cool, without weeds, and the meadow by it was dry enough to sit down in. When I looked up casually toward the crescent of snow, I would mistake it for the sky, a white glowing sky or cloud, it was so high, while the dark earth or mountain side above it passed for a dark cloud.

In the course of the afternoon, we heard, as we thought, a faint shout, and it occurred to me that B——, for whom I had left a note at the Glen House, might possibly be looking for me, but soon Wentworth decided that it must be a bear, for they make a noise like a woman in distress. He has caught many of them. Nevertheless we shouted in return, and waved a light coat on the meadow. After an hour or two had elapsed, we heard the voice again nearer, and saw two men. I went up the stream to meet B—— and B——, wet, ragged, and bloody from black flies. I had told B—— to look out for a smoke and a white tent. We had made a smoke sure enough. They were on the edge of the ravine when they shouted, and heard us answer, about a mile distant, over all the roar of the stream. They also saw our coat waved and ourselves. We slept five in the tent that night, and found it quite warm. It rained in the night, putting out the fire we had set. The woodthrush, which Wentworth called the nightingale, sang at evening and in the morning, and the same bird which I heard on Monadnock, I think, and then thought might be the Blackburnian warbler; also the veery.

July 9, 1858. Walked to Hermit Lake some forty rods northeast. It was clear and cold, with scarcely a plant in it, of perhaps half an acre. H—— tried in vain for trout here. From a low ridge east of it was a fine view of the ravine. Heard a bull-frog in the lake, and afterwards saw a large toad part way up the ravine. Our camp was about on the limit of trees, and may have been from twenty-five hundred to three thousand feet below the summit. I was here surprised to discover, looking down through the fir-tops, a large, bright, downy, fair weather cloud, covering the lower world far beneath us, and there it was the greater part of the time we were there, like a lake, while the snow and alpine summit were to be seen above us on the other side at about the same angle. The pure white crescent of snow was our sky, and the dark mountain side above, our permanent cloud. — We had the *Fringilla hiemalis* with its usual note about our camp. Wentworth said it was common, and bred about his house. I afterwards saw it in the valleys about the mountains. I had seen the white-throated sparrow near his house. This also, he said, commonly bred there on the ground. — The wood we were in was fir and spruce. Along the brook grew the *Alnus viridis, Salix Torneyana* (?), canoe birch, red cherry, mountain ash, etc. . . . I ascended the stream in the afternoon and got out of the ravine at its head, after dining on chiogenes tea, which plant I could gather without moving from my log seat. We liked it so well that B—— gathered a parcel to carry home. In most places it was scarcely practicable to get out of the ravine on either side on account of the precipices. I judged it to be one thousand or fifteen hundred feet deep. With care you could ascend by some slides. I found we might have camped in the scrub firs above the edge of the ravine, though it would have been cold and windy and comparatively unpleasant there, for we should have been most of the time in a cloud. The dense patches of dwarf fir and spruce scarcely rose above the rocks which they concealed. At a glance, looking over, or even walking over this dense shrubbery, you would think it nowhere more than a foot or two deep, and the trees at most only an inch or two in diameter, but by searching you would find hollow places in it six or eight feet deep, where the firs were from six to ten inches in diameter. By clearing a space here with your hatchet you could find a shelter for your tent, and also fuel, and water was close by above the head of the ravine. The strong wind and the snow are said to flatten these trees down thus. I noticed that this shrubbery just above the ravine as well as in it was principally fir, while the yet more dwarfish and prostrate portion on the edge was spruce.

Returning I sprained my ankle in jumping down the brook, so that I could not sleep that night, nor walk the next day. — We had commonly clouds above and below us, though it was clear where we were. They commonly reached about down to the edge of the ravine. — The

black flies which pestered us till into evening
were of various sizes, the largest more than one
eighth of an inch long. There were scarcely
any mosquitoes, it was so cool.

A small owl came in the evening and sat
within twelve feet of us, turning its head this
way and that, and peering at us inquisitively.

July 10, 1858. . . . When I tasted the water
under the snow arch . . . I was disappointed
at its warmth, though it was in part melted snow,
but half a mile lower down it tasted colder.
Probably the air being cooled by the neighborhood of the snow, it seemed thus warmer by
contrast. . . . The most peculiar and memorable
songster was the one with a note like that I heard
on Monadnock, keeping up an exceedingly brisk
and lively strain. It was remarkable for its incessant twittering flow. Yet we never got sight
of the bird, at least while singing, so that I could
not identify it, and my lameness prevented my
pursuing it. I heard it afterwards even in the
Franconia Notch. It was surprising from its
steady, uninterrupted flow, for, when one stopped,
another appeared to take up the strain. It reminded me of a fine corkscrew stream issuing
with incessant tinkle from a cork, flowing rapidly,
and I said he had pulled out the spile and left
it running. That was the rhythm, but with a
sharper tinkle of course. It had no more variety

than that, and was more remarkable for its con-
tinuance and monotony than any other bird's note
I ever heard. It evidently belongs only to cool
mountain sides high up amid the fir and spruce.
I saw ever flitting through the fir tops restlessly
a small white and dark bird, sylvia-like, which
may have been it. Sometimes they appeared to
be attracted by our smoke. The note was so incessant that at length you only noticed when it
ceased.

The black flies were of various sizes, much
larger than I noticed in Maine. They compelled
me most of the time to sit in the smoke, which
I preferred to wearing a veil. They lie along
your forehead in a line where your hat touches
it, or behind your ears, or about your throat if
not protected by a beard, or get into the rims of
the eyes or between the fingers, and there suck
till they are crushed. But fortunately they do
not last far into the evening, and a wind or a fog
disperses them. I did not mind them much, but
I noticed that men working on the highway made
a fire to keep them off. Anything but mosquitoes by night. I find many black flies accidentally pressed in my botany and plant books. A
botanist's books, if he has ever visited the primitive northern woods, will be pretty sure to contain such specimens.

H—— found, near the edge of the ravine

above, *Rhododendron lapponicum*, some time out of bloom, in the midst of empetrum and moss, according to Durand, at 68° in Greenland, *Arctostaphylos alpina* going to seed, *Polygonum viviparum*, in prime according to Durand, at all Kane's stations, and *Salix harbacea*, according to Durand, at 73° in Greenland, a pretty, trailing, roundish-leaved willow going to seed, but apparently not as early as the *Salix uva ursi.*

July 11, 1858. . . . One of the slender spruce trees by our camp, which we cut down, twenty-eight feet high, and only six and a half inches in diameter, though it looked young and thrifty, had about 80 rings, and the firs were at least as old. . . .

After some observation I concluded that it was true, as Wentworth had intimated, that the lower limbs of the spruce slanted downward more generally than those of the fir.

July 12, 1858. It having cleared up, we shouldered our packs and commenced our descent by a path two and a half or three miles to carriage road, not descending a great deal. . . . Trees at first, fir and spruce, then canoe birches increased, and, after two miles, yellow birch began.

I had noticed that the trees of the ravine camp, fir and spruce, did not stand firmly. Two

or three of us could have pulled down one thirty
feet high and six or seven inches thick. They
were easily rocked, lifting their horizontal roots
each time, which reminded me of what is said
about the Indians, that they sometimes bend
over a young tree, burying a chief under its
roots and letting it spring back, for his monu-
ment and protection. — In the afternoon, we rode
along, three of us, northward and northwestward
on our way round the mountains, going through
Gorham. We camped one and a half miles west
of Gorham by the roadside on the bank of Moose
River.

July 13, 1858. This morning it rained, keeping us in camp till near noon, for we did not
wish to lose the view of the mountains as we rode
along. . . .

I noticed, as we were on our way in the afternoon, that when finally it began to rain hard,
the clouds settling down, we had our first distinct view of the mountain outline for a short
time. . . . It rained steadily and soakingly the
rest of the afternoon as we kept on through Randolph and Kilkenny to Jefferson Hill, so that
we had no clear view of the mountains. We
put up at a store just opposite the town hall on
Jefferson Hill. It cleared up at sunset after
two days' rain, and we had a fine view, repaying
us for our journey and wetting. . . . When the

sun set to us, the bare summits were of a delicate rosaceous color, passing through violet into the deep, dark-blue or purple of the night, which already invested the lower parts. This night-shadow was wonderfully blue, reminding me of the blue shadows on snow. There was an after-glow in which these tints and variations were repeated. It was the grandest mountain view I ever got. In the meanwhile, white clouds were gathering again about the summits, first about the highest, appearing to form there, but sometimes to send off an emissary to initiate a cloud upon a lower neighboring peak. You could tell little about the comparative distance of a cloud and a peak till you saw that the former actually impinged on the latter.

July 14, 1858. This forenoon we rode on through Whitefield to Bethlehem, clouds for the most part concealing the higher mountains. . . . Camped half a mile up the side of Lafayette.

July 15. Continued the ascent of Lafayette. It is perhaps three and a half miles from the road to the top by path along a winding ridge. . . . At about one mile or three quarters below the summit, just above the limit of trees, we came to a little pond, may be of a quarter of an acre (with a yet smaller one near by), one of the sources of the Pemigewasset. . . . The out-

let of this pond was considerable, but soon lost
beneath the rocks.

In the dwarf fir thickets above and below this
pond were the most beautiful linnæas I ever
saw. They grew quite densely, full of rose purple flowers (deeper reddish-purple than ours,
which are pale), perhaps nodding over the brink
of a spring. Altogether the finest mountain
flowers I saw, lining the side of the narrow horse
track through the fir scrub. Just below the top,
reclined on a dense bed of *Salix uva ursi*, five
feet in diameter by four or five inches deep, a
good spot to sit on, mixed with a rush, amid
rocks. This willow was generally showing its
down. — We had fine weather on the mountain,
and from the summit a good view of Mount
Washington and the rest, though it was a little
hazy in the horizon. It was a wild mountain
and forest scene from south-southeast round
eastwardly to north-northeast. On the northwest and down as far as Monadnock, the country
was half cleared, the " leopard "-spotted land.

Boiled tea for our dinner by the little pond,
the head of the Pemigewasset. . . . We made
our fire on the moss and lichens by a rock amid
the shallow fir and spruce, burning the dead fir
twigs, or " deer's horns." I cut off a flourishing
fir three feet high and not flattened at the top
yet. This was one and a quarter inches in di-

ameter, and had thirty-four rings. Another
flourishing one fifteen inches high had twelve
rings at ground. . . . Another, three feet high,
fresh and vigorous, without a flat top as yet, had
its woody part one and an eighth inches in diameter, the bark being one eighth inch thick, and
sixty-one rings. There were no signs of decay,
though it was, as usual, mossy or covered with
lichens. . . .

When half way down the mountain amid the
spruce, we saw two pine grossbeaks, male and
female, and looked for a nest, but in vain. They
were remarkably tame. . . . The male flew near
inquisitively, uttering a low twitter, and perched
fearlessly within four feet of us, eyeing us and
pluming himself, and plucking and eating the
leaves of the *Amelanchier oligocarpa* on which
he sat for several minutes. The female, mean-
time, was a rod off. They were evidently breeding there, yet neither Wilson nor Nuttall speak
of their breeding in the United States.

At the base of the mountain over the road
heard singing, and saw at the same place where
I heard him the evening before, a splendid rose-
breasted grossbeak. I had before mistaken him
at first for a tanager, then for a red-eye, but was
not satisfied. Now with my glass I distinguished
him sitting quite still high above the road at
the entrance of the mountain path, in the deep

woods, and singing steadily for twenty minutes.
Its note was much more powerful than that of
the tanager or red-eye. It had not the hoarse-
ness of the tanager's, and more sweetness and
fullness than that of the red-eye. . . . Rode on
and stopped at Morrison's (once Tilton's) Inn
in West Thornton.

July 16, 1858. Continue on through Thornton and Campton. The butternut is first noticed
in these towns, a common tree.

About the mountains were wilder and rarer
birds, more or less arctic, like the vegetation. I
did not even *hear* the robin in them, and when
I had left them a few miles behind, it was a
great change and surprise to hear the lark, the
wood-pewee, the robin, and the bobolink (for the
last had not done singing). On the mountains,
especially at Tuckerman's Ravine, the notes of
even familiar birds sounded strange to me. I
hardly knew the wood-thrush and veery and
oven-bird at first. They sing differently there.
. . . We were not troubled at all by black flies
after leaving the Franconia Notch. It is only
apparently in primitive woods that they work.

Saw chestnuts first and frequently in Franklin
and Boscawen, about 43½° north, or half a degree
higher than Emerson puts it. . . . Of oaks I
saw and heard only of the red in northern New
Hampshire. The witch-hazel was very abundant

and large there and about the mountains. Lodged at tavern in Franklin, west side of river.

July 17, 1858. Passed by Webster's place, three miles this side of the village; some half dozen houses there, no store, nor public buildings. Very quiet; road lined with elms and maples. Railroad between house and barn. The farm apparently a level and rather sandy interval. Nothing particularly attractive about it. A plain, public grave-yard within its limits. Saw the grave of Ebenezer Webster, Esq., who died 1806, aged sixty-seven, and of Abigail, his wife, who died 1816, aged seventy-six, probably Webster's father and mother. . . . Webster was born two or more miles northwest, house now gone. . . . Reached Weare, and put up at a quiet and agreeable house, without any sign or bar-room. Many Friends in this town. Pillsbury and Rogers known here. The former lived in Henniker, the next town.

July 18, 1858. Keep on through New Boston, etc., to Hollis, . . . and at evening to Pepperell. A marked difference when we enter Massachusetts in roads, farms, houses, trees, fences, etc.; a great improvement, showing an older settled country. In New Hampshire there is a great want of shade trees; the roads bleak or sunny, from which there is no escape. What barbarians we are! The convenience of the traveler is very little consulted. He merely has the privilege of crossing somebody's farm by a particular narrow and may be unpleasant path. The individual retains all the rights as to trees, fruit, wash of the road, etc. On the other hand, these should belong to mankind inalienably. The road should be of ample width and adorned with trees expressly for the use of the traveler. There should be broad recesses in it, especially at springs and watering-places, where he can turn out, and rest or camp, if he will. I feel commonly as if I were condemned to drive through somebody's cow-yard or huckleberry pasture by a narrow lane, and if I make a fire by the roadside to boil my hasty pudding, the farmer comes running over to see if I am not burning up his stuff.

July 19, 1858. Got home at noon. . . . We might easily have built us a shed of spruce bark at the foot of Tuckerman's Ravine. I thought that I might in a few moments strip off the bark of a spruce a little bigger than myself and seven feet long, letting it curl, as it naturally would, then crawl into it and be protected from any rain. Wentworth said that he had sometimes stripped off birch bark two feet wide, and put his head through a slit in the middle, letting the ends fall down before and behind as he walked.

— The slides in Tuckerman's Ravine appeared
to be a series of deep gullies side by side, where
sometimes it appeared as if a very large rock
had slid down without turning over, plowing this
deep furrow all the way, only a few rods wide.
Some of the slides were streams of rocks a rod
or more in diameter each. In some cases which
I noticed, the ravine side had evidently been
undermined by water on the lower side.

It is surprising how much more bewildering
is a mountain top than a level area of the same
extent. Its ridges and shelves and ravines add
greatly to its apparent extent and diversity.
You may be separated from your party by stepping only a rod or two out of the path. We
turned off three or four rods to the pond on our
way up Lafayette, knowing that H—— was behind, and so we lost him for three quarters of
an hour, and did not see him again till we
reached the summit. One walking a few rods
more to the right or left is not seen over the
ridge of the summit, and, other things being
equal, this is truer the nearer you are to the
apex. If you take one side of a rock, and your
companion another, it is enough to separate you
sometimes for the rest of the ascent.

On these mountain summits or near them, you
find small and almost uninhabited ponds, apparently without fish, sources of rivers, still and

cold, strange and weird as condensed clouds, of
which, nevertheless, you make tea! surrounded
by dryish bogs in which, perchance, you may detect traces of the bear or *loup cervier*.

We got the best views of the mountains from
Conway, Jefferson, Bethlehem, and Campton.
Conway combines the Italian (?) level and soft-
ness with Alpine peaks around. — Jefferson
offers the completest view of the range a dozen
or more miles distant, the place from which to
behold the manifold varying lights of departing
day on the summits. — Bethlehem also afforded
a complete but generally more distant view of
the range, and, with respect to the highest summits, more diagonal.

Campton afforded a fine distant view of the
pyramidal Franconia Mountains, with the lump-
ish Profile Mountain. The last view, with its
smaller intervals and partial view of the great
range far in the north, was somewhat like that
from Conway. . . .

It is remarkable that what you may call trees
on the White Mountains (*i. e.*, the forest), cease
abruptly, with those about a dozen or more feet
high, and then succeeds a distinct kind of
growth, quite dwarfish and flattened, and confined almost entirely to fir and spruce, as if it
marked the limit of almost perpetual snow, as if
it indicated a zone where the trees were peculi-

arly oppressed by the snow, cold, wind, etc. The transition from these flattened firs and spruces to shrubless rocks is not nearly so abrupt as from upright or slender trees to these dwarfed thickets.

July 3, 1840. When Alexander appears, the Hercynian and Dodonean woods seem to wave a welcome to him. Do not thoughts and men's lives enrich the earth and change the aspect of things as much as a new growth of wood?

What are Godfrey and Gonsalve unless we breathe a life into them, and reënact their exploits as a prelude to our own? The past is only so heroic as we see it; it is the canvas on which our conception of heroism is painted, the dim prospectus of our future field. We are dreaming of what we are to do.

The last sunrise I witnessed seemed to outshine the splendor of all preceding ones, and I was convinced it behoved man to dawn as freshly, and with equal promise and steadiness advance into the career of life, with as lofty and serene a countenance to move onward, through his midday, to a yet fairer and more promising setting. Has the day grown old when it sets? and shall man wear out sooner than the sun? In the crimson colors of the west I discern the budding lines of dawn. To my western brother it is rising pure and bright as it did to me, but the evening exhibits in the still rear of day the beauty which through morning and noon escaped me. When we are oppressed by the heat and turmoil of the noon, let us remember that the sun which scorches us with brazen beams is gilding the hills of morning, and awaking the woodland choirs for other men.

We will have a dawn and noon and serene sunset in ourselves.

What we call the gross atmosphere of evening is the accumulated deed of the day, which absorbs the rays of beauty, and shows more richly than the naked promise of the dawn. By earnest toil in the heat of the noon, let us get ready a rich western blaze against the evening of our lives.

. . . The sky is delighted with strains [of music] which the connoisseur rejects. It seems to say "Now is this my own earth." In music are the centripetal and centrifugal forces. The universe only needed to hear a divine harmony that every star might fall into its proper place and assume a true sphericity.

July 3, 1852. . . . The *Chimaphila umbellata,* winter-green, must have been in blossom some time. The back side of its petals, " cream-colored, tinged with purple," which is turned toward the beholder, while the face is toward the earth, is the handsomer. It is a very pretty little chandelier of a flower, fit to adorn the forest floor. Its buds are nearly as handsome. They appear to be long in unfolding.

The pickers have quite thinned the crop of early blueberries where Stow cut off the trees winter before last. When the woods on some hill-side are cut off, the *Vaccinium Pennsylvanicum* springs up or grows more luxuriantly, being exposed to light and air, and by the second year its stems are weighed to the ground with clusters of blueberries covered with bloom, and much larger than they commonly grow, also with a livelier taste than usual, as if remembering some primitive mountain side given up to them anciently. Such places supply the villagers with the earliest berries for two or three years, or until the rising wood overgrows them, and they withdraw into the bosom of Nature again. They flourish during the few years between one forest's fall and another's rise. Before you had prepared your mind or made up your mouth for the berries, thinking only of small green ones, earlier by ten days than you had expected, some child of the woods is at your door with ripe blueberries, for did not you know that Mr. Stow cut off his wood-lot winter before last. It is an ill wind that blows nobody any good, and thus it happens that when the owner lays bare and deforms a hill-side, and alone appears to reap any

advantage from it by a crop of wood, all the villagers and the inhabitants of distant cities ob-
tain some compensation in the crop of berries
that it yields. They glean after the woodchop-
per, not faggots, but full baskets of blueberries. . . . Bathed beneath Fair Haven. How
much food the muskrats have at hand! They
may well be numerous. At this place the bottom in shallow water at a little distance from
the shore is thickly covered with clams, half
buried and on their ends, generally a little
aslant. Sometimes there are a dozen or more
side by side within a square foot, and I think
that over a space twenty rods long and one wide
(I know not how much farther they reach into
the river), they would average three to a square
foot. This would give 16,335 clams to twenty
rods of shore, on one side of the river, and I
suspect there are many more. No wonder that
muskrats multiply, and that the shores are covered with the shells left by them. In bathing
here I can hardly step without treading on them,
sometimes half a dozen at once, and often I cut
my feet pretty severely on their shells. They
are partly covered with mud and the short weeds
at the bottom, and they are of the same color
themselves, but stooping down over them where
the soil has subsided, I can see them now at 5.30
P. M. with their mouths (?) open, an inch long

and quarter of an inch wide, with a waving
fringe about it, and another smaller opening
close to it without any fringe, through both of
which I see distinctly into the white interior of
the fish. When I touch one, he instantly closes
his shell, and, if taken out quickly, spurts water
like a salt-water clam. Evidently taking in their
food and straining it with short waving motion
of the ciliæ, there they lie both under the pads
and in the sun. . . . The common carrot by the
roadside, *Daucus carota*, is in some respects an
interesting plant. Its umbel, as Bigelow says,
is shaped like a bird's nest, and its large pin-
natifid involucre, interlacing by its fine seg-
ments, resembles a fanciful ladies' work-basket.

July 3, 1853. The oven-bird's nest in Laurel
Glen is near the edge of an open pine wood
under a fallen pine twig and a heap of dry oak
leaves. Within these on the ground is the nest
with a dome-like top and an arched entrance of
the whole height and width on one side. Lined
within with dry pine needles. . . . The chestnut behind my old house site is fully out, and
apparently has been partly so for several days.

Black huckleberries. — Tansy on the causeway.

July 3, 1854. I hear the purple finch these
days about the houses, *à twitter witter weeter
wee, à witter witter wee.*

P. M. To Hubbard's Bridge by boat. . . .
The river and shores with their pads and weeds
are now in their midsummer and hot weather
condition, now when the pontederias have just
begun to bloom. The seething river is confined
within two burnished borders of pads, gleaming
in the sun for a mile, and a sharp snap is heard
from them from time to time. Next stands the
upright phalanx of dark-green pontederias. —
When I have left the boat for a short time, the
seats become intolerably hot. What a luxury to
bathe now. It is gloriously hot, the first of this
weather. I cannot get wet enough. I must let
the water soak into me. When you come out,
it is rapidly dried on you, or absorbed into your
body, and you want to go in again. I begin to
inhabit the planet, and see how I may be natu-
ralized at last. — As I return from the river, the
sun westering, I admire the silvery light on the
tops and extremities of the now densely-leaved
golden willows, and swamp white oaks and maples, from the under-side of the leaves. They
have so multiplied that you cannot see through
the trees; these are solid depths of shade on
the surface of which the light is variously reflected.

July 3, 1856. P. M. To Assabet River. In
the main stream at the Rock I am surprised to
see flags and pads laying the foundation of an

islet in the middle where I had thought it deep before. Apparently a hummock, lifted by ice, sunk there in the spring, and this may be the way in which many an island has been formed in the river.

July 3, 1859. . . . P. M. To Hubbard's Grove. . . . The *Mitchella repens*, so abundantly in bloom now in the northwest part of this grove, emits a strong, astringent, cherry-like scent as I walk over it, which is agreeable to me, spotting the ground with its downy-looking white flowers.

July 3, 1860. . . . Looked at the marsh-hawk's nest (of June 16) in the Great Meadows. It was in the very midst of the sweet gale (which is three feet high) occupying an opening only a foot or two across. We had much difficulty in finding it again, but at last nearly stumbled upon a young hawk. There was one as big as my fist resting on the bare flat nest in the sun, with a great head, staring eyes, and open, gaping, or pouting mouth, yet mere down, grayish-white down as yet; but I detected another which had crawled a foot one side amid the bushes for shade or safety, more than half as large again, with small feathers, and a yet more angry, hawk-like look. How naturally anger sits on the young hawk's head. It was 3.30 P. M., and the old birds were gone and saw us not. Meanwhile their callow young lie panting under the sweet gale and rose-bushes in the swamp, waiting for their parents to fetch them food.

June is an up-country month when our air and landscape is most like that of a mountain-ous region, full of freshness, with the scent of fern by the wayside.

July 4, 1840. 4 A. M. The Townsend Light Infantry encamped last night in my neighbor's enclosure.— The night still breathes slumberously over field and wood when a few soldiers gather about one tent in the twilight, and their band plays an old Scotch air with bugle and drum and fife attempered to the season. It seems like the morning hymn of creation. The first sounds of the awakening camp mingled with the chastened strains which so sweetly salute the dawn, impress me as the morning prayer of an army. And now the morning gun fires. . . . I am sure none are cowards now. These strains are the roving dreams which steal from tent to tent, and break forth into distinct melody. They are the soldier's morning thought. Each man awakes himself with lofty emotions, and would do some heroic deed. You need preach no homily to him. He is the stuff they are made of.

We may well neglect many things, provided we overlook them.

When to-day I saw the "Great Ball" rolled

majestically along, it seemed a shame that man could not move like it. All dignity and grandeur has something of the undulatoriness of the sphere. It is the secret of majesty in the rolling gait of the elephant, and of all grace in action and in art. The line of beauty is a curve.

Each man seems striving to imitate its gait, and keep pace with it, but it moves on regardless, and conquers the multitude with its majesty. What shame that our lives which should be the source of planetary motion, and sanction the order of the spheres, are full of abruptness and angularity, so as not to roll nor move majestically.

July 4, 1852. 3 A. M. To Conantum, to see the lilies open. I hear an occasional crowing of cocks in distant barns, as has been their habit for how many thousand years. It was so when I was young, and it will be so when I am old. I hear the croak of a tree-toad as I am crossing the yard. I am surprised to find the dawn so far advanced. There is a yellowish segment of light in the east, paling a star, and adding sensibly to the light of the waning and now declining moon. . . . I hear a little twittering and some clear singing from the seringo and the song-sparrow as I go along the back road, and now and then the note of a bull-frog from the river. The light in the east has acquired a reddish tinge near the horizon. Small wisps of cloud are already fuscous and dark, seen against the light, as in the west at evening. It being Sunday morning I hear no early stirring farmer driving over a bridge. . . . The sound of a whippoorwill is wafted from the woods. Now in the Corner road the hedges are alive with twittering sparrows, a blue-bird or two, etc. The daylight now balances the moonlight. How short the nights! The last traces of day have not disappeared much before 10 o'clock, or perchance 9.30, and before 3 A. M. you see them again in the east (probably 2.30), leaving about five hours of solid night, the sun so soon coming round again. The robins sing, but not so long and loud as in the spring. I have not been awakened by them latterly in the mornings. Is it my fault? Ah, those mornings when you are awakened by the singing, the matins of the birds! . . . Methinks I saw the not yet extinguished lights of one or two fireflies in the darker ruts in the grass in Conant's meadow. The moon yields to the sun, she pales even in the presence of the dawn. It is chiefly the spring birds that I hear at this hour, and in each dawn the spring is thus revived. The notes of the sparrows, and the blue-birds and the robin, have a prominence now which they have not by day. The light is more and more general, and some low bars begin to look bluish as well

as reddish. Elsewhere the sky is wholly clear
of clouds. The dawn is at this stage far lighter
than the brightest moonlight ; I write by it. Yet
the sun will not rise for some time. Those bars
are reddening more above one spot. They grow
purplish, or lilac rather.

White and whiter grows the light in the eastern sky. And now descending to the Cliff by
the river side, I cannot see the low horizon and
its phenomena.

I love to go through these old apple orchards
so irregularly set out, sometimes two trees standing close together. The rows of grafted fruit
will never tempt me to wander amid them like
these. A bittern leaves the shore at my approach. A night-hawk squeaks and booms before sunrise. . . . I hear the blackbird's *con-
queree*, and the kingfisher darts away with his
alarum and outstretched neck. Every lily is
shut. Sunrise. I see it gilding the top of the
hill behind me, but the sun itself is concealed
by the hills and woods on the east shore. A
very slight fog begins to rise now in one place
on the river. There is something serenely glorious and memorable to me in the sight of the
first cool sunlight now gilding the eastern ex-
tremity of the bushy island in Fair Haven, that
wild lake. The subdued light and the repose
remind me of Hades. In such sunlight there

is no fever. It is such an innocent pale yellow
as the spring flowers. It is the pollen of the
sun fertilizing plants. The color of the earliest
spring flowers is as cool and innocent as the first
rays of the sun in the morning, falling on woods
and hills. The fog not only rises upward about
two feet, but at once there is a motion from the
sun over the surface. . . .

And now I see an army of skaters advancing
in loose array, chasseurs or scouts, as Indian
allies are drawn in old books. Now the rays of
the sun have reached my seat, a few feet above
the water. Flies begin to buzz, mosquitoes to
be less troublesome. A humming-bird hums by
over the pads up the river, as if looking, like
myself, to see if lilies have blossomed. The
birds begin to sing generally, and if not loudest,
at least most noticeably on account of the quiet-
ness of the hour, a few minutes before sunrise.
They do not sing so incessantly and earnestly,
as a regular thing, half an hour later. — Carefully looking both up and down the river, I
could perceive that the lilies began to open
about fifteen minutes after the sun from over
the opposite bank fell on them, perhaps three-
quarters of an hour after sunrise, which is about
4.30, and one was fully expanded about twenty
minutes later. When I returned over the bridge
about 6.15, there were perhaps a dozen open

ones in sight. It was very difficult to find one
not injured by insects. Even the buds which
were just about to expand were frequently bored
quite through, and the water had rotted them.
You must be on hand early to anticipate insects.
I bring home a dozen perfect lily buds, all I can
find within many rods, which have never yet
opened. I prepare a large pan of water, and
cutting their stems quite short, I turn back their
calyx leaves with my fingers, so that they may
float upright; then, touching the points of their
petals, and breathing or blowing on them, I toss
them in. They spring open rapidly, or gradually expand in the course of an hour, all but
one or two. — At 12.30 p. m. I perceive that
the lilies in the river have begun to shut up.
. . . I go again at 2.30 p. m. and every lily is
shut.

I will here tell the history of my rosaceous
lilies, plucked the 1st of July. They were buds
at the bottom of a pitcher of water all the 2d,
having been kept in my hat part of the day
before. On the morning of the 3d I assisted
their opening, and put them in water, as I have
described. They did not shut up at noon, like
those on the river, but at dark, their petals, at
least, quite close. They all opened again in the
course of the forenoon of the 4th, but had not
shut up at 10 o'clock p. m., though I found them

shut on the morning of the 5th. May it be that they can bear only a certain amount of light, and so, being in the shade, remained open longer (I think not, for they shut up on the river that quite cloudy day, July 1), or is their vitality too little to allow them to perform their regular functions?

Can that meadow fragrance come from the purple summits of the eupatorium?

July 4, 1860. Standing on J. P. B——'s land, south side, I observed his rich and luxuriant uncut grass lands northward, now waving under the easterly wind. It is a beautiful camilla, sweeping like waves of light and shade over the whole breadth of his land, like a low steam curling over it, imparting wonderful life to the landscape, like the light and shade of a changeable garment. . . . It is an interesting feature, very easily overlooked, and suggests that we are wading and navigating at present in a sort of sea of grass which yields and undulates under the wind like water, and so perchance the forest is seen to do from a favorable position. . . . Early there was that flashing light of waving pines in the horizon, now the camilla on grass and grain.

July 5, 1840. Go where we will, we discover infinite change in particulars only, not in generals.

You cannot rob a man of anything which he will miss.

July 5, 1852. I know a man who never speaks of the sexual relation but jestingly, though it is a subject to be approached only with reverence and affection. What can be the character of that man's love? It is ever the subject of a stale jest, though his health or his dinner can be seriously considered. The glory of the world is seen only by a chaste mind. To whomsoever this fact is not an awful, but beautiful mystery, there are no flowers in Nature.

White lilies continue to open in the house in the morning and shut in the night, for five or six days, until their stamens have shed their pollen, and they turn rusty, and begin to decay. Then the beauty of the flower is gone, and its vitality, so that it no longer expands with the light.

How perfect an invention is glass! There is a fitness in glass windows which reflect the sun morning and evening; windows the doorways of light thus reflecting its rays with a splendor only second to itself. . . . The sun rises with a salute, and leaves the world with a farewell to our windows. To have, instead of opaque shutters, or dull horn or paper, a material like solidified air, which reflects the sun thus brightly. It is inseparable from our civilization and enlight-

enment. It is encouraging that this intelligence
and brilliancy or splendor should belong to the
dwellings of men, and not to the cliffs and
micaceous rocks and lakes exclusively. . . .

P. M. To Second Division Brook.

There is a meadow on the Assabet, just above
Derby's bridge (it may contain an acre, bounded
on one side by the river, on the other by alders
and a hill), completely covered with small hummocks which have lodged on it in the winter,
covering it like the mounds in a graveyard,
at pretty regular intervals. Their edges are
rounded, and they and the paths between them
are covered with a firm, short, green sward, with
here and there hard-hacks springing out of them,
so that they make excellent seats, especially in
the shade of an elm that grows there. They
are completely united with the meadow, forming
little oblong hillocks from one to ten feet long.
. . . I love to ponder the natural history thus
written on the banks of the stream ; for every
higher freshet and intenser frost is recorded by
it. The stream keeps a faithful journal of every
event in its experience, whatever race may settle
on its banks. It purls past this natural graveyard with a storied murmur, and no doubt it
could find endless employment for an Old Mortality in renewing its epitaphs.

The progress of the season is indescribable.

It is growing warm again, but the warmth is different from that we have had. We lie in the shade of a locust-tree. Haymakers go by in a hay-rigging. I am reminded of berrying. I scent the sweet fern and the dead or dry pine leaves. Cherry-birds alight on a neighboring tree. The warmth is something more normal and steady. Nature offers fruits now as well as flowers. We have become accustomed to the summer. It has acquired a certain eternity. The earth is dry. Perhaps the sound of the locust expresses the season as well as anything. I might make a separate season of those days when the locust is heard. That is our torrid zone. This dryness and heat are necessary for the maturing of fruits.

How cheering it is to behold a full spring bursting forth directly from the earth, like this of Tarbell's, from clean gravel, copiously in a thin sheet; for it descends at once, where you see no opening, cool from the caverns of the earth, and making a considerable stream. . . . I lie almost flat, resting my hands on what offers, to drink at this water where it bubbles, at the very udders of Nature, for man is never weaned from her breast while life lasts.

We are favored in having two rivers flowing into one, whose banks afford different kinds of scenery, the streams being of different characters, one a dark, muddy, dead stream, full of animal and vegetable life, with broad meadows, and black, dwarf willows and weeds, the other comparatively pebbly and swift, with more abrupt banks and narrower meadows. To the latter I go to see the ripple and the varied bottom with its stones and sands and shadows; to the former for the influence of its dark water resting on invisible mud, and for its reflections. It is a factory of soil, depositing sediment. . . .

Some birds are poets and sing all summer. They are the true singers. Any man can write verses in the love season. I am reminded of this while we rest in the shade . . . and listen to a wood-thrush now just before sunset. We are most interested in those birds that sing for the love of the music and not of their mates ; who meditate their strains and amuse themselves with singing; the birds whose strains are of deeper sentiment, — not bobolinks that lose their bright colors and their song so early, — the robin, the red-eye, the veery, the wood-thrush, etc. The wood-thrush's is no opera music, it is not so much the composition as the strain, the tone that interests us, cool bars of melody from the atmosphere of everlasting morning or evening. It is the quality of the sound, not the sequence. In the pewee's note there is some sultriness, but in the thrush's, though heard at noon, there is the liquid coolness of things drawn from the bottom of springs. The thrush's alone declares the immortal wealth and vigor that is in the forest. Here is a bird in whose strain the story is told. Whenever a man hears it, he is young, and Nature is in her spring. Wherever he hears it, there is a new world and a free country, and the gates of heaven are not shut against him. Most other birds sing, from the level of my ordinary cheerful hours, a carol, but this bird never fails to speak to me out of an ether purer than that I breathe, of immortal vigor and beauty. He deepens the significance of all things seen in the light of his strain. He sings to make men take higher and truer views. . . . He sings to amend their institutions, to relieve the slave on the plantation and the prisoner in his dungeon, the slave in the house of luxury and the prisoner of his own low thoughts.

How fitting to have every day, in a vase of water on your table, the wild flowers of the season which are just blossoming. Can any house be said to be furnished without them? Shall we be so forward to pluck the fruits of Nature and neglect her flowers? These are surely her finest influences. So may the season suggest the thoughts it is fitted to suggest. . . . Let me know what picture Nature is painting, what poetry she is writing, what ode composing now.

The sun has set. . . . The dew is falling fast. Some fine clouds, which have just escaped being condensed in dew, hang on the skirts of day, and make the attraction in our western sky, that part of day's gross atmosphere which has escaped the clutches of the night, and is not enough condensed to fall to earth, soon to be gilded by the sun's parting rays; remarkably finely divided clouds, a very fine mackerel sky, or rather as if one had sprinkled that part of the sky with a brush, the outline of the whole being that of several large sprigs of fan coral. They grow darker and darker, and now are reddened, while dark-blue bars of cloud of a wholly different character lie along the northwest horizon.

July 5, 1854. . . . P. M. To White Pond. . . . The blue curls and fragrant life-everlasting with their refreshing aroma show themselves now pushing up in dry fields, bracing to the thought. — On Lupine Knoll picked up a dark-colored spear head three and a half inches long, lying on the bare sand, so hot that I could not long hold it tight in my hand. Now the earth begins to be parched, the corn curls, and the four-leaved loosestrife, etc., wilt and wither.

July 5, 1856. The large evening primrose below the foot of our garden does not open till sometime between 6.30 and 8 P. M., or sundown. It was not open when I went to bathe, but freshly out in the cool of the evening at sundown, as if enjoying the serenity of the hour.

July 6, 1840. All this worldly wisdom was once the unamiable heresy of some wise man. — I observe a truly wise practice on every hand, in education, in religion, and the morals of society, enough embodied wisdom to have set up many an ancient philosopher. This society, if it were a person to be met face to face, would not only be tolerated but courted, with its so impressive experience and admirable acquaintance with things. — Consider society at any epoch, and who does not see that heresy has already prevailed in it ?

Have no mean hours, but be grateful for every hour, and accept what it brings. The reality will make any sincere record respectable. No day will have been wholly misspent, if any sincere, thoughtful page has been written. Let the daily tide leave some deposit on these pages, as it leaves sand and shells on the shore, so much increase of terra firma. This may be a calendar of the ebbs and flows of the soul, and on these sheets, as a beach, the waves may cast up pearls and seaweed.

July 6, 1851. I walked by night last moon, and saw its disk reflected in Walden Pond, the broken disk, now here, now there, a pure and memorable flame, unearthly bright. . . . Ah!

but that first faint tinge of moonlight on the gap seen some time ago, a silvery light from the east before day had departed in the west. What an immeasurable interval there is between the first tinge of moonlight which we detect, lighting with mysterious, silvery, poetic light the western slopes, like a paler grass, and the last wave of daylight on the eastern slopes. It is wonderful how our senses ever span so vast an interval ; how, from being aware of the one, we become aware of the other. . . . It suggests an interval equal to that between the most distant periods recorded in history. The silver age is not more distant from the golden than moonlight is from sunlight. I am looking into the west where the red clouds still indicate the course of departing day. I turn and see the silent, spiritual, contemplative moonlight shedding the softest imaginable light on the western slopes, . . . as if, after a thousand years of polishing, their surfaces were just beginning to be bright, a pale, whitish lustre. Already the crickets chirp to the moon a different strain, and the night wind rustles the leaves of the wood. . . . Ah, there is the mysterious light which for some hours has illustrated Asia and the scene of Alexander's victories, now at length, after two or three hours spent in surmounting the billows of the Atlantic, come to shine on America. There on that illustrated sand bank was revealed an antiquity beside which Nineveh is young, such a light as sufficed for the earliest ages. . . . Even at midday I see the full moon shining in the sky. What if in some vales only its light is reflected! What if there are some spirits which walk in its light alone still! . . . I passed from dynasty to dynasty, from one age of the world to another, . . . from Jove, perchance, back to Saturn. What river of Lethe was there to run between! I bade farewell to that light setting in the west, and turned to salute the new light rising in the east.

There is some advantage in being the humblest, cheapest, least dignified man in the village, so that the very stable boys shall damn you. Methinks I enjoy that advantage to an unusual extent. There is many a coarsely well-meaning fellow, who knows only the skin of me, who addresses me familiarly by my Christian name. I get the whole good of him, and lose nothing myself. There is " Sam," the jailer (whom I never call " Sam," however), who exclaimed last evening, " Thoreau, are you going up the street pretty soon? Well, just take a couple of these handbills along, and drop one on H——'s piazza, and one at H——'s, and I'll do as much for you another time." I am not above being abused sometimes.

July 6, 1852. 2.30 P. M. To Beck Stow's, thence to Sawmill Brook, and return by Walden. — Now for the shade of oaks in pastures. The witnesses attending court sit on the benches in the shade of the great elm. The cattle gather under the trees. The pewee is heard in the heat of the day, and the red-eye (?). The pure white cymes (?) of the elder are very conspicuous along the edges of meadows, contrasting with the green above and around. . . . From the lane in front of Hawthorne's, I see dense beds of tufted vetch, *Vicia cracca*, for some time, taking the place of the grass in the low grounds, blue inclining in spots to lilac like the lupines. This, too, was one of the flowers that Proserpine was gathering ; yellow lilies, also. It is affecting to see such an abundance of blueness in the grass. It affects the eyes, this celestial color. I see it afar . . . in masses on the hill-sides near the meadow, so much blue, laid on with so heavy a hand ! — In selecting a site in the country, let a lane near your house, grass-grown, cross a sizable brook where is a watering-place. — I see a pickerel in the brook showing his whitish, greedy upper lips projecting over the lower. How well concealed he is. He is generally of the color of the muddy bottom, or the decayed leaves and wood that compose it, and the longitudinal light stripe on his back, and the transverse ones on his

sides are the color of the yellowish sand here and
there exposed. He heads up stream and keeps
his body perfectly motionless, however rapid the
current, chiefly by the motion of his narrow pectoral fins, though also by the waving of his other
fins and tail as much as is necessary, a motion
which a frog might mistake for that of weeds.
Thus concealed by his color and stillness, like a
stake, he lies in wait for frogs and minnows. Now
a frog leaps in, and he darts forward three or four
feet.

Pastinaca sativa, parsnip. How wholesome
and edible smells its sweet root. — Tansy, *tana-
cetum vulgare*, just begins.

H—— is haying, but inclined to talk as usual.
. . . I am disappointed that he, the most intelli-
gent farmer in Concord, and perchance in Mid-
dlesex, who admits that he has property enough
for his use without accumulating more, and talks
of leaving off hard work, letting his farm, and
spending the rest of his days easier and better,
cannot yet think of any method of employing
himself except in work for his hands. Only he
would have a little less of it. Much as he is
inclined to speculate in conversation, giving up
any work to it for the time, and long-headed as
he is, he talks of working for a neighbor for a
day now and then, and taking his dollar. "He
would not like to spend his time sitting on the

22

Mill Dam " [*i. e.*, in the village]. He has not even planned an essentially better life. . . .

Sometime: the swampy vigor in large doses proves rank poison to the sensitively bred man, as where dogwood grows. How far he has departed from the rude vigor of Nature, that he cannot assimilate and transmute her elements. The morning air may make a debauchee sick. No herb is friendly to him. All at last are poisons, and yet none are medicines to him, and so he dies ; the air kills him. . . .

I heard a solitary duck on Goose Pond making a doleful cry, though its ordinary one, just before sundown, as if caught in a trap or by a fox, and creeping silently through the bushes, I saw it, probably a wood duck, sailing rapidly away. But it still repeated its cry as if calling for a mate. When the hen hatches ducks, they do not mind her clucking. They lead the hen. — Chickens and ducks are well set on the earth. What great legs they have ! This part is early developed. A perfect Antæus is a young duck in this respect, deriving a steady stream of health and strength from the earth, for he rarely gets off it, ready either for land or water. Nature is not on her last legs yet. A chick's stout legs ! If they were a little larger, they would injure the globe's tender organization with their scratching. Then, for digestion, consider their crops

and what they put into them in the course of a
day. Consider how well fitted to endure the
fatigue of a day's excursion. A young chick
will run all day in pursuit of grasshoppers, and
occasionally vary its exercise by scratching, go
to bed at night with protuberant crop, and get
up early in the morning ready for a new start.

July 6, 1856. P. M. To Assabet bath. . . .
I hear the distressed or anxious peet of a peet-
weet, and see it hovering over its young, half-
grown, which runs beneath, and suddenly hides
securely in the grass when but a few feet from
me.

G. Emerson says the sweetbrier was doubtless introduced, yet according to Bancroft, Gos-
nold found it on the Elizabeth Isles.

July 6, 1859. . . . P. M. To Lee's Cliff. . . .
The heart-leaf flower is now very conspicuous
and pretty in that pool westerly of the old Conantum house. Its little, white, five-petalled
flower, about the size of a five-cent piece, looks
like a little white lily. Its perfectly heart-shaped
floating leaf, an inch or more long, is the smallest kind of pad. There is a single pad to each
slender stem which is from one to several feet
long in proportion to the depth of the water, and
these padlets cover sometimes, like an imbrica-
tion, the whole surface of a pool. Close underneath each leaf or pad is concealed an umbel of

from ten to fifteen flower buds of various sizes, and of these, one at a time (and sometimes more) curls upward between the lobes of the base and expands its corolla to the light and air, about half an inch above the water, and so on successively till all have flowered. Over the whole surface of the shallow pool you see thus each little pad with its pretty lily between its lobes turned toward the sun. It is simply leaf and flower.

July 7, 1840. I have experienced such simple joy in the trivial matters of fishing and sporting formerly as might inspire the muse of Homer or Shakespeare. And now when I turn over the pages and ponder the plates of the " Angler's Souvenir," I exclaim with the poet,

> " Can these things be, and overcome us like
> A summer's cloud? "

When I hear a sudden burst from a horn, I am startled, as if one had provoked such wildness as he could not rule nor tame. He dares make the echoes which he cannot put to rest.

July 7, 1851. The intimations of the night are divine, methinks. Men might meet in the morning and report the news of the night, what divine suggestions have been made to them. I find that I carry with me into the day often some such hint derived from the gods, such impulses to purity, to heroism, to literary effort, even, as are never day-born.

One of those mornings which usher in no day, but rather an endless morning, a protracted auroral season, for clouds prolong the twilight the livelong day.

Now that there is an interregnum in the blossoming of the flowers, so is there in the singing of the birds. The golden robin, the bobolink, etc., are rarely heard.

I rejoice when in a dream I have loved virtue and nobleness.

Where is Grecian History? Is it when in the morning I recall the intimations of the night?

The moon is now more than half full. When I come through the village at ten o'clock this cold night, cold as in May, the heavy shadows of the elms, covering the ground with their rich tracery, impress me as if men had got so much more than they bargained for, — not only trees to stand in the air, but to checker the ground with their shadows. At night they lie along the earth. They tower, they arch, they droop over the streets like chandeliers of darkness.

With a certain wariness, but not without a slight shudder at the danger oftentimes, I perceive how near I had come to admitting into my mind the details of some trivial affair, as a case

at court, and I am astonished to observe how
willing men are to lumber their minds with
such rubbish, to permit idle rumors, tales, incidents, even of an insignificant kind, to intrude
upon what should be the sacred ground of the
thoughts. Shall the temple of our thoughts be
a public arena where the most trivial affair of
the market and the gossip of the tea-table is dis-
cussed, a dusty, noisy, trivial place? or shall it
be a quarter of the heavens itself, consecrated
to the service of the gods, a hypæthral temple?
I find it so difficult to dispose of the few facts
which to me are significant, that I hesitate to
burden my mind with the most insignificant,
which only a divine mind can illustrate. Such
is, for the most part, the news in newspapers
and conversation. It is important to preserve
the mind's chastity in this respect. Think of
admitting the details of a single case at the
criminal court into the mind to stalk profanely
through its very *sanctum sanctorum* for an hour,
— aye, for many hours; to make a very bar-room
of your mind's inmost apartment, as if for a moment the dust of the street had occupied you, —
aye, the very street itself, with all its travel, had
poured through your very mind of minds, your
thought's shrine, with all its filth and bustle.
Would it not be an intellectual suicide? By all
manner of boards and traps threatening the ex-

treme penalty of the divine law, excluding tres-
passers from these grounds, it behoves us to preserve the purity and sanctity of the mind. It is
so hard to forget what it is worse than useless to
remember. If I am to be a channel or thor-
oughfare, I prefer that it be of the mountain
brooks, the Parnassian streams, and not of the
city sewers. There is inspiration, the divine
gossip which comes to the attentive mind from
the Courts of Heaven, there is the profane and
stale revelation of the bar-room and the police
court. The same ear is fitted to receive both
communications. Only the character of the individual determines to which source chiefly it
shall be open, and to which closed. I believe
that the mind can be profaned by the habit of
attending to trivial things, so that all our
thoughts shall be tinged with triviality. They
shall be dusty as stones in the street. Our very
minds shall be paved and macadamized, their
foundation broken into fragments for the wheels
of travel to roll over. If you would know what
will make the most durable pavements, surpassing
rolled stones, spruce blocks, and asphaltum, you
have only to look into some mens' minds. If we
have thus desecrated ourselves, the remedy will
be by circumspection and wariness, by aspiration
and devotion to consecrate ourselves, to make a
fane of the mind. I think we should treat our

minds as innocent and ingenuous children whose guardians we are, be careful what objects and what subjects are thrust on their attention. I think even the facts of science may dust them by their dryness, unless they are in a sense effaced each morning, or rather rendered fertile by the dews of fresh and living truth. Every thought which passes through the mind helps to wear and tear it, and to deepen the ruts, which, as in the streets of Pompeii, evince how much it has been used. How many things there are concerning which we might well deliberate whether we had better know them. Routine, conventionality, manners, etc.; how insensibly an undue attention to these dissipates and impoverishes the mind, robs it of its simplicity and strength, emasculates it.

Knowledge does not come to us by details, but by *lieferungs* from the gods.

Only thought which is expressed by the mind in repose, or, as it were, lying on its back and contemplating the heavens, is adequately and fully expressed. What are sidelong, transient, passing half views? The writer expressing his thoughts must be as well seated as the astronomer contemplating the heavens. He must not occupy a constrained position. The facts, the experience we are well poised upon! which secure our whole attention!

The senses of children are unprofaned. Their whole body is one sense, they take a physical pleasure in riding on a rail. So does the unviolated, the unsophisticated mind derive an inexpressible pleasure from the simplest exercise of thought.

I can express adequately only the thought which I love to express.

All the faculties in repose but the one you are using, the whole energy concentrated in that.

Be so little distracted, your thoughts so little confused, your engagements so few, your attention so free, your existence so mundane, that in all places and in all hours you can hear the sound of crickets in those seasons when they are to be heard. It is a mark of serenity and health of mind when a person hears this sound much in streets of cities as well as in fields. Some ears can never hear this sound ; are called deaf. Is it not because they have so long attended to other sounds?

July 7, 1852. 4 A. M. The first (?) really foggy morning. Yet before I rise, I hear the song of birds from out it like the bursting of its bubbles with music. . . . Their song gilds thus the frost work of the morning. . . . I came near waking this morning. I am older than last year. The mornings are further between. The days are fewer. Any excess, to have drunk too much

water even the day before, is fatal to the morning's clarity. But in health, the sound of a cow
bell is celestial music. O might I always wake
to thought and poetry, regenerated! Can it be
called a morning, if our senses are not clarified
so that we perceive more clearly ? if we do not
rise with elastic vigor ?

How wholesome these fogs which some fear.
They are cool, medicated vapor baths mingled
by Nature, which bring to our senses all the
medical properties of the meadows; the touch-
stones of health. Sleep with all your windows
open, and let the mist embrace you.

To the Cliffs. The fog condenses into foun-
tains and streams of music, as in the strain of
the bobolink which I hear, and runs off so. The
music of the birds is the tinkling of the rills
that flow from it. I cannot see twenty rods. . . .

There is everywhere dew on the cobwebs, little
gossamer veils or scarfs as big as your hand
dropped from the shoulders of fairies that danced
on the grass the past night. . . . The to me
beautiful rose-colored spikes of the hardhack,
Spiræa tomentosa; one is out. — I think it was
this thin vapor that produced a kind of mirage
when I looked over the meadow from the railroad last night toward Trillium wood, giving to
the level meadow a certain liquid, sea-like look.
Now the heads of herd's grass, seen through the
dispersing fog, look like an ocean of grass.

6 P. M. To Hubbard's Bathing Place. Pogonias are still abundant in the meadows, but
arethusas I have not lately seen. . . . The blue-
eyed grass shuts up before sunset. . . . The very
handsome "pink-purple" flowers of the *Calopogon! pulchellus* enrich the grass all around
the edge of Hubbard's blueberry swamp, and
are now in their prime. The *Arethusa bulbosa*,
" crystalline purple," *Pogonia ophioglassoides*,
snake-mouthed [tongued] arethusa, "pale purple," and the *Calopogon pulchellus*, grass pink,
" pink-purple," make one family in my mind
(next to the purple orchis, or with it), being
flowers *par excellence*, all flower, naked flowers,
and difficult, at least the calopogon, to preserve.
But they are flowers, excepting the first, at least,
without a name. Pogonia! Calopogon!! They
would blush still deeper if they knew what
names man had given them. The first and the
last interest me most, for the pogonia has a
strong, snaky odor. The first may perhaps
retain its name, arethusa, from the places in
which it grows, and the other two deserve the
names of nymphs, perhaps of the class called
Naiades. How would the *Naiad Ægle* do for
one ? . . . To be sure, in a perfect flower, there
will be proportion between the flowers and leaves,
but these are fair and delicate, nymph-like. . . .
When the yellow lily flowers in the meadows,
and the red in dry lands and by wood-paths, then,

methinks, the flowering season has reached its height. They surprise me as perhaps no more can. Now I am prepared for anything.

July 7, 1857. . . . Some of the inhabitants of the Cape think that the Cape is theirs, and all occupied by them, but, in my eyes, it is no more theirs than it is the blackbirds', and in visiting the Cape there is hardly more need of my regarding or going through the villages than of going through the blackbirds' nests. I leave them both on one side, or perchance I just glance into them to see how they are built and what they contain. I know that they have *spoken for* the whole Cape, and lines are drawn on the maps accordingly, but I know that these are imaginary, having perambulated many such, and they would have to get me or one of my craft to find them for them. For the most part, indeed with very trifling exceptions, there were no human beings there, only a few imaginary lines on a map.

July 8, 1838.

CLIFFS.

The loudest sound that burdens here the breeze
Is the wood's whisper ; 't is when we choose to list,
Audible sound, and when we list not,
It is calm profound. Tongues were provided
But to vex the ear with superficial thoughts.
When deeper thoughts up swell, the jarring discord
Of harsh speech is hushed, and senses seem
As little as may be to share the ecstasy.

July 8, 1840. Doubt and falsehood are yet good preachers. They affirm soundly while they deny partially.

I am pleased to learn that Thales was up and stirring by night not unfrequently, as his astronomical discoveries prove.

It was a saying of Solon that "it is necessary to observe a medium in all things." The golden mean in ethics as in physics is the centre of the system, that about which all revolve, and though to a distant and plodding planet it is the uttermost extreme, yet when that planet's year is complete, it will be found central. They who are alarmed lest virtue run into extreme good have not yet wholly embraced her, but described only a small arc about her, and from so small a curvature you can calculate no centre whatever. Their mean is no better than meanness, nor their medium than mediocrity. If a brave man observes strictly this golden mean, he may run through all extremes with impunity, like the sun which now appears in the zenith, now in the horizon, and again is faintly reflected from the moon's disk, and has the credit of describing an entire great circle, crossing the equinoctial and solstitial colures, without detriment to his steadfastness.

Every planet asserts its own to be the centre of the system.

Only meanness is mediocre, moderate ; the true medium is not contained within any bounds, but is as wide as the ends it connects.

When Solon endeavored to prove that Salamis had formerly belonged to the Athenians, and not to the Megarians, he caused the tombs to be opened, and showed that the inhabitants of Salamis turned the faces of their dead to the same side with the Athenians, but the Megarians to the opposite side. So does each fact bear witness to all, and the history of all the past may be read in a single grain of its ashes.

July 8, 1851. . . . I am struck by the cool, juicy, pickled-cucumber green of the potato-fields now. How lusty these vines look. The pasture naturally exhibits at this season no such living green as the cultivated fields. . . . Here are mulleins covering a field where three years ago none were noticeable, but a smooth, uninterrupted pasture sod. Two years ago it was ploughed for the first time for many years, and millet and corn and potatoes planted. Now, where the millet grew, these mulleins have sprung up. Who can write the history of these fields? The millet does not perpetuate itself, but the few seeds of the mullein which perchance were brought here with it are still multiplying the race. . . .

Here are some rich rye-fields waving over all
the land, their heads nodding in the evening
breeze, with an apparently alternating motion,
i. e., they do not all bend at once, by ranks, but
separately, and hence this agreeable alterna-
tion. How rich a sight this cereal fruit, now
yellow for the cradle, *flavus.* It is an impenetrable phalanx. I walk for half a mile, looking
in vain for an opening. . . . This is food for
man. The earth labors not in vain. It is bearing its burden. The yellow, waving, rustling
rye extends far up and over the hills on either
side, a kind of pinafore to Nature, leaving only
a narrow and dark passage at the bottom of a
deep ravine. How rankly it has grown! How
it hastes to maturity! I discover that there is
such a goddess as Ceres. . . . The small trees
and shrubs seen dimly in its midst are over-
whelmed by the grain as by an inundation.
They are seen only as indistinct forms of bushes
and green leaves, mixed with the yellow stalks.
There are certain crops which give me the idea
of bounty, of the *Alma Natura.* They are the
grains. Potatoes do not so fill the lap of earth.
This rye excludes everything else, and takes
possession of the soil. The farmer says, next
year I will raise a crop of rye, and he proceeds
to clear away the brush, and either ploughs it,
or, if it is too uneven or stony, burns and harrows

it only and scatters the seed with faith. And all winter the earth keeps his secret, unless it did leak out somewhat in the fall, and in the spring this early green on the hillsides betrays him. When I see this luxuriant crop spreading far and wide, in spite of rock and bushes and unevenness of ground, I cannot help thinking that it must have been unexpected by the farmer himself, and regarded by him as a lucky accident for which to thank fortune. This to reward a transient faith the gods had given.

July 8, 1852. P. M. Down river in boat to the Holt. . . . It is perhaps the warmest day yet. We held on to the abutments under the Red Bridge to cool ourselves in the shade. No better place in hot weather, the river rippling away beneath you, and the air rippling through between the abutments, if only in sympathy with the river, while the planks afford a shade, and you hear all the travel and the travelers' talk without being seen or suspected. . . . There is generally a current of air circulating over water, always, methinks, if the water runs swiftly, as if it put the air in motion. There is quite a breeze here this sultry day. Commend me to the subpontean, the under-bridge life.

I am inclined to think bathing almost one of the necessaries of life, but it is surprising how indifferent some are to it. What a coarse, foul, busy life we lead compared even with the South Sea Islanders in some respects. Truant boys steal away to bathe, but the farmers, who most need it, rarely dip their bodies into the streams or ponds. M—— was telling me last night that he had thought of bathing when he had done his hoeing, of taking some soap and going down to Walden, and giving himself a good scrubbing, but something had occurred to prevent, and now he will go unwashed to the harvesting, aye, even till the next hoeing is over. Better the faith and practice of the Hindoos, who worship the sacred Ganges. We have not faith enough in the Musketaquid to wash in it even after hoeing. Men stay on shore, keep themselves dry, and drink rum. Pray what were rivers made for? One farmer, who came to bathe in Walden one Sunday while I lived there, told me it was the first bath he had had for fifteen years. Now what kind of religion could his be? or was it any better than a Hindoo's?

July 8, 1853. . . . Toads are still heard occasionally at evening. To-day I heard a hylodes peep (perhaps a young one), which have so long been silent.

July 8, 1854. Full moon. By boat to Hubbard's Bend. There is wind, making it cooler and keeping off fog. Delicious on water. The moon reflected from the rippled surface like a

stream of dollars. I hear a few toads still. . . .
The bull-frogs trump from time to time. . . .
The whippoorwills are heard, and the baying of
dogs.

The *Rosa nitida*, I think, has some time done;
lucida generally now ceasing, and the *Carolina* (?) just begun.

July 8, 1857. . . . Counted the rings of a
white-pine stump sawed off last winter at Laurel
Glen. It is three and a half feet in diameter
and has one hundred and twenty-six rings.

July 9, 1840. In most men's religion the lig-
ature which should be the umbilical cord con-
necting them with the source of life is rather
like that thread which the accomplices of Cylon
held in their hands when they went abroad from
the temple of Minerva, the other end being attached to the statue of the goddess. Frequently,
as in their case, the thread breaks, being
stretched, and they are left without an asylum.

The value of many traits in Grecian history
depends not so much on their importance as history, as on the readiness with which they accept
a wide interpretation, and illustrate the poetry
and ethics of mankind. When they announce
no particular truth, they are yet central to all
truth. . . . Even the isolated and unexplained
facts are like the ruins of the temples which in
imagination we restore, and ascribe to some
Phidias or other master.

The Greeks were boys in the sunshine; the Romans were men in the field; the Persians, women in the house; the Egyptians, old men in the dark.

He who receives an injury is an accomplice of the wrong-doer.

July 9, 1851. When I got out of the cars at Porter's, Cambridge, this morning, I was pleased to see the handsome blue flowers of the succory or endive, *Cichorium intybus*, which reminded me that within the hour I had been whirled into a new botanical region. They must be extremely rare, if they occur at all in Concord. This weed is handsomer than most garden flowers. . . .

Coming out of town willingly as usual, when I saw that reach of Charles River just above the Depot, the fair, still water this cloudy evening suggesting the way to eternal peace and beauty, whence it flows, the placid, lake-like fresh water so unlike the salt brine, affected me not a little. I was reminded of the way in which Wordsworth so coldly speaks of some natural visions or scenes "giving him pleasure." This is perhaps the first vision of elysium on the route from Boston. And just then I saw an encampment of Penobscots, their wigwams appearing above the railroad fence, they, too, looking up the river as they sat on the ground, and enjoying the scene. What can be more impressive than to look up a noble river just at evening, — one, perchance, which you have never explored, — and behold its placid waters, reflecting the woods and sky, lapsing inaudibly toward the ocean, to behold it as a lake, but know it as a river, tempting the beholder to explore it and his own destiny at once, haunt of water-fowl. This was above the factories, all that I saw. That water could never have flowed under a factory. How *then* could it have reflected the sky?

July 9, 1852. 4 A. M. To Cliffs. . . . An aurora fading into a general saffron color. At length the redness travels over partly from east to west, before sunrise, and there is little color in the east. The birds all unite to make the morning choir, sing rather faintly, not prolonging their strains. The crickets appear to have received a reinforcement during the sultry night.

There is no name for the evening red corresponding to aurora. It is the blushing foam about the prow of the sun's boat, and at eve, the same in its wake. — I do not often hear the bluebird now except at dawn. — I think we have had no clear winter skies, no skies the color of a robin's egg and pure amber . . . for some months. — These blueberries on Fair Haven have a very innocent, ambrosial taste, as if made of the ether itself, as they plainly are colored with it. . . .

How handsome the leaves of the shrub oak, so
clear and unspotted a green, so firm and enduring, glossy, uninjured by the wind, meed for
mighty conquerors, lighter on the under-side,
which contrast is important. . . . It must be
the cuckoo that makes that half-throttled sound
at night, for I saw one while he made it this
morning, as he flew from an apple-tree when I
disturbed him. — Those white water-lilies, what
boats! I toss one into the pan half unfolded,
and it floats upright like a boat. It is beautiful
when half open, and also when fully expanded.

Morton, in his "Crania Americana," says,
referring to Wilkinson as his authority, that vessels of porcelain of Chinese manufacture have
of late been repeatedly found in the catacombs
of Thebes in Egypt, some as old as the Phara-
onic period, and the inscriptions on them "have
been read with ease by Chinese scholars, and in
three instances record the following legend,
'The flower opens, and lo! another year."
There is something sublime in the fact that some
of the oldest written sentences should thus celebrate the coming in of spring. How many
times have the flowers opened and a new year
begun! Hardly a more cheering sentence could
have come down to us. How old is spring, a
phenomenon still so fresh! Do we perceive any
decay in Nature? How much evidence is con-

tained in this short and simple sentence respecting the former inhabitants of this globe! It is a sentence to be inscribed on vessels of porcelain, suggesting that so many years had gone before, an observation as fit then as now.

3 P. M. To Clematis Brook. The heat of to-day, as yesterday, is furnace-like. It produces a thickness almost amounting to vapor in the near horizon. The railroad men cannot work in the Deep Cut, but have come out on to the causeway, where there is a circulation of air. They tell, with a shudder, of the heat reflected from the rails, yet a breezy wind, as if it were born of the heat, rustles all leaves. — Those piles of clouds in the north, assuming interesting forms of unmeasured rocky mountains or unfathomed precipices, light-colored and even downy above, but with watery bases, portend a thunder-shower before night. Well, I can take shelter in some barn or under a bridge. It shall not spoil my afternoon. — I have scarcely heard one strain from the telegraph harp this season. Its string is rusted and slackened, relaxed, and now no more it encourages the walker. So is it with all sublunary things. Every poet's lyre loses its tension. It cannot bear the alternate contraction and expansion of the seasons. — How intense and suffocating the heat under some sunny woodsides where no breeze circulates!

The red lily with its torrid color and sun-freckled spots, dispensing, too, with the outer garment of a calyx, its petals so open and wide apart that you can see through it in every direction, tells of hot weather. It is of a handsome bell shape, so upright, and the flower prevails over every other part. It belongs not to spring.

It is refreshing to see the surface of Fair Haven rippled with wind. The waves break here quite as on the sea shore, and with like effects. This little brook makes great sands comparatively at its mouth, which the waves of the pond wash up and break upon like a sea.

Bathing is an undescribed luxury. To feel the wind blow on your body, and the water flow upon you and lave you, is a rare physical enjoyment this hot day. . . .

Low hills or even hillocks which are stone-capped (have rocky summits), as this near James Baker's, remind me of mountains, which in fact they are on a small scale, — the brows of earth, round which the trees and bushes trail like the hair of eyebrows, outside bald places, templa, primitive places where lichens grow. I have some of the same sensations as if I sat on the top of the Rocky Mountains. Some low places thus give a sense of elevation.

July 9, 1854. . . . Examined a lanceolate thistle which has been pressed and has lain by a year. The papers being taken off, its head sprang up more than an inch, and the downy seeds began to fly off.

July 9, 1857. . . . P. M. Up Assabet with S——. There is now but little black willow down left on the trees. I think I see how this tree is propagated by its seeds. Its countless, minute, brown seeds, just perceptible to the naked eye in the midst of their cotton, are wafted with the cotton to the water (most abundantly about a fortnight ago), and then they drift and form a thick white scum together with other matter, especially against some alder or other fallen or drooping shrub where there is less current than usual. There within two or three days a great many germinate and show their two little roundish leaves, more or less tinging with green the surface of the scum, somewhat like grass seed in a tumbler of cotton. Many of these are drifted in amid the button-bushes, willows, and other shrubs, and the sedge along the river side, and the water falling just at this time when they have put forth little fibres, they are deposited on the mud just left bare in the shade, and thus probably a great many of them have a chance to become perfect plants. But if they do not drift into sufficiently shallow water, and are not left on the mud just at the right time, probably they perish. The mud in many such places

is now green with them, though perhaps the seed
has often blown thither directly through the air.
— I am surprised to see dense groves of young
maples an inch or more high from seed of this
year. They have sprung in pure sand where the
seed has been drifted and moisture enough sup-
plied, at the water's edge. The seed, now effete,
commonly lies on the surface, having sent down
its rootlet into the sand.

July 10, 1840. To myself I am as pliant as
an osier, and my courses seem not so easy to be
calculated as that of Encke's comet, but I am
powerless to bend the character of another. He
is like iron in my hands. I could tame a hyena
more easily than my friend. He is material
which no tool of mine will work. A naked savage will fell an oak with a firebrand, and wear
a hatchet out of the rock, but I cannot hew the
smallest chip out of the character of my fellow
to beautify or deform it.

Nothing was ever so unfamiliar and startling
to me as my own thoughts.

We know men through their eyes. You might
say that the eye was always original and unlike
another. It is the feature of the individual, and
not of the family ; in twins, still different. All
a man's privacy is in his eye, and its expression
he cannot alter more than he can alter his character. So long as we look a man in the eye, it

seems to rule the other features, and make them
too original. When I have mistaken one person
for another, observing only his form and carriage and inferior features, the unlikeness seemed
of the least consequence, but when I caught his
eye and my doubts were removed, it seemed to
pervade every feature. The eye revolves on an
independent pivot which we can no more control
than our own will. Its axle is the axle of the
soul, as the axis of the earth is coincident with
the axis of the heavens.

July 10–12, 1841. . . . A slight sound at
evening lifts me up by the ears, and makes life
seem inexpressibly serene and grand. It may
be in Uranus, or it may be in the shutter. It is
the original sound of which all literature is the
echo. It makes all fear superfluous. Bravery
comes from further than the sources of fear.

July 10, 1851. A gorgeous sunset after rain,
with horizontal bars of cloud, red sashes to the
western window, barry clouds hanging like a curtain over the window of the west, damask. First
there is a low arch of the storm clouds, under
which is seen the clearer, fairer, serener sky and
more distant sunset clouds, and under all, on the
horizon's edge, heavier, massive dark clouds not
to be distinguished from the mountains. How
many times I have seen this kind of sunset, the
most gorgeous sight in Nature. From the hill

behind Minot's I see the birds flying against this red sky; one looks like a bat. Now between two stupendous mountains of the low stratum under the evening red, clothed in slightly rosaceous, amber light, through a magnificent gorge, far, far away, as perchance may occur in pictures of the Spanish coast viewed from the Mediterranean, I see a city, the eternal city of the West, the phantom city, in whose streets no traveler has trod, over whose pavement the horses of the sun have already hurried, some Salamanca of the imagination. But it lasts only for a moment, for now the changing light has wrought such changes in it that I see the resemblance no longer. A softer amber sky than in any picture. The swallows are improving this short day, twittering as they fly, the huckleberry-bird repeats his jingling strain, and I hear the notes of the song-sparrow more honest-sounding than most. — I am always struck by the centrality of the observer's position. He always stands fronting the middle of the arch, and does not suspect at first that a thousand observers from a thousand hills behold the sunset sky from equally favorable positions.

And now I turn and observe the dark masses of the trees in the east, not green, but black. While the sun was setting in the west, the trees were rising in the east.

I perceive that the low stratum of dark clouds under the red sky all dips one way, and to a remarkable degree presents the appearance of the butt ends of cannons slanted towards the sky. Such uniformity on a large scale is unexpected, and pleasant to detect, evincing the simplicity of the laws of their formation. Uniformity in the shapes of clouds of a single stratum is always to be detected, the same wind shaping clouds of the same consistency and in like positions. No doubt an experienced observer could discover the states of the upper atmosphere by studying the forms and characters of the clouds. I traced the distinct form of the cannon in seven instances, stretching over the whole length of the cloud many a mile in the horizon.

July 10, 1852. Another day, if possible, still hotter than the last. We have already had three or four such, and still no rain. The soil under the sward in the yard is dusty as an ash-heap for a foot in depth, and the young trees are suffering and dying.

2 P. M. To the North River, in front of Major Bassett's. It is with a suffocating sensation, and a slight pain in the head, that I walk the Union Turnpike where the heat is reflected from the road. The leaves of the elms on the dry highways begin to roll up. I have to lift my hat to let the air cool my head. But I find a re-

freshing breeze from over the river and meadow. In the hottest day you can be comfortable in the shade on the open shore of a pond or river, where a zephyr comes over the water sensibly cooled by it ; that is, if the water is deep enough to cool it. I find the white melilot, *Melilotus leucantha*, a fragrant clover, in blossom by the roadside. We turn aside by a large rye-field near the old Lee place. The rye-fields are now quite yellow and ready for the sickle. Already there are many flavous colors in the landscape, much maturity of small seeds. The nodding heads of the rye make an agreeable maze to the eye. I hear now the huckleberry bird, the red-eye, and the oven-bird. The robin, methinks, is oftener heard of late, even at noon. . . . The long, narrow, open intervals in the woods near the Assabet are quite dry now, in some parts yellow with the upright loosestrife. One of these meadows, a quarter of a mile long, by a few rods wide, narrow and winding, and bounded on all sides by maples showing the under-sides of their leaves, swamp white-oaks, with their glossy dark-green leaves, birches, etc., and full of meadow-sweet just coming into bloom, and cranberry vines, and a dry kind of grass, is a very attractive place to walk in. We undressed on this side, carried our clothes down in the stream a considerable distance, and

finally bathed in earnest from the opposite side.
The heat tempted us to prolong this luxury.
. . . I made quite an excursion up and down
the river in the water, a fluvial . . . walk. It
seemed the properest highway for this weather,
now in water a foot or two deep, now suddenly
descending through valleys up to my neck, but
all alike agreeable. Sometimes the bottom
looked as if covered with large, flat, sharp-edged
rocks. I could break off cakes three or four
inches thick, and a foot or two square. It was
a conglomeration . . . of sand and pebbles, as
it were cemented with oxide of iron (?), quite
red with it, iron colored to the depth of an inch
on the upper-side, a hard kind of pan covering
or forming the bottom in many places. . . .
There are many interesting objects of study, as
you walk up and down a clear river like this in
the water, where you can see every inequality in
the bottom, and every object on it. The breams'
nests are interesting and even handsome, and
the shallow water in them over the sand is so
warm to my hand that I think their ova will
soon be hatched; also, the numerous heaps of
stones, made I know not certainly by what fish,
many of them rising above the surface. There
are weeds on the bottom which remind you of
the sea; the radical leaves of the floating heart
which I have never seen mentioned, very large,

five inches long and four wide, dull claret (and
green when freshest), pellucid, with waved edges,
in large tufts or dimples on the bottom, oftenest
without the floating leaves, like lettuce, or some
kelps, or carrageen moss (?). The bottom is
also scored with furrows made by the clams
moving about, sometimes a rod long, and always
the clam lies at one end. So this fish can change
its position, and get into deeper and cooler water.
I was in doubt before whether the clam made
these furrows; for one, apparently fresh, that I
examined, had a " mud clam " at the end, but
these, which were very numerous, had living
clams. — There are but few fishes to be seen.
They have, no doubt, retreated to the deepest
water. In one somewhat muddier place close
to the shore I came upon an old pout cruising
with her young. She dashed away at my approach, but the fry remained. They were of
various sizes, from one third of an inch to one
and a half inches, quite black and pout-shaped,
except that the head was most developed in the
smallest. They were constantly moving about
in a somewhat circular or rather lenticular
school, about fifteen or eighteen inches in diameter, and I estimated that there were at least
one thousand of them. Presently the old pout
came back and took the lead of her brood, which
followed her, or rather gathered about her, like

chickens about a hen; but this mother had so
many children she did n't know what to do.
Her maternal yearnings must be on a great
scale. When one half of the divided school
found her out they came down upon her and
completely invested her like a small cloud. She
was soon joined by another smaller pout, apparently her mate, and all, both old and young,
began to be very familiar with me. They came
round my legs and felt them with their feelers,
and the old pouts nibbled my toes, while the
fry half concealed my feet. Probably if I had
been standing on the bank, with my clothes on,
they would have been more shy. Ever and
anon the old pouts dashed aside to drive away
a passing bream or perch. The larger one kept
circling about her charge as if to keep them
together within a certain compass. If any of
her flock were lost or drowned she would hardly
have missed them. I wondered if there was
any calling of the roll at night; whether she,
like a faithful shepherdess, ever told her tale
under some hawthorn in the river dales. Ever
ready to do battle with the wolves that might
break into her fold. The young pouts are protected then for a season by the old. Some had
evidently been hatched before the others. One
of these large pouts had a large velvet black
spot which included the right pectoral fin, — a

kind of disease which I have often observed on them. — I wonder if any Roman emperor ever indulged in such a luxury as this — of walking up and down a river in torrid weather with only a hat to shade the head. What were the baths of Caracalla to this? Now we traverse a long watery plain some two feet deep; now we descend into a dark river valley, where the bottom is lost sight of and the water rises to our armpits; now we go over a hard iron pan; now we stoop and go under a low bough of the *Salix nigra;* now we slump into soft mud, amid the pads of the *Nymphœa odorata,* at this hour shut. On this road there is no other traveler to turn out for. We finally return to the dry land and recline in the shade of an apple-tree on a bank overlooking the meadow. When I first came out of the water the short, wiry grass was burning hot to my feet, and my skin was soon parched and dry in the sun. — I still hear the bobolink. . . . The stones lying in the sun on this hillside, where the grass has been cut, are as hot to the hand as an egg just boiled, and very uncomfortable to hold; so do they absorb the heat. Every hour do we expect a thunder-shower to cool the air, but none comes. We say they are gone down the river.

. . . St. John's-wort is perhaps the prevailing flower now. Many fields are very yellow with

24

it.   In one such I was surprised to see rutabaga
turnips growing well and showing no effects of
drouth, and still more surprised when the farmer
. . . showed me, with his hoe, that the earth was
quite fresh and moist there only an inch beneath
the surface.   This he thought was the result of
keeping the earth loose by cultivation.

July 10, 1853. . . . The bream poised over
its sandy nest on waving fin — how aboriginal!
So it was poised here and watched its ova before
the new world was known to the old.   Still I
see the little cavities of their nests along the
shore.

July 10, 1854. . . . The singing birds at present are (villageous) robin, chip-bird, warbling
vireo, swallows; (rural) song-sparrow, seringo,
flicker, king-bird, goldfinch, link of bobolink;
cherry-bird; (sylvan) red-eye, tanager, wood-
thrush, chewink, veery, oven-bird, all even at
mid-day, cat-bird (full strain), whippoorwill,
crows.

July 10, 1856. . . . 5 P. M.   Up Assabet.
As I was bathing under the swamp white-oaks at
6 P. M. heard a suppressed sound, often repeated,
like perhaps the working of beer through a bung-
hole, which I already suspected to be produced
by owls.   I was uncertain whether it was far or
near.   Proceeding a dozen rods up stream on
the south side, toward where a cat-bird was inces-

santly mewing, I found myself suddenly within
a rod of a gray screech-owl, sitting on an alder
bough, with horns erect, turning its head from
side to side, and up and down, and peering at
me in that same ludicrously solemn and com-
placent way that I had noticed in one in cap-
tivity. Another, more red, also horned, repeated
the same warning sound, an apparent call to its
young, about the same distance off, in another
direction, on an alder. When they took to
flight, they made some noise with their wings.
With their short tails and squat figures they
looked very clumsy, all head and shoulders.
Hearing a fluttering under the alders, I drew
near and found a young owl, a third smaller
than the red, all gray, without obvious horns,
only four or five feet distant. It flitted along
two rods, and I followed it. I saw at least two
or more young. . . . These birds kept opening
their eyes when I moved, as if to get a clearer
sight of me. The young were very quick to
notice any motion of the old, and so betrayed
their return by looking in that direction when
they returned, though I had not heard it.
Though they permitted me to come near with
so much noise, as if bereft of half their senses,
they at once noticed the coming and going of
the old birds, even when I did not. There were
four or five owls in all. I have heard a some-

what similar note further off, and louder, in the night.

July 10, 1860. . . . This cloudy, cool after-noon I was exhilarated by the mass of cheerful, bright yellowish light reflected from the sedge, *Carex Pennsylvanica* growing densely on hill-sides laid bare within a year or two. It is of a distinct, cheerful, yellow color, even this over-cast day, as if it were reflecting a bright sun-light, though no sun is visible. It is surprising how much this will light up a hillside, or upland hollow or plateau, and when, in a clear day, you look toward the sun over it late in the afternoon, the scene is incredibly bright and elysian.

INDEX.

376 INDEX.

Standard and Popular Library Books

SELECTED FROM THE CATALOGUE OF

HOUGHTON, MIFFLIN AND COMPANY.

JOHN ADAMS and Abigail Adams.
Familiar Letters of, during the Revolution. 12mo, $2.00.

Oscar Fay Adams.
Handbook of English Authors. 16mo, 75 cents.
Handbook of American Authors. 16mo, 75 cents.

Louis Agassiz.
Methods of Study in Natural History. Illus. 16mo, $1.50.
Geological Sketches. Series I. and II., each 16mo, $1.50.
A Journey in Brazil. Illustrated. 8vo, $5.00.

Thomas Bailey Aldrich.
Story of a Bad Boy. Illustrated. 12mo, $1.50.
Marjorie Daw and Other People. 12mo, $1.50.
Prudence Palfrey. 12mo, $1.50.
The Queen of Sheba. 16mo, $1.50.
The Stillwater Tragedy. 12mo, $1.50.
From Ponkapog to Pesth. 16mo, $1.25.
Cloth of Gold and Other Poems. 12mo, $1.50.
Flower and Thorn. Later Poems. 12mo, $1.25.
Poems, Complete. Illustrated. 8vo, $5.00.
Mercedes, and Later Lyrics. Crown 8vo, $1.25.

American Commonwealths.
Virginia. By John Esten Cooke.
Oregon. By William Barrows.
(*In Preparation.*)
South Carolina. By Hon. W. H. Trescot.
Kentucky. By N. S. Shaler.
Maryland. By Wm. Hand Browne.
Pennsylvania. By Hon. Wayne MacVeagh.

Connecticut. By Alexander Johnston.
Kansas. By Leverett W. Spring.
Tennessee. By James Phelan.
California. By Josiah Royce.
    Each volume, 16mo, $1.25.
        Others to be announced hereafter.

American Men of Letters.

Washington Irving. By Charles Dudley Warner.
Noah Webster. By Horace E. Scudder.
Henry D. Thoreau. By Frank B. Sanborn.
George Ripley. By O. B. Frothingham.
J. Fenimore Cooper. By Prof. T. R. Lounsbury.
Margaret Fuller Ossoli. By T. W. Higginson.
        (*In Preparation.*)
Ralph Waldo Emerson. By Oliver Wendell Holmes
Nathaniel Hawthorne. By James Russell Lowell.
Edmund Quincy. By Sidney Howard Gay.
William Cullen Bryant. By John Bigelow.
Bayard Taylor. By J. R. G. Hassard.
William Gilmore Simms. By George W. Cable.
Benjamin Franklin. By John Bach McMaster.
Edgar Allan Poe. By George E. Woodberry.
    Each volume, with Portrait, 16mo, $1.25.
        Others to be announced hereafter.

American Statesmen.

John Quincy Adams. By John T. Morse, Jr.
Alexander Hamilton. By Henry Cabot Lodge
John C. Calhoun. By Dr. H. von Holst.
Andrew Jackson. By Prof. W. G. Sumner.
John Randolph. By Henry Adams.
James Monroe. By Pres. D. C. Gilman.
Thomas Jefferson. By John T. Morse, Jr.
Daniel Webster. By Henry Cabot Lodge.
Albert Gallatin. By John Austin Stevens.
        (*In Preparation.*)
John Adams. By John T. Morse, Jr.
James Madison. By Sidney Howard Gay.

Henry Clay. By Hon. Carl Schurz.
Samuel Adams. By John Fiske.
Martin Van Buren. By Hon. Wm. Dorsheimer.
Each volume, 16mo, $1.25.
Others to be announced hereafter.

Mrs. Martha Babcock Amory.
Life of John Singleton Copley. 8vo, $3.00.

Hans Christian Andersen.
Complete Works. 10 vols. 12mo, each $1.50.

Francis, Lord Bacon.
Works. Collected and edited by Spedding, Ellis, and Heath.
15 vols. crown 8vo, $33.75.
Popular Edition. With Portraits and Index. 2 vols. crown
8vo, $5.00.
Promus of Formularies and Elegancies. 8vo, $5.00.
Life and Times of Bacon. Abridged. By James Spedding.
2 vols. crown 8vo, $5.00.

Maturin M. Ballou.
Due West. Crown 8vo, $1.50.

E. D. R. Bianciardi.
At Home in Italy. 16mo, $1.25.

William Henry Bishop.
The House of a Merchant Prince. A Novel. 12mo, $1.50.
Detmold. A Novel. 18mo, $1.25.

Björnstjerne Björnson.
Norwegian Novels. 7 vols. 16mo, each $1.00 ; the set, $6.00.

Anne C. Lynch Botta.
Handbook of Universal Literature. 12mo, $2.00.

British Poets.
Riverside Edition. Crown 8vo, each $1.75 ; the set, 68 vols.,
$100.00.

John Brown, M. D.
Spare Hours. 3 vols. 16mo, each $1.50

Robert Browning.
Poems and Dramas, etc. 15 vols. 16mo, $22.00.
Complete Works. *New Edition.* 7 vols. crown 8vo, $12.00.
Jocoseria. New Poems. 16mo, $1.00. Crown 8vo, $1.00.

William Cullen Bryant.
Translation of Homer. The Iliad. 1 vol. crown 8vo, $3.00.
2 vols. royal 8vo, $9.00 ; crown 8vo, $4.50.
The Odyssey. 1 vol. crown 8vo, $3.00. 2 vols. royal 8vo,
$9.00 ; crown 8vo, $4.50.

Sara C. Bull.
Life of Ole Bull. Portrait and illustrations. 8vo, $2.50.

John Burroughs.
Works. 5 vols. 16mo, each $1.50.

Thomas Carlyle.
- Essays. With Portrait and Index. 4 vols. 12mo, $7.50.
Popular Edition. 2 vols. 12mo, $3.50.

Alice and Phœbe Cary.
Poems. *Household Edition.* 12mo, $2.00.
Library Edition. Including Memorial by Mary Clemmer.
Portraits and 24 illustrations. 8vo, $4.00.

Lydia Maria Child.
Looking toward Sunset. 12mo, $2.50.
Letters. With Biography by Whittier. 16mo, $1.50.

James Freeman Clarke.
Ten Great Religions. 8vo, $3.00.
Ten Great Religions. Part II. Comparison of all Relig-
ions. 8vo, $3.00.
Common Sense in Religion. 12mo, $2.00.
Memorial and Biographical Sketches. 12mo, $2.00.

James Fenimore Cooper.
Works. *Household Edition.* Illustrated. 32 vols. 16mo,
each $1.00 ; the set, $32.00.
Globe Edition. Illustrated. 16 vols. 16mo, $20.00.

Charles Egbert Craddock.
In the Tennessee Mountains. 16mo, $1.25.

F. Marion Crawford.
To Leeward. 16mo, $1.25.
A Roman Singer. 16mo, $1.25.

M. Creighton.
The Papacy during the Reformation. 2 vols. 8vo, $10.00.

Richard H. Dana.
To Cuba and Back. 16mo, $1.25.
Two Years before the Mast. 16mo, $1.50.

Thomas De Quincey.
Works. *Riverside Edition.* 12 vols. 12mo, each $1.50 ; the
set, $18.00.

Madame De Staël.
Germany. 12mo, $2.50.

Charles Dickens.
Works. *Illustrated Library Edition.* With Dickens Dic-
tionary. 30 vols. 12mo, each $1.50 ; the set, $45.00.
Globe Edition. 15 vols. 16mo, each $1.25 ; the set, $18.75.

J. Lewis Diman.
The Theistic Argument, etc. Crown 8vo, $2.00.
Orations and Essays. Crown 8vo, $2.50.

F. S. Drake.
Dictionary of American Biography. 8vo, $6.00.

Charles L. Eastlake.
Hints on Household Taste. Illustrated. 8vo, $3.00.
Notes on the Louvre and Brera Galleries. Small 4to, $2.00.

George Eliot.
The Spanish Gypsy. A Poem. 16mo, $1.00.

Ralph Waldo Emerson.
Works. *Riverside Edition.* 11 vols. each $1.75.
"Little Classic" Edition. 11 vols. 18mo, each, $1.50.
Parnassus. *Household Edition.* 12mo, $2.00.
Library Edition. 8vo, $4.00.

Edgar Fawcett.
A Hopeless Case. 18mo, $1.25.
A Gentleman of Leisure. 18mo, $1.00.
An Ambitious Woman. 12mo, $1.50.

F. de S. de la Motte Fénelon.
Adventures of Telemachus. 12mo, $2.25.

James T. Fields.
Yesterdays with Authors. 12mo, $2.00 ; 8vo, $3.00.
Underbrush. 18mo, $1.25.
Ballads and other Verses. 16mo, $1.00.
The Family Library of British Poetry. Royal 8vo, $5.00.
Memoirs and Correspondence. 8vo, $2.00.

John Fiske.
Myths and Myth-Makers. 12mo, $2.00.
Outlines of Cosmic Philosophy. 2 vols. 8vo, $6.00.
The Unseen World, and other Essays. 12mo, $2.00.
Excursions of an Evolutionist. 12mo, $2.00.
Darwinism and Other Essays. 12mo, $2.00.

Dorsey Gardner.
Quatre Bras, Ligny, and Waterloo. 8vo, $5.00.

John F. Genung.
Tennyson's In Memoriam. A Study. Crown 8vo, $1.25.

Johann Wolfgang von Goethe.
Faust. Part First. Translated by C. T. Brooks. 16mo, $1.25.
Faust. Translated by Bayard Taylor. 1 vol. crown 8vo,
$3.00. 2 vols. royal 8vo, $9.00 ; 12mo, $4.50.

Correspondence with a Child. 12mo, $1.50.
Wilhelm Meister. Translated by Carlyle. 2 vols. 12mo, $3.00.

Anna Davis Hallowell.

James and Lucretia Mott. Crown 8vo, $2.00.

Arthur Sherburne Hardy.

But Yet a Woman. *Nineteenth Thousand.* 16mo, $1.25.

Bret Harte.

Works. *New Edition.* 5 vols. Crown 8vo, each $2.00.
Poems. *Household Edition.* 12mo, $2.00. *Red-Line Edition.* Small 4to, $2.50. *Diamond Edition,* $1.00.

Nathaniel Hawthorne.

Works. *"Little Classic"* Edition. Illustrated. 25 vols. 18mo, each $1.00 ; the set $25.00.
New Riverside Edition. Introductions by G. P. Lathrop. 11 Etchings and Portrait. 12 vols. crown 8vo, each $2.00.

John Hay.

Pike County Ballads. 12mo, $1.50.
Castilian Days. 16mo, $2.00.

George S. Hillard.

Six Months in Italy. 12mo, $2.00.

Oliver Wendell Holmes.

Poems. *Household Edition.* 12mo, $2.00.
Illustrated Library Edition. 8vo, $4.00.
Handy-Volume Edition. 2 vols. 18mo, $2.50.
The Autocrat of the Breakfast-Table. Crown 8vo, $2.00.
Handy-Volume Edition. 18mo, $1.25.
The Professor at the Breakfast-Table. Crown 8vo, $2.00.
The Poet at the Breakfast-Table. Crown 8vo, $2.00.
Elsie Venner. Crown 8vo, $2.00.
The Guardian Angel. Crown 8vo, $2.00.
Medical Essays. Crown 8vo, $2.00.
Pages from an old Volume of Life. Crown 8vo, $2.00.
John Lothrop Motley. A Memoir. 16mo, $1.50.

Augustus Hoppin.

A Fashionable Sufferer.   12mo, $1.50.
Recollections of Auton House.   4to, $1.25.

Blanche Willis Howard.

One Summer.   18mo, $1.25.   Sq. 12mo, $2.50.
One Year Abroad.   18mo, $1.25.

William D. Howells.

Venetian Life.   12mo, $1.50.
Italian Journeys.   12mo, $1.50.
Their Wedding Journey.   Illus.   12mo, $1.50 ; 18mo, $1.25.
Suburban Sketches.   Illustrated.   12mo, $1.50.
A Chance Acquaintance.   Illus.   12mo, $1.50 ; 18mo, $1.25.
A Foregone Conclusion.   12mo, $1.50.
The Lady of the Aroostook.   12mo, $1.50.
The Undiscovered Country.   12mo, $1.50.
Poems.   18mo, $1.25.
Out of the Question.   A Comedy.   18mo, $1.25.
A Counterfeit Presentment.   18mo, $1.25.
Choice Autobiography.   8 vols.   18mo, each $1.25.

Thomas Hughes.

Tom Brown's School-Days at Rugby.   16mo, $1.00.
Tom Brown at Oxford.   16mo, $1.25.
The Manliness of Christ.   16mo, $1.00 ; paper, 25 cents.

William Morris Hunt.

Talks on Art.   Series I. and II.   8vo, each $1.00.

Thomas Hutchinson.

Diary and Letters.   8vo, $5.00.

Henry James, Jr.

A Passionate Pilgrim and other Tales.   12mo, $2.00.
Transatlantic Sketches.   12mo, $2.00.
Roderick Hudson.   12mo, $2.00.
The American.   12mo, $2.00.
Watch and Ward.   18mo, $1.25.

The Europeans. 12mo, $1.50.
Confidence. 12mo, $1.50.
The Portrait of a Lady. 12mo, $2.00.

Mrs. Anna Jameson.
Writings upon Art Subjects. 10 vols. 18mo, each $1.50.

Sarah Orne Jewett.
Deephaven. 18mo, $1.25.
Old Friends and New. 18mo, $1.25.
Country By-Ways. 18mo, $1.25.
Play-Days. Stories for Children. Square 16mo, $1.50.
The Mate of the Daylight. 18mo, $1.25.
A Country Doctor. 16mo, $1.25.

Rossiter Johnson.
Little Classics. Eighteen handy volumes containing the
choicest Stories, Sketches, and short Poems in English
Literature. Each in one vol. 18mo, $1.00 ; the set, $18.00.
9 vols. square 16mo, $13.50. (*Sold only in sets.*)

Samuel Johnson.
Oriental Religions: India, 8vo, $5.00. China, 8vo, $5.00.
Persia, 8vo. (*In Press.*)
Lectures, Essays, and Sermons. Crown 8vo, $1.75.

Charles C. Jones, Jr.
History of Georgia. 2 vols. 8vo, $10.00.

T. Starr King.
Christianity and Humanity. With Portrait. 16mo, $2.00.
Substance and Show. 16mo, $2.00.

Lucy Larcom.
Poems. 16mo, $1.25.   An Idyl of Work. 16mo, $1.25.
Wild Roses of Cape Ann and other Poems. 16mo, $1.25.
Breathings of the Better Life. 16mo, $1.25.

George Parsons Lathrop.
A Study of Hawthorne. 18mo, $1.25.
An Echo of Passion. 16mo, $1.25.

Henry C. Lea.
Sacerdotal Celibacy. 8vo, $4.50.

Charles G. Leland.
The Gypsies.   Crown 8vo, $2.00.

George Henry Lewes.
The Story of Goethe's Life.   Portrait.   12mo, $1.50.
Problems of Life and Mind.   5 vols. 8vo, $14.00.

J. G. Lockhart.
Life of Sir W. Scott.   3 vols. 12mo, $4.50.

Henry Cabot Lodge.
Studies in History.   Crown 8vo, $1.50.

Henry Wadsworth Longfellow.
Poetical Works.   *Cambridge Edition.*   4 vols. 12mo, $9.00.
Poems.   *Octavo Edition.*   Portrait and 300 illustrations. $8.00.
Household Edition.   Portrait.   12mo, $2.00.
Red-Line Edition.   Portrait and 12 illus.   Small 4to, $2.50.
Diamond Edition. $1.00.
Library Edition.   Portrait and 32 illustrations.   8vo, $4.00.
Christus.   *Household Edition,* $2.00 ; *Diamond Edition,* $1.00.
Prose Works.   *Cambridge Edition.*   2 vols. 12mo, $4.50.
Hyperion.   16mo, $1.50.   Kavanagh.   16mo, $1.50.
Outre-Mer.   16mo, $1.50.   In the Harbor.   16mo, $1.00.
Michael Angelo : a Drama.   Illustrated.   Folio, $7.50.
Twenty Poems.   Illustrated.   Small 4to, $4.00.
Translation of the Divina Commedia of Dante.   1 vol.
   . cr. 8vo, $3.00.   3 vols. royal 8vo, $13.50 ; cr. 8vo, $6.00.
Poets and Poetry of Europe.   Royal 8vo, $5.00.
Poems of Places.   31 vols., each $1.00 ; the set, $25.00.

James Russell Lowell.
Poems.   *Red-Line Edition.*   Portrait.   Illus.   Small 4to, $2.50.
Household Edition.   Portrait.   12mo, $2.00.
Library Edition.   Portrait and 32 illustrations.   8vo, $4.00.
Diamond Edition. $1.00.
Fireside Travels.   12mo, $1.50.
Among my Books.   Series I. and II.   12mo, each $2.00.
My Study Windows.   12mo, $2.00.

Thomas Babington Macaulay.
Complete Works. 8 vols. 12mo, $10.00.

Harriet Martineau.
Autobiography. Portraits and illus.   2 vols. 8vo, $6.00.
Household Education.   18mo, $1.25.

Owen Meredith.
Poems. *Household Edition.* Illustrated.   12mo, $2.00.
Library Edition. Portrait and 32 illustrations.   8vo, $4.00.
Lucile. *Red-Line Edition.* 8 illustrations.   Small 4to, $2.50.
Diamond Edition. 8 illustrations. $1.00.

J. W. Mollett.
Illustrated Dictionary of Words used in Art and Archæ-
ology.   Small 4to, $5.00.

Michael de Montaigne.
Complete Works. Portrait.   4 vols. 12mo, $7.50.

William Mountford.
Euthanasy.   12mo, $2.00.

T. Mozley.
Reminiscences of Oriel College, etc.   2 vols. 16mo, $3.00.

Elisha Mulford.
The Nation.   8vo, $2.50.
The Republic of God.   8vo, $2.00.

T. T. Munger.
On the Threshold.   16mo, $1.00.
The Freedom of Faith.   16mo, $1.50.

J. A. W. Neander.
History of the Christian Religion and Church, with Index
volume, 6 vols. 8vo, $20.00 ; Index alone, $3.00.

Joseph Neilson.
Memories of Rufus Choate.   8vo, $5.00.

Charles Eliot Norton.
Notes of Travel and Study in Italy.   16mo, $1.25.
Translation of Dante's New Life.   Royal 8vo, $3.00.

James Parton.

Life of Benjamin Franklin. 2 vols. 8vo, $4.00.
Life of Thomas Jefferson. 8vo, $2.00.
Life of Aaron Burr. 2 vols. 8vo, $4.00.
Life of Andrew Jackson. 3 vols. 8vo, $6.00.
Life of Horace Greeley. 8vo, $2.50.
General Butler in New Orleans. 8vo, $2.50.
Humorous Poetry of the English Language. 8vo, $2.00.
Famous Americans of Recent Times. 8vo, $2.00.
Life of Voltaire. 2 vols. 8vo, $6.00.
The French Parnassus. 12mo, $2.00 ; crown 8vo, $3.50.
Captains of Industry.

Blaise Pascal.

Thoughts. 12mo, $2.25.   Letters. 12mo, $2.25.

Elizabeth Stuart Phelps.

The Gates Ajar. 16mo, $1.50.
Beyond the Gates. 16mo, $1.25.
Men, Women, and Ghosts. 16mo, $1.50.
Hedged In. 16mo, $1.50.
The Silent Partner. 16mo, $1.50.
The Story of Avis. 16mo, $1.50.
Sealed Orders, and other Stories. 16mo, $1.50.
Friends : A Duet. 16mo, $1.25.
Doctor Zay. 16mo, $1.25.

Carl Ploetz.

Epitome of Universal History. 12mo, $3.00.

Adelaide A. Procter.

Poems. *Diamond Ed.* $1.00. *Red-Line Ed.* Sm. 4to, $2.50.

Abby Sage Richardson.

History of Our Country. 8vo, $4.50.
Songs from the Old Dramatists. 4to, $2.50.

C. F. Richardson.

Primer of American Literature. 18mo, 30 cents.

Henry Crabb Robinson.

Diary, Reminiscences, etc. Crown 8vo, $2.50.

A. P. Russell.

Library Notes. Crown 8vo, $2.00.
Characteristics. Crown 8vo, $2.00.

Edgar E. Saltus.

Balzac. Crown 8vo, $1.25.

John Godfrey Saxe.

Poems. *Red-Line Edition.* Illustrated. Small 4to, $2.50.
Diamond Edition. $1.00. *Household Edition.* 12mo, $2.00.

Sir Walter Scott.

Waverley Novels. *Illustrated Library Edition.* 25 vols.
12mo, each $1.00 ; the set, $25.00.
Globe Edition. 100 illustrations. 13 vols. 16mo, $16.25.
Tales of a Grandfather. 3 vols. 12mo, $4.50.
Poems. *Red-Line Edition.* Illustrated. Small 4to, $2.50.
Diamond Edition. $1.00.

Horace E. Scudder.

The Bodley Books. Illus. 7 vols. small 4to, each $1.50.
The Dwellers in Five-Sisters' Court. 16mo, $1.25.
Stories and Romances. 16mo, $1.25.

W. H. Seward.

Works. 5 vols. 8vo, $15.00.
Diplomatic History of the War. 8vo, $3.00.

John Campbell Shairp.

Culture and Religion. 16mo, $1.25.
Poetic Interpretation of Nature. 16mo, $1.25.
Studies in Poetry and Philosophy. 16mo, $1.50.
Aspects of Poetry. 16mo, $1.50.

William Shakespeare.

Works. Edited by R. G. White. *Riverside Edition.* 3 vols.
crown 8vo, $7.50.
The Same. 6 vols. 8vo, $15.00.

Dr. William Smith.

Bible Dictionary. *American Edition.* The set, 4 vols. 8vo,
$20.00.

Edmund Clarence Stedman.

Poems. *Farringford Edition.* Portrait. 16mo, $2.00.
Household Edition. Portrait. 12mo, $2.00.
Victorian Poets. 12mo, $2.00.
Poetry of America. (*In Press.*)
. Edgar Allan Poe. An Essay. Vellum, 18mo, $1.00.

Harriet Beecher Stowe.

Agnes of Sorrento. 12mo, $1.50.
The Pearl of Orr's Island. 12mo, $1.50.
The Minister's Wooing. 12mo, $1.50.
The May-flower, and other Sketches. 12mo, $1.50.
Nina Gordon. 12mo, $1.50.
Oldtown Folks. 12mo, $1.50.
Sam Lawson's Fireside Stories. Illustrated. 12mo, $1.50.
Uncle Tom's Cabin. 100 illustrations. 12mo, $3.50.
Popular Edition. 12mo, $2.00.

Jonathan Swift.

Works. *Edition de Luxe.* 19 vols. 8vo, each $4.00.

Bayard Taylor.

Poetical Works. *Household Edition.* 12mo, $2.00.
Dramatic Works. 12mo, $2.25.

Alfred Tennyson.

Poems. *Household Edition.* Portrait and illus. 12mo, $2.00.
Illustrated Crown Edition. 2 vols. 8vo, $5.00.
Library Edition. Portrait and 60 illustrations. 8vo, $4.00.
Red-Line Edition. Portrait and illus. Small 4to, $2.50.
Diamond Edition. $1.00.

Celia Thaxter.

Among the Isles of Shoals. 18mo, $1.25.
Poems. Small 4to, $1.50.   Drift-Weed. 18mo, $1.50.
Poems for Children. Illustrated. Small 4to, $1.50.

Henry D. Thoreau.

Works. 9 vols. 12mo, each $1.50 ; the set, $13.50.

George Ticknor.

History of Spanish Literature. 3 vols. 8vo, $10.00.
Life, Letters, and Journals. Portraits. 2 vols. 12mo, $4.00.

J. T. Trowbridge.
A Home Idyl. 16mo, $1.25.   The Vagabonds. 16mo, $1.25.
The Emigrant's Story. 16mo, $1.25.

Herbert Tuttle.
History of Prussia. Crown 8vo, $2.25.

Jones Very.
Poems. With Memoir. 16mo, $1.50.

F. M. A. de Voltaire.
History of Charles XII. 12mo, $2.25.

Lew Wallace.
The Fair God. A Novel. 12mo, $1.50.

Charles Dudley Warner.
My Summer in a Garden. 16mo, $1.00.
Illustrated Edition. Square 16mo, $1.50.
Saunterings. 18mo, $1.25.
Back-Log Studies. Illustrated. Square 16mo, $1.50.
Baddeck, and that Sort of Thing. 18mo, $1.00.
My Winter on the Nile. Crown 8vo, $2.00.
In the Levant. Crown 8vo, $2.00.
Being a Boy. Illustrated. Square 16mo, $1.50.
In the Wilderness. 18mo, 75 cents.
A Roundabout Journey. 12mo, $1.50.

William A. Wheeler.
Dictionary of Noted Names of Fiction. 12mo, $2.00.

Edwin P. Whipple.
Essays. 6 vols. crown 8vo, each $1.50.

Richard Grant White.
Every-Day English. 12mo, $2.00.
Words and their Uses. 12mo, $2.00.
England Without and Within. 12mo, $2.00.
The Fate of Mansfield Humphreys. 16mo, $1.25.

Mrs. A. D. T. Whitney.
Faith Gartney's Girlhood. 12mo, $1.50.

Hitherto. 12mo, $1.50.
Patience Strong's Outings. 12mo, $1.50.
The Gayworthys. 12mo, $1.50.
Leslie Goldthwaite. Illustrated. 12mo, $1.50.
We Girls. Illustrated. 12mo, $1.50.
Real Folks. Illustrated. 12mo, $1.50.
The Other Girls. Illustrated. 12mo, $1.50.
Sights and Insights. 2 vols. 12mo, $3.00.
Odd or Even. 12mo, $1.50.
Boys at Chequasset. 12mo, $1.50.
Mother Goose for Grown Folks. 12mo, $1.50.
Pansies. Square 16mo, $1.50.
Just How. 16mo, $1.00.

John Greenleaf Whittier.

Poems. *Household Edition.* Portrait. 12mo, $2.00.
Cambridge Edition. Portrait. 3 vols. 12mo, $6.75.
Red-Line Edition. Portrait. Illustrated. Small 4to, $2.50.
Diamond Edition. $1.00.
Library Edition. Portrait. 32 illustrations. 8vo, $4.00.
Prose Works. *Cambridge Edition.* 2 vols. 12mo, $4.50.
The Bay of Seven Islands. Portrait. 16mo, $1.00.
John Woolman's Journal. Introduction by Whittier. $1.50.
Child Life in Poetry. Selected by Whittier. Illustrated.
12mo, $2.25. Child Life in Prose. 12mo, $2.25.
Songs of Three Centuries. Selected by J. G. Whittier.
Household Edition. 12mo, $2.00. *Library Edition.* 32
illustrations. 8vo, $4.00.

J. A. Wilstach.

Translation of Virgil's Works. 2 vols. cr. 8vo, $5.00.

Justin Winsor.

Reader's Handbook of American Revolution. 16mo, $1.25.

HOUGHTON, MIFFLIN AND COMPANY,
4 Park St., Boston.   11 East 17th St., New York.